Breakthroughs
in
Antipsychotic
Medications

*A Guide for
Consumers,
Families, and
Clinicians*

*A Publication
of the
National Alliance
for the
Mentally Ill*

Breakthroughs in Antipsychotic Medications

A Guide for Consumers, Families, and Clinicians

Peter J. Weiden, M.D.

Patricia L. Scheifler, M.S.W.

Ronald J. Diamond, M.D.

Ruth Ross, M.A.

W. W. Norton & Company

New York • London

For information about permission to reproduce
selections from this book, write to
Permissions, W. W. Norton & Company, Inc., 500 Fifth Avenue,
New York, NY 10110

Composition by Ken Gross
Manufacturing by Hamilton Printing
Book design by Charlotte Staub

Library of Congress Cataloging-in-Publication Data
Breakthroughs in antipsychotic medications : a guide for consumers, families, and clinicians / Peter J. Weiden . . . [et al.].
      p.   cm.
      Includes bibliographical references.
      ISBN 0-393-70303-7 (pbk.)
      1. Schizophrenia—Chemotherapy—Technological innovations.
2. Psychotics—Treatment—Technological innovations. 3. Schizophrenia—Treatment—Technological innovations. 4. Psychopharmacology—Technological innovations. 5. Consumer education.
I. Weiden, Peter J.
RC514.B6835   1999
616.89'82061—dc21   99-17205   CIP

W. W. Norton & Company, Inc., 500 Fifth Avenue, New York, NY 10110
www.wwnorton.com

W. W. Norton & Company Ltd., 10 Coptic Street, London WC1A 1PU

1 2 3 4 5 6 7 8 9 0

Contents

Foreword

Nearly 15 years ago, my daughter was first hospitalized with a serious mental illness. Her symptoms were upsetting and my family struggled to understand her needs. Information about my daughter's medications and treatment was confusing and hard to understand.

Since that frightening time, there has been a revolution in treatment. People diagnosed with schizophrenia, bipolar disorder, or other psychoses have new hope. Many individuals have achieved remarkable stability and made real progress toward recovery. While we still have no cure, atypical antipsychotic medications are making a big difference. My daughter, like thousands of others, has a dramatically better quality of life than ever before possible.

But so many new treatment choices can be confusing. That's why this book was written. Our goal is to help you think about your situation and consider all the options available to help. I believe an informed and active partnership with a treatment professional can truly make a difference in your care. Our book is designed to share science-based information in a format you can understand and use to assess your needs and get the treatment you decide is best.

NAMI, the nation's voice on mental illness, is an aggressive advocacy organization. I hope that *Breakthroughs in Antipsychotic Medications* will serve as a kind of road map through a complex set of medical and personal decisions. I also hope you will join NAMI in promoting education and advocacy for people with mental illness and their families. Together we can create a brighter future!

— Laurie Flynn, Executive Director
NAMI (National Alliance for the Mentally Ill)

The Keys to Recovery

Imagine you're locked in a room with no windows and only one door. You have a ring of keys. What would you do? Of course, you'd use the keys to try to unlock the door. If the first key didn't work, would you give up? No, of course not. You'd try another key. Would you keep trying the same key over and over again if it didn't work? No, you'd give it a good try, then try the next key. Would you try only two or three keys and give up? Not if you were locked in a room and wanted to get out—you'd try every key on the ring, wouldn't you?

That's how it is with mental illness. The illness locks you in. It keeps you from going places, doing things, and achieving goals. Antipsychotic medications are the keys. You don't know which medication might be the key that unlocks the door. The only way out is to try every key. Don't give up if the first medication doesn't work. Don't keep taking the same medication for years if it doesn't work. There are other medications to try. Medications are the keys to recovery.

Acknowledgments

We thank Laurie Flynn of the National Alliance for the Mentally Ill (NAMI) for her continued encouragement and support in moving this project from an idea into a reality. Susan Munro and Regina Ardini at W. W. Norton have been wonderful in turning a manuscript that showed up on Norton's doorstep in the fall of 1998 into a finished book in early 1999. We thank Patricia Deegan for allowing us to present some ideas from her forthcoming book *Using Medications as Part of the Recovery Process: A Workbook for Consumers*, in Chapter 3 of our book. Dr. Weiden gratefully acknowledges the help provided by Bruce Link and Sharon Schwartz of the Psychiatric Epidemiology Training Fellowhip program at the Columbia School of Public Health while he was working on this project as a third year "PET" fellow (Training Grant MH 13043).

We would also like to say a word about financial support and potential conflicts of interest. In a variety of ways, all the authors of *Breakthroughs in Antipsychotic Medications* have received, and continue to receive, financial support from the pharmaceutical companies that make these medications. However, financial support for the writing of this book was provided solely by a grant from NAMI, and the authors did not receive any other financial support for this project. All royalties from sales of *Breakthroughs* will go directly to NAMI.

Introduction

You are probably reading this because your life is touched by serious mental illness. Perhaps you have schizophrenia, or someone you love has it. Or, perhaps you are a mental health professional treating schizophrenia. If so, you already know that severe mental illness causes tremendous hardships for the affected person and affects the lives of everyone in the person's social network.

If you've dealt with this illness, or spoken with doctors, you probably already know that medications are important. Even if you don't like the idea of taking medication, chances are good that your doctor is recommending medications for you or your loved one.

This book is about psychiatric medications known as antipsychotics. As their name suggests, antipsychotics help control symptoms of psychosis. For a person with schizophrenia, antipsychotics do much more. When an illness like schizophrenia strikes, these medications are a cornerstone of rehabilitation and the illness recovery process.

Antipsychotics have been around for almost 50 years. For most of those years, no new medications came along. Over the last 10 years, a series of new antipsychotics have been developed. While still not a cure, these newer medications have been breakthroughs for many people with schizophrenia. Many people feel better and recover to an extent that had hardly been thought possible.

These new medications have made life easier and better for lots of people with schizophrenia and other psychotic illnesses. Many people who continue to hear voices or have other psychotic symptoms on the older medications find that their symptoms are controlled better by one of the newer medications. The newer medications work better on parts of the schizophrenic illness that do not respond well to the older medications, such as lack of motivation or problems with concentration. Finally, the side effects of the newer medications are much easier for most people to live with than those of the older medications.

With all these advantages, why isn't everyone on one of the new medications? Because these medications are so new, many patients and family members don't know about them. Or, even if they know about the medications, they don't know whether to try one. For similar reasons, many doctors aren't certain about whether to recommend the new medications. Some doctors are reluctant to use them or are not sure how to go about switching patients from one medication to another.

We have written this book to give people more information so they can make better decisions about their treatment. We hope that it will help consumers and their families talk to psychiatrists and other clinicians about the advantages and problems of switching to an atypical antipsychotic. Although this book was written primarily for people who have schizophrenia or schizoaffective disorder, anyone who needs to take antipsychotics or has a family member who does may also find it helpful. The new medications are not for everyone who takes an antipsychotic medication, but everyone who takes antipsychotic medication should at least know about them.

The older antipsychotic medications are much more like each other than they are different. However, the newer medications are not only different from the older medications, but also quite different from one another. Although not much research has yet been done on this, it seems that some people respond better to one of the new antipsychotics than to another. This means that if the first medication does not work, it is worth trying a second and even a third. We hope this book will help consumers, their families, and their clinicians learn something about all the new medications. We also hope it will encourage them to keep trying to find the right medication.

Organization   This book is divided into six sections.

1. *Consumer Guide.* The consumer guide discusses the advantages and disadvantages of the new antipsychotic medications. It goes into detail about how to switch from an older antipsychotic to a new antipsychotic medication. It covers things to think about, why to switch, why not to switch, and how to do it. It is designed to be very practical and to answer many of the questions that people switching medication typically ask. We have done our best to avoid jargon without overly simplifying the material. Although it's written "for consumers," many families will also want to read this section to get answers to the questions they have about the new antipsychotics.

2. *Technical Information.* The second section is more technical. It gives more specific information about each of the new medications, side effects, and some of the technical issues involved in switching medications. It is designed for use by clinicians as well as by family members and consumers with more background in these topics. Referring to the glossary will help non-professionals use this section more easily. We expect that the information in this section will also be useful to mental health professionals in educating patients and their family members about the new medications.

3. *Paying for Medications.* The third section discusses some different ways to pay for the new antipsychotic medications. Although the atypical medications have some very definite advantages over the older ones, they are also much more expensive.

4. *Glossary.* This section provides definitions in simple, clear language for the more technical terms used in the book.

5. *Resources.* This section lists helpful books, articles, and videos. It also provides information concerning organizations, helplines, and Internet resources that provide information and support for patients and families.

6. *Handouts.* This section provides a set of handouts that consumers, their families, and their clinicians can copy and use.

How to Use this Book

This book is not meant to be read cover to cover. People with different needs, agendas, and knowledge backgrounds will be looking at this book. Where you start and how you use it depend on your needs.

- *If you are taking antipsychotic medications.* If you have been on one medication for a long time and don't know much about other options, start with the Consumer Guide. It will walk you through the process of deciding whether you should stay on your current medication or change medications.

  If you already know about the new medications but don't know much about what to expect from switching medications, start with chapter 5 in the Consumer Guide. Should you have more questions after reading the Consumer Guide, read the parts of the Technical Information section that address your questions or concerns. You can use the Glossary to look up any unfamiliar words or terms.

- *If you know someone on antipsychotic medication.* If a family member only recently developed psychosis, you may be new to this whole area of treatment. Your life may be in turmoil right now, and it would not be surprising if you are overwhelmed with questions and concerns. If so, you may find a basic orientation helpful. You might want to start with the Glossary to get familiar with the medical language and then move on to the Consumer Guide and then the "Overview of the Treatment of Schizophrenia" in the Handouts section.

If you are a family member of someone who has been ill for a long time, chances are good that you already know the basics of medications and psychosis. You might want to go straight to the Technical Information section and look up the specific areas that address your concerns. If you want to try to understand the issues from your relative's point of view, you might read the Consumer Guide.

- *If you are a prescribing physician.* The Technical Information section provides an update on the psychopharmacology of the new agents. The one-page-per-issue formatting allows for easy photocopying for patient and staff education. The Handouts can be used to supplement patient teaching and psychoeducation about the newer medications.

- *If you are a mental health clinician.* Providing up-to-date information about antipsychotic medication is a basic part of psychoeducation for patients and families. The Consumer Guide uses plain English to explain the medications and can be used as a template for teaching these topics. Photocopying the Handouts for consumers and families will help to reinforce the material. The "Knowledge Assessment" handout can be used either to evaluate the effectiveness of the psychoeducation or as a way to reinforce the material.

This book is meant to help patients and families understand some of the issues in deciding whether to try a new medication, and what they might expect during and after switching medication. Please remember that no author can know all the facts about you or your loved one, and no advice or suggestions offered here can substitute for your own treatment plan. Nevertheless, we hope that this book helps you know what to ask for or look for should you decide to change medications.

Breakthroughs
in
Antipsychotic
Medications

A Guide for Consumers, Families, and Clinicians

Part I

Consumer Guide

What is this guide about?

This guide was written to help you understand

- What antipsychotic medications do
- Some of the differences between antipsychotic medications
- How switching to an atypical antipsychotic medication might help you
- How to decide with your family and your treatment team if it's a good idea for you to switch medications
- How to tell when it's a good time to switch medications
- What problems you might have if you switch medications
- How switching is usually done

How can this guide help me?

We hope you'll use what you learn to be an active partner in making decisions about your recovery. The more you understand about your illness and your medication, the more confidently you can talk with mental health professionals. You can work *with* your treatment team. You can make educated suggestions about what might help you. You can help make decisions that can make your life better.

> *Knowledge can help me be an active partner in making decisions about my recovery.*

1 What Are Antipsychotic Medications and What Do They Do?

Antipsychotic medications are used to treat a number of different kinds of symptoms. This chapter describes the types of symptoms for which these medications may be prescribed and how medication can help.

What Are Antipsychotic Medications?

The prefix *anti* means "to stop or block." For example, if a group is anti-discrimination, they work to stop or block discrimination.

The word *psychotic* is used to describe odd or unusual changes in a person's perceptions (five senses), thoughts, feelings, and behavior. Some common examples of psychotic symptoms are hallucinations, delusions, and thought disorder.

So, *antipsychotic* medications work to stop or block unusual changes in a person's perceptions, thoughts, feelings, and behavior. Antipsychotic medications help stop the psychotic symptoms of mental illness.

What's the difference between psychotic symptoms and a psychiatric diagnosis?

Doctors use the word *symptoms* to mean something that alerts the patient or a doctor that there may be a problem. But a symptom doesn't tell the doctor the diagnosis. For example, a fever is a symptom. Having a fever means there is a problem, but the fever doesn't pinpoint the exact cause of the problem. There are many causes of fever: infection, flu, and medication reactions, to name a few. Psychosis is a symptom. There are many different causes of psychosis, including schizophrenia, mood disorders, medical problems, drug reactions, and severe stress. Antipsychotics treat psychotic symptoms, no matter what the cause.

> *Antipsychotic medications help stop psychotic symptoms.*

What symptoms are treated with antipsychotic medications?

Antipsychotic medications are used to treat psychotic symptoms that occur in psychiatric disorders such as schizophrenia and mood disorders (bipolar and major depressive disorders). In this book, we focus on the use of antipsychotics to treat schizophrenia and schizophrenia-like illnesses. If you don't have a diagnosis of schizophrenia or schizoaffective disorder, talk to your treatment team about if and how the information in this book applies to your illness.

What about Other Psychiatric Medications?

Many people on antipsychotic medications are also treated with medications to counteract the neurologic side effects of these medications. The side-effect medications are called *anticholinergics* or *antiparkinson* medications. Examples include Cogentin (benztropine), Artane (trihexyphenidyl), and Symmetrel (amantadine). Sometimes Inderal (propranolol) is given to counteract a feeling of restlessness, known as akathisia, which is caused by medications.

Keep in mind that there are several other major classes of psychiatric medications:

- *Antidepressants* are used for the treatment of depression. Examples include Prozac (fluoxetine), Zoloft (sertraline), and Tofranil (imipramine).
- *Mood stabilizers* are used in the treatment of bipolar (manic-depressive) disorders. Examples of mood stabilizing medications include lithium, Depakote (divalproex), and Tegretol (carbamazepine).
- *Antianxiety medications* are used to help reduce anxiety or to treat insomnia. Examples of antianxiety medications include Ativan (lorazepam), Klonopin (clonazepam), and BuSpar (buspirone).

Many people are treated with several classes of medications. This book only briefly describes these other classes of medications; you will need to refer to other books if you want more information on these kinds of medications.

What Are the Symptoms of Schizophrenia?

Many of the symptoms of schizophrenia can be divided into two groups: (1) positive symptoms and (2) negative symptoms. There can be other symptoms as well, but positive and negative symptoms happen to almost every person with schizophrenia.

What Are Positive Symptoms?

Positive symptoms are the changes that mental illness makes in a person's perceptions (five senses), thoughts, feelings, and behavior. Used this way, "positive" doesn't mean good. Rather, it describes symptoms that should not be there. Positive symptoms are often called *psychotic symptoms*.

Which of these positive symptoms do you experience?

__ Hallucinations (changes in your senses, such as hearing voices or seeing unusual things)

__ Delusions (believing things that no one else believes, such as an unshakable belief that the CIA is following you when no one else thinks that this is happening, or believing that you are Jesus)

__ Thought disorder (changes in how you think, such as having trouble thinking clearly, becoming easily confused, or having trouble concentrating)

__ Paranoia (feeling fearful about troubling or worrisome perceptions and thoughts)

__ None of these positive symptoms applies to me.

What causes psychotic symptoms?

Research suggests that people with schizophrenia (and other similar illnesses) have a chemical imbalance in the brain. People with these illnesses who experience psychotic symptoms appear to have too much of a chemical called dopamine in their brain. Drugs that increase dopamine in the brain cause people to become psychotic, and medications that stop or block dopamine in the brain decrease psychotic symptoms.

What is dopamine?

Dopamine is a neurotransmitter. *Neuro* means brain. A *transmitter* sends messages. So a *neurotransmitter* is a chemical messenger in the brain that nerve cells use to communicate with each other. Dopamine is one of the brain's chemical messengers. Psychotic symptoms appear to be related to having too much dopamine in certain areas of the brain.

What happens when there's too much dopamine?

Too much dopamine makes your brain play tricks on you. When dopamine gets out of balance, it tricks your brain by sending weird messages. Too much dopamine can alter your senses, create voices, confuse your thinking, convince you of false ideas, and make your mind do lots of other strange things. When dopamine gets out of balance, your perceptions (five senses), thoughts, feelings, and behaviors change.

> *Medications that stop or block dopamine in the brain decrease psychotic symptoms.*

What Are Negative Symptoms?

Negative symptoms are the abilities or motivation that people lose when they have a mental illness. People with negative symptoms often have problems doing normal, everyday things that used to be easy. It becomes hard for them to do even simple things like taking a shower, talking to a friend, or filling out a job application, even if it is something that the person very much wants to do. People with negative symptoms often keep to themselves more.

What are some examples of negative symptoms?

There are lots of different negative symptoms. You can tell positive symptoms from negative symptoms by doing the "don't" test. If the word "don't" fits in front of the symptom, then it's probably a negative symptom. The ability or motivation is taken away by the illness. Mental illness subtracts abilities and motivation. Some of the most common negative symptoms are listed below.

Which negative symptoms do you have?

__ I don't take a bath, shower, brush my teeth, or wear clean clothes as often as I used to.

__ I don't smile, joke, or laugh at funny things.

__ I don't enjoy things, don't feel good, don't feel pleasure anymore.

__ I don't talk unless someone talks to me first.

__ I don't have much to say to people (I only say a word or two when people ask me questions because I can't think of anything else to say).

__ I don't have the energy or interest to go places anymore (church, stores, friends' homes).

__ I don't do anything most of the time (just stay in bed, sit around, or stare at the TV unless someone tells me to do something).

__ I don't cook, clean house, do laundry, or do yardwork.

__ None of these negative symptoms applies to me.

> *Negative symptoms take away the person's capabilities and motivation.*

Many people think negative symptoms are just a sign of laziness, but that isn't true. When people have negative symptoms, it is because their brains don't work right, which makes it hard for them to do the things they used to do.

Which of the following things do you have trouble with?

__ Thinking about what needs to be done

__ Planning ahead

___ Concentrating

___ Finishing things

___ Pulling together enough energy to get things done

___ Enjoying things

___ Thinking of things to say or do

___ I don't have trouble with any of the things listed.

> *Negative symptoms are caused by a brain disorder, not laziness.*

Has anyone ever called you lazy because of negative symptoms?

How did you feel?

What did you say or do?

Which of the symptoms listed above bother you the most?

What problems do they cause for you?

> *Note to friends and family members: Because negative symptoms are "invisible," it can be difficult to understand just how hard it is to do anything. Think back to the last time you were in bed with the flu. Remember how hard it was to get dressed? To get up to go to the bathroom? To see visitors? Having negative symptoms is like having the flu, but unlike the flu they don't go away.*

Do negative symptoms go away on their own?

The answer is both yes and no. Many problems can look like negative symptoms in the short run. For example, a bad flu can cause all the negative symptoms. Or depression or medication side effects can make the person seem to have negative symptoms. Things that look like negative symptoms, if they are caused by flu, depression, or side effects, go away.

But persistent negative symptoms don't go away. They continue, usually for years. If you have a diagnosis of schizophrenia and your negative symptoms have been around for a long time, it is unlikely that the negative symptoms will completely go away on their own.

What causes negative symptoms?

This is a new area of brain research and we don't have many of the answers yet. It is possible that negative symptoms may be related to a different chemical imbalance than positive symptoms. The two types of chemical imbalance may even be in different parts of the brain.

So far, research has shown the following:

- People with negative symptoms may have chemical imbalances in certain areas of the brain.
- Negative symptoms may have to do with too little dopamine in certain parts of the brain.
- Because the older antipsychotics lower dopamine levels, they often don't work well for negative symptoms.
- The newer medications seem to do a better job of balancing all of the brain chemicals, including dopamine and serotonin. This can help decrease negative symptoms while still controlling positive symptoms.
- When negative symptoms decrease, people can regain some of their ability to do many of the normal, everyday things they used to do before they became ill.

Do Antipsychotic Medications Help Reduce Symptoms?

Yes. Antipsychotic medication corrects the chemical imbalance in the brain and helps get rid of symptoms. That's the medication's job. When medication does a good job, it helps stop or control your symptoms.

> *Antipsychotics help stop or reduce symptoms by correcting the chemical imbalance in the brain.*

Will medication stop all my symptoms?

Many people find that their antipsychotic medication doesn't get rid of all their symptoms—it only does part of the job. The medicine controls some, but not all, of the symptoms. Sometimes a medication just decreases a person's symptoms. The symptoms don't bother the person as much as they used to, but they're still there. Other people find that the medication decreases how often they have symptoms. Instead of having symptoms most of the time, with medication there might be periods when the symptoms go away.

How well does your medicine work?

__ The medication I take does an excellent job. It gets rid of all my symptoms.

__ The medication I take does part of the job.

    __ It gets rid of some, but not all, of my symptoms. Some are gone and some are not.

    __ It decreases some of my symptoms. The symptoms are still there, but they don't bother me as much as they used to.

    __ It works for my positive symptoms, not my negative symptoms.

__ The medication I take doesn't work at all. It doesn't seem to do anything. I still have all the same symptoms. None of them have gone away.

__ I'm not sure how well the medication I take is working. (You might want to ask your doctor, therapist, or family for their opinion.)

2 What Kinds of Antipsychotic Medications Are Available and How Are They Different?

Two kinds of antipsychotic medications are available: (1) older "conventional" antipsychotics and (2) newer "atypical" antipsychotics. Look at the *antipsychotic medication charts* below. Table 2.1 lists the older antipsychotic medications. Table 2.2 lists the new antipsychotics we have now, plus one that is expected to be available soon. There are lots of medications to choose from. Look at the charts and find the medication you are taking now. Is it an old or a new antipsychotic?

Table 2.1. Conventional Antipsychotics

Brand Name	Generic Name	Usual Dosage Range Adults (mg/day)
Haldol	haloperidol	2–20
Loxitane	loxapine	25–100
Mellaril	thioridazine	150–600
Moban	molindone	50–225
Navane	thiothixene	5–30
Prolixin	fluphenazine	2–20
Serentil	mesoridazine	75–300
Stelazine	trifluoperazine	5–30
Thorazine	chlorpromazine	200–800
Trilafon	perphenazine	8–64

Table 2.2. Atypical Antipsychotics

Brand Name	Generic Name	Usual Dosage Range Adults (mg/day)
Clozaril	clozapine	300–800
Risperdal	risperidone	3–6
Seroquel	quetiapine	300–750
Zeldox*	ziprasidone	40–160
Zyprexa	olanzapine	10–20

*Currently in development

Do All Antipsychotic Medications Work about the Same?

No. The new antipsychotic medications work differently than the old ones. They seem to work in different ways. For many people, the newer medications do some jobs better than the older medications. The newer medications cause fewer side effects involving muscle and body movements. And, for some people, they work better on positive and/or negative symptoms. Some people also find that the newer medications work better for depression and anxiety, or help them think more clearly.

What Are the "Conventional" Antipsychotics?

"Conventional" antipsychotic medications (see Table 2.1) have been around for a long time. The oldest one (Thorazine) has been used since the 1950s. All the conventional antipsychotics are closely related to each other. They work in similar ways. The conventional antipsychotics all do about the same job in the brain. They all correct brain chemistry by working on the dopamine systems in the brain.

Which of the conventional antipsychotic medications have you taken?

What Are the "Atypical" Antipsychotics?

All the *"atypical" antipsychotic medications* listed in Table 2.2 are available now, except Zeldox, which is currently in development. Other new antipsychotics are being tested and will be ready for use soon. You may know of some more new antipsychotic medications that have come out since this book was written. The more medications there are to choose from, the greater the chances of finding one that works well for you.

Have you ever taken an atypical antipsychotic? If so, which one(s)?

__ Clozaril (clozapine)

__ Risperdal (risperidone)

__ Seroquel (quetiapine)

__ Zeldox (ziprasidone)

__ Zyprexa (olanzapine)

__ I have never taken an atypical antipsychotic.

__ Not sure (Look on the inside back cover of this book to see if you recognize pictures of the new medications.)

How long did you take the medication? A few days? A few weeks? A few months? If you were on a medication for less than a month, you may not have taken it long enough to tell whether it works for you. See chapter 8.

How well did the new medication(s) work for you?

What problems did you have?

Why are the new antipsychotic medications called "atypical"?

Atypical means something different or unusual. In this case, something different also means something better. The newer antipsychotic medicines are often called "atypical" because they work on different neurotransmitters (chemical messengers in the brain) than the old medications do. The side effects of conventional antipsychotics often make people feel uncomfortable. This is much less likely when people take the new medications. Also, the conventional antipsychotics often *don't* work very well for negative symptoms while the newer ones often work better.

> *Atypical antipsychotic medications*
> *work on different chemical messengers in the brain.*

Pretty soon we'll have to come up with a new name for this group of medications because they are being used a lot more often. In the years to come, there will be many more new antipsychotics to choose from. They won't be so unusual anymore.

What's different about the new antipsychotic medications?

Many people who are taking the new atypical antipsychotics find that they are doing better in ways that seemed impossible when they were taking one of the older, conventional antipsychotic medications. They are able to function better and they feel better. They often find that they can do things they enjoy again for the first time in a long time. Most important, they often feel more "normal" than they did while taking one of the older antipsychotics. Instead of spending most of their time and energy dealing with their illness, they are able to put their energy into goals that are important to them. This happens because the new "atypical" medications are different than the old "conventional" antipsychotics in several ways.

> *New antipsychotic medications*
> *often work better for*
> *both positive and negative symptoms.*

The new atypical antipsychotics

- Work on positive symptoms while doing a better job on negative symptoms
- Help you think more clearly and focus better
- Are less likely to make you restless, make your hands shake, make your muscles stiff, or make your mouth dry
- Will probably help you get more of your life back, the longer you take them

Don't the old antipsychotics do as good a job on negative symptoms?

Usually not. One of the most important differences between old and new antipsychotic medications is that new atypical antipsychotics do a better job of controlling negative symptoms. For most people with schizophrenia, the old antipsychotics don't work as well on negative symptoms.

> *Atypical antipsychotic medications often do a better job than the older ones of reducing negative symptoms.*

What Are the Side Effects?

Side effects refer to a medication's *unwanted* effects. Any medication can have side effects. Here, we'll describe some of the more common and bothersome side effects that can happen with antipsychotic medications. There are extrapyramidal side effects, anticholinergic side effects, as well as other kinds. Keep in mind that this list does not cover every side effect, and also keep in mind that everyone is different; some people may get many side effects, and other people may not have any side effects problems at all!

What are extrapyramidal side effects?

There are two kinds of cells in the brain that control muscle movements. The first kind of cell is shaped like a pyramid. These are called pyramidal cells. The other kind of cells are called extrapyramidal cells. The older antipsychotic medications affect these extrapyramidal cells and can cause the muscle-movement side effects listed below. This is the reason these side effects are called extrapyramidal side effects (EPS). Some kinds of EPS can cause problems that look just like the person's psychiatric symptoms. When that happens, it is sometimes hard to figure out whether the problem is from the person's symptoms or the medication used to treat those symptoms. The new antipsychotics have only a very small effect on the extrapyramidal cells and so are much less likely to cause EPS.

The older antipsychotics often cause EPS. These include

- Akathisia—feeling restless and unable to sit still, legs bouncing up and down
- Akinesia—feeling slowed down "like a zombie"
- Tremor—hands shaking
- Muscle rigidity—muscles becoming stiff or tight, or drawing up
- Dystonia—muscle spasms that feel like writer's cramp or a charley horse

Many of these EPS can be treated with side-effect medications called anticholinergics. However, anticholinergics have their own side effects.

What are anticholinergic side effects?

Choline is a chemical that nerve cells use to communicate. Many of the medications used to treat EPS work by blocking this brain chemical. This is the reason why many of the side effect medications are called *anti-cholinergics*. Commonly used anticholinergic medications include Cogentin (benztropine), which is often used in the United States, and Akineton (biperiden), which is often used in Europe. Also, some of the antipsychotics have built-in anticholinergic effects. Examples of antipsychotics that are also anticholinergic include Mellaril (thioridazine), Thorazine (chlorpromazine), and Clozaril (clozapine).

Anticholinergic side effects usually disrupt normal body secretions, like saliva or tears. Common and predictable ones are

- dry mouth
- blurry vision
- constipation
- difficulty urinating

If you have any of these problems, chances are they are from the medications you are taking.

What are some other side effects?

1. *Amenorrhea and galactorrhea.* Some antipsychotic medications can cause high levels of the hormone prolactin. High prolactin levels fool a woman's hormonal system into believing she is pregnant, which causes her to miss menstrual periods. This is referred to as amenorrhea. High prolactin levels can also cause abnormal breast milk leakage, which is called galactorrhea.

2. *Sedation (sleepiness).* Both the newer and older antipsychotics can cause sedation—make people feel more sleepy and tired. Sedation is most likely to happen when the medication is started or the dose is raised. Some of the medications are more likely to cause sedation than others. Higher doses are also more likely to cause sleepiness. Sometimes the sleepiness is temporary and goes away on its own.

3. *Weight gain.* Antipsychotics can cause people to gain weight or make it harder for them to lose weight. Some of the antipsychotic medications are more likely to cause weight gain than others. Unfortunately, while the newer medications are better for EPS problems, weight gain is a more common problem with the newer antipsychotics than with the older conventional antipsychotics.

4. *Sexual difficulties.* Antipsychotic medications can cause many kinds of sexual difficulties, for both men and women. However, there are many causes of sexual problems. It often is hard to figure out whether a sexual problem is due to the medication or another reason. Very little is known about how often antipsychotics cause sexual problems or whether the newer medications are less likely to cause sexual problems.

What about tardive dyskinesia?

Tardive dyskinesia (TD) causes uncontrolled mouth, tongue, and muscle movements or exaggerated eye blinking. Each year about 4 or 5 people out of a 100 who take the older medications get TD. It's not certain, but the new antipsychotics may be less likely to cause TD. Fewer people seem to get TD while taking the newer antipsychotics. Your chance of getting TD on the newer medications is probably less than half that of getting it on the older medications.

Do the new antipsychotic medications have side effects?

Yes. All medications have side effects, including the new ones. If you expect not to have *any* side effects from a new medication, chances are you'll be disappointed! Talk with your treatment team about what side effects to watch for with the new medication you're considering. (You can also read about the most common side effects of the new antipsychotics in the *Medication Fact Sheets.*)

What are the side–effect differences between the older and newer medications?

The most important side effect benefit from the newer medications is that they are much less likely to cause EPS (but some EPS can still happen, even on the newer medications). This is a major advantage for many people, and one of the reasons that the new medications are breakthroughs. An extra benefit from fewer EPS is that the anticholinergic side-effect medications are less likely to be needed, so there may be fewer anticholinergic side effects to contend with. Another side-effect benefit from most of the newer medications is that women continue to have normal menstrual cycles.

Probably the biggest problem with the newer medications is weight gain. The new medications are more likely to cause weight gain, and more people have weight problems on the newer medications than on the older medications.

> The atypical antipsychotics are much less likely to cause EPS.

Should I Change Medications? If you are interested in trying a new antipsychotic medication, you need to consider the six important questions listed below. Each question is discussed in detail in the chapter shown in parentheses.

1. How do I know if trying a new medication might be a good idea for me? *(Chapter 3)*

2. How do I know if switching might *not* be a good idea for me? *(Chapter 4)*

3. When is the best time to change medications? *(Chapter 5)*

4. Which medication should I switch to? *(Chapter 6)*

5. How is switching done? *(Chapter 7)*

6. What will happen after I switch? *(Chapter 8)*

Discussing and answering these six questions will help you, your family, and your treatment team figure out if the new medications are right for you. We know that the newer medications *are* better for some people. You need to figure out if they might be better for you. You also need to know how to switch medications safely and successfully.

Are you interested in trying one of the new medications?

___ Yes, because

___ No, because

I'm Already on One of the Newer Medications. Does This Material Still Apply to Me?

Much of the time, the issues are the same for people on the older medications as they are for people on the newer medications. The most important thing is how well the medication works for you. If you've already been on one of the newer medications for a while (over 6 months) but have not had a satisfactory response, you should consider the pros and cons of switching to another atypical medication in exactly the same way you would if you were taking an older, conventional medication. Or, if you are on a newer medication and you have some bothersome and persistent side effects, you might want to think of switching, as each of the atypicals has a somewhat different side-effect profile. We'll cover the specifics of all the newer medications later on.

3 How Do I Know If Switching Might Be a Good Idea for Me?

This question is very hard to answer. The atypical medications are so new that there isn't much research to give us clues about which medication might work well for you. Doctors don't fully understand who is most likely to do well on one of the newer medications. However, we know from experience that many people need to try several different antipsychotic medications before they find one medication, or a combination of medications, that works best for them.

What Are Some Reasons for Switching?

Many people find the newer antipsychotic medications do a better job of treating positive (psychotic) symptoms that the older medications have not controlled. The atypical medications also work much better on negative symptoms. The new medications are also less likely to cause extrapyramidal side effects (such as restlessness, shaking hands, and a "zombie-like" feeling). The atypical antipsychotics may be less likely to cause tardive dyskinesia (TD) than the conventional antipsychotics (but this has not been proven). Finally, most of the newer medications don't disrupt the hormones in a way that may interfere with the normal menstrual cycle (periods).

> *Switching is a good idea for some people.*

What reasons do you have for switching?

__ The antipsychotic medication I'm taking now only controls some of my positive symptoms even though I take it the right way, every day.

__ My symptoms are interfering with

    __ My relationships/friendships

    __ My ability to work

    __ My ability to live where I want to live

__ My ability to take care of myself

__ My ability to enjoy life

__ My goals (work, school, etc.)

__ My doctor says that the problems I'm having with my medication can't be fixed by changing the dose or waiting a little longer.

__ I have negative symptoms that bother me or keep me from reaching my goals.

__ I have extrapyramidal side effects (EPS) (see p. 31) that bother me.

__ I've gained a lot of weight on one of the new medications that can't be controlled by diet or exercise.

__ There's a realistic chance that one of the new antipsychotic medications will work better for me and I want to try it.

__ My menstrual periods have stopped because of my medication, and this really bothers me.

__ I'm sleepy all the time because of my medication.

__ I have other reasons for switching, such as _____.

Doctors call these reasons to switch *indications*. Because lots of people who take antipsychotic medications for mental illness still have some symptoms of the illness or some side effects, most people can find an indication to switch. The hard part is figuring out if switching is worth the *risk*.

How many of those statements applied to you?

__ I marked _____ of the reasons for switching. The most important one is

__ None of those statements fits my situation. I don't really have any reasons for switching.

__ I'm not sure how well these statements apply to me.

If you marked one or more of the reasons for switching, you might want to talk to your family and treatment team about the possibility of switching antipsychotic medications—*remember, though, it's very important not to make any changes in your medication without talking to your doctor.* This book can only help teach and guide you. Your doctor has the skills and knowledge to help you with your individual situation.

> *It's very important not to make any changes in your medication without talking to your doctor.*

Do you think switching might be a possibility for you?

___ Yes, because

___ No, because

How Do I Know If Switching Is Worth the Risk?

To figure out if you should consider switching to a new medication, you also need to think about the possible risks. You, your family, and your treatment team need to decide whether or not switching is worth the risks involved.

No one can tell for sure ahead of time whether a new medication will work for you, or whether you'll be more comfortable on a new medication. With that in mind, the chances of success depend in part on your past treatment history, the reason(s) for switching, and what medication you'll be trying.

- If you are on an older medication and are switching because of EPS side effects, chances are pretty good that one of the newer atypical antipsychotics can do a better job than the medication you're taking right now.
- If you are thinking of switching because of other side effects, such as sexual problems, loss of menstrual periods, or weight gain, you will need to ask your doctor about the differences between the side effects of the medication you're on right now and the one you're trying.
- If you want to switch because of positive symptoms that don't go away, there is a fair chance that a new medication may help. The single best medication for continued positive symptoms is clozapine and that is more likely to work for you than any of the others.
- If you are switching because of negative symptoms that don't go away, don't expect any medication to completely cure your negative symptoms! All of the newer medications seem to help negative symptoms for many people, but they work gradually and slowly over a long period of time.

Chapter 4 goes over risks and reasons for *not* switching medication. If something there applies to you, weigh the pros and cons of switching with your family and treatment team.

> *You can never know for sure whether a new medication will work better for you.*

4 How Do I Know If Switching Might *Not* Be a Good Idea for Me?

There are a number of good reasons for staying on your current medication. Many people worry that if they change medications they might have a symptom flare-up (their symptoms might get worse instead of better). This is a very realistic concern. Probably the biggest risk in switching antipsychotic medications is that your symptoms could get worse. Old symptoms that have been controlled by your current medication could reappear. Sometimes it might feel like the changes in medication are shaking up your whole nervous system. You might become more anxious or tense.

> *Switching* isn't *a good idea for some people.*

Some people have an increase in symptoms while switching medications. However, many people switch without having a symptom flare-up. Unfortunately, there is no way to tell ahead of time who will and who won't get extra symptoms while switching. When symptom flare-ups do happen, if you stick it out and finish switching medications, the symptoms usually decrease again with time.

What Are Some Reasons for Not Switching?

Listed below are some good reasons for staying on the medication you're taking now. Do any of these fit your situation?

__ *I'm satisfied with my medication.* I don't have any symptoms that are troublesome or side effects that particularly bother me. I'd rather put up with the symptoms I have.

__ *I'm dealing with stress, conflicts, or other problems right now.* My symptoms are worse because of the problems I'm having. My treatment team and I think I'll feel better once I've solved my other problems (no medication can fix personal problems).

__ *I don't want to take a chance of relapsing right now.* The last time my symptoms got worse was awful! I'm in the middle of something important (for example, school, a job, a relationship) and I can't afford to rock the boat right now.

__ *I don't want to put up with the side effects (such as weight gain) that I might get from atypical medications.* I'm really worried about the possibility of gaining weight. I know I wouldn't stick with a diet or exercise program to keep my weight down. I'm not gaining weight with the medication I'm taking now.

__ *I'm not sure I'll be able to afford the new medication.* Do any of the statements below fit your situation?

> __ How would I pay for it? I don't have any insurance and the new medications are expensive.
>
> __ I have Medicaid, but I don't know if it covers any of the new medications.
>
> __ I have Medicare, but it doesn't pay for medications, and I can't afford to pay for one of the new medications myself.
>
> __ My family pays for my medication and I'm not sure they can afford the new medications.
>
> If you have concerns about affording the new medication, read Part III of this book, "Paying for Medications," or talk with someone on your treatment team who can help you figure out how you might be able to pay for the new medication.

> *If you're not sure*
> *about how to pay for the newer medications,*
> *read "Paying for Medications" on p. 151.*

__ I'm not sure I'll be able to keep taking a new medication for other reasons, such as:

Are There Other Good Reasons for Not Switching?

Yes. Listed below are examples of times when switching may *not* be a good idea. Do any of these apply to you?

__ *I've just gotten over a relapse and I haven't been stable for very long.* Don't switch just after a relapse. Be patient and let your brain chemistry stabilize. If you still want to switch medications a few months from now, talk it over with your treatment team. It is much safer to switch medications after you've been stable for a few months.

__ *My family is against the idea.* If someone in your family is strongly against your switching medication, it's a good idea to put off switching until you know their concerns. Often the person is worried that you might get your worst symptoms back. *If your doctor wants you to switch and someone in your family is against it, tell your doctor about your family's concerns.* It is much better to work these issues out ahead of time and be sure everyone is on the same wavelength.

__*I haven't been out of the hospital very long.* If you've been discharged from the hospital in the past few months, then switching probably isn't a good plan. The medication you're taking helped you get out of the hospital. Changing now could cause a relapse and you might end up in the hospital again. It is much safer to switch medications after you've been out of the hospital for about 6 months.

__*I'm taking a long-acting shot (Haldol [haloperidol] or Prolixin [fluphenazine]), and the shots have helped me more than pills.* None of the atypical antipsychotics currently come in long-acting shots. If long-acting injections have helped you more than pills, it may be better to stay on the shots. Ask your doctor or treatment team how important they think it is for you to be on the shots. If they really think the shots are better for you, they might be reluctant to switch you to pills.

> *None of the new antipsychotics currently comes in long-acting shots.*

__*I've already switched to a new medication, but I haven't taken it long enough to see if it will work for me.* It takes up to 3 months to figure out whether a new medication is better for you. If you're doing better on a new medication but still have some symptoms, you should probably wait at least a year before switching a second time.

__*I'm doing better on Clozaril (clozapine) but I don't like getting the weekly blood tests done or I'm having troublesome side effects.* Think twice before trying to change from Clozaril. The chances of relapse— getting sick again—are much higher for people being switched from Clozaril. Consider waiting until more is learned about the safest way to switch from Clozaril to other medications.

__*I'm drinking alcohol pretty often or I'm taking street drugs.* Using street drugs or drinking more than just one beer every so often will make your symptoms worse and keep your medication from working. Changing your medication while you're still drinking or using street drugs won't help you very much. You're probably better off getting help for the alcohol or drug problem before you switch medications. At the very least, you need to be honest with your treatment team. They need to know what's going on.

> *No antipsychotic medication*
> *can fully help your mental illness*
> *while you're drinking or drugging.*

— *My doctor doesn't think it is a good idea to change medications right now.* It goes without saying that your doctor is a key participant in the decision about whether or not to change medications. Not only is your doctor the only one who can prescribe medications but your doctor is also responsible for monitoring your symptoms and side effects during the switch. If you and your doctor don't see eye to eye on this idea, you should ask your doctor about the rationale for not changing medications. It may have to do with one of the reasons in this list. Your doctor may want to try something else first, such as adjusting your medication dose or prescribing a new medication (such as an antidepressant or a mood stabilizer) to take along with your old antipsychotic. Or, perhaps you doctor is not comfortable with the new antipsychotics or does not have enough time to change your medications (it takes more time to prescribe a new medication than to continue the one you're on). If you disagree with your doctor's advice, you could ask for a consultation or see another qualified psychiatrist for a second opinion.

Do you think switching would be a good idea for you?

— Yes, because

— No, because

What If It *Is* a Good Idea for Me to Switch, But I'm Worried about Having a Symptom Flare-Up?

Many people who take antipsychotic medications face the same problem. They're not totally satisfied with the medication they're taking, but they're worried about getting worse if they try a new medicine. Fortunately, there are things that can be done to decrease the risks of having a symptom flare-up while you're changing medications. Chapter 5 ("When Is the Best Time to Switch?") will help you choose a time that can increase your chances of switching successfully. Chapter 7 ("The Six Steps in Making the Switch") will explain how and why doctors do a "medication crossover" when switching.

> *Balance hope with realism.*
> *No medication is guaranteed*
> *to work better for you.*

Can I Count on Getting Better If I Switch Medications?

You need to balance hope with realism. No medication is guaranteed to work better for you. Even if it does a good job for many other people, it may not work well for you. Switch medications with the *hope* that the new medication will work better. Realize it may take trying more than one new medication to find one that works for you.

If you're still having symptoms on the medicine you're taking now, you might continue to have some symptoms after switching medications. The newer medication might work better than the one you are on now, but it might not control all your symptoms.

> *Even if the new medication*
> *does a much better job,*
> *it cannot cure schizophrenia.*

Should I Stop Taking Medication If the One I'm Taking Isn't Working Well?

No. Studies have shown beyond a shadow of doubt that, for the vast majority of people with serious mental illness, *staying on antipsychotic medication is* necessary *to move toward recovery.*

> *If you decide not to switch,*
> *continue your current medication,*
> *even if there are problems.*

Have you ever quit taking your antipsychotic medication?

What happened?

> *Stopping antipsychotics*
> *almost always causes a relapse*
> *for people with schizophrenia.*

5 When Is the Best Time to Switch?

Let's assume that you, your family, and your treatment team have agreed that switching to a new antipsychotic medication is a good idea. The next job is timing the switch. Choosing the right time to switch can increase your chances of success.

What Makes One Time Better than Another for Switching Medications?

The pointers listed below can help you, your family, and your treatment team figure out if this is a good time for you to switch. Are most or all of the statements true for you?

___ I've been pretty stable for a while, but I'm still having bothersome symptoms or side effects that just don't go away.

___ I can make switching a priority over other things for a few months.

___ My family and I are willing to put up with some hassles and the possibility of some extra symptoms for the next few months.

___ I don't have other stressful things coming up (such as a new job, starting school, taking exams, moving, or changing treatment programs).

___ I'm able to see my doctor, therapist, or case manager more often for the next few months.

___ There are people (such as doctor, therapist, case manager, and family members) I can depend on who can be around and see me through the switching period.

___ I won't be going away on a trip or vacation for the next few months.

Is it a good idea to switch *right after* recovering from a relapse?

Not usually. When you've just recovered from a relapse, your brain is struggling to keep itself in balance. This is a time when your brain is most sensitive to chemical changes. Switching medications during this time can throw it out of balance again and you'd run the risk of another relapse. After a relapse or hospitalization, you should wait about 6 months before switching to a new antipsychotic.

> *It's usually a good idea to wait about 6 months*
> *after getting over a relapse*
> *before switching to a new antipsychotic.*

Is it *always* a bad idea to switch *right after* a relapse?

No. Adding one of the new medications after a relapse might make sense if you relapsed because the old medication wasn't working very well. Then, there's a good chance the old medication won't help your brain chemistry stay in balance enough to keep you stable down the road. You may do better if your doctor adds one of the new medications to your old medication, then slowly decreases the old medicine for several months before stopping it.

It might also make sense to slowly switch to a new medication if your old medication was causing a lot of side effects. This would be especially true if you relapsed because your side effects were so bad you quit taking your medicine.

When was your last hospitalization or relapse?

> *Sometimes it makes sense*
> *to start a new antipsychotic after a relapse,*
> *especially if you stopped your medication*
> *because of side effects.*

Do I need to be hospitalized to switch medication?

No. Switching medications is almost always done out of the hospital. If your treatment team is available and you are willing to stick it out, the new medication can be started safely and monitored while you are an outpatient. The reasons people need hospitalization have more to do with whether or not they are safe at home and their symptoms are under control.

I'm in the hospital right now. Is it a good idea to switch in the hospital?

It depends. Actually, one of the few good things about being hospitalized is that it is often easier to change someone's medications while they are in the hospital. The hassles of the medication adjustments are taken care of by the nurses, and side effects are carefully monitored.

Whether or not it's a good idea for you to switch depends on *why* you are in the hospital. If you are in the hospital because the medication you've been taking hasn't worked well enough to keep you out of the hospital, then switching medications makes sense. Or if it's hard for you to switch medications when you're at home, then you might want to consider switching while you're in the hospital.

> *Sometimes it's a good idea to switch while you're in the hospital.*

I was just in the hospital for a few days. Now I'm home and I'm taking my old medication and a new medication. What's going on?

The doctors in the hospital were probably starting to switch you from your old medication to one of the newer ones, but they didn't finish the switch by the time you were discharged. That's because hospitalizations are shorter these days, and the goal is often to get you home as soon as possible.

It's very important to make sure that your outpatient doctor knows that you are taking *two* antipsychotic medications. Most of the time the goal is to get you on one antipsychotic medication. If you don't know what the plan is, ask!

> *If you are taking two antipsychotic medications, make sure your outpatient doctor knows.*

Isn't it up to my doctor to pick the best time to switch my medication?

Not completely. You need to help make that decision. Your doctor might not know about all the things going on in your life. It's a good idea to talk with your treatment team and discuss the pointers on pages 35 and 38 if you're thinking about changing antipsychotic medications. For example, if you don't tell your treatment team you are planning to move, they won't know it isn't a good time to switch.

> *Work with your family and treatment team to pick a good time for switching.*

> *Note to friends and family members: Hospitalizations are often very brief these days. The person may be discharged before he or she is fully recovered from a psychotic episode. If the person is in the middle of a medication change or adjustment when he or she is discharged, it might be a good idea to go along to the first few outpatient appointments to help sort out the medication plan.*

6 Which Medication Should I Switch To?

If you've decided to try a new medication, most experts recommend trying one of the newer medications rather than one of the older ones. Experts don't agree on *which* of the newer medicines should be tried first, or how many you should try. Therefore, the next step is deciding which atypical antipsychotic to take. It is important to ask your doctor about the differences between the new medications and to decide together which one may be the best for you.

Are the New Medications All Pretty Much the Same?

No. The new medications are *not* all the same. It would be great if doctors could tell *ahead of time* which medication would work best for you. Unfortunately, there's no way to know which of the medications will work best for you. We also don't have much experience or research comparing the new medications with each other. *The good news is that different medications work for different people. In other words, even if one medication doesn't work for you, the next one might work very well!* You just have to try each medication to find one that does a good job for you.

> *The new medications aren't all the same.*

What medications have worked well for you in the past?

What medications have not done a good job for you?

What side effects have bothered you in the past?

What symptoms kept bothering you even though you took your medication the right way, every day?

What Are the Differences Between the New Medications?

Most of the differences between the new antipsychotics have to do with side effects. Some of the differences are listed below.

1. *Clozaril* (clozapine) is the only medication that has been proven to work on "refractory symptoms." Refractory symptoms are symptoms that you continue to have even after you try a number of different medications. So Clozaril is probably the best medication to switch to when nothing else has worked well for you. Even so, most doctors suggest trying one or more of the other atypical antipsychotics first, before switching to Clozaril. This is because Clozaril has many more serious side effects than the other atypical antipsychotic medications. One advantage of Clozaril is that it may help women whose menstrual periods have stopped on other medications resume their periods.

2. *Risperdal* (risperidone). One advantage of Risperdal is that it has been used longer than any of the other atypical antipsychotics, except Clozaril. Many doctors have more experience with Risperdal than with the other atypical medications. Risperdal has very few extrapyramidal side effects (EPS) at lower doses. However, one disadvantage of Risperdal is that it is likely to cause EPS at higher doses. If you are someone who needs higher doses of medication and are switching mainly because of EPS side effects, you should think of trying one of the other antipsychotic medications.

3. *Seroquel* (quetiapine). One advantage of Seroquel is that it is probably less likely to cause EPS than Risperdal or Zyprexa (Clozaril also has lower EPS rates but can cause other serious side effects). The disadvantage of Seroquel is that it needs to be started slowly and the dose raised over the first week or two, you have to take it twice a day, and you might need to get an occasional eye exam. One advantage of Seroquel is that it may help women whose menstrual periods have stopped on other medications resume their periods.

4. *Zeldox* (ziprasidone). A medication that is currently being tested and might be available soon—check with your doctor to see if it is available now. One of the best things about Zeldox is that it doesn't cause as much weight gain as other atypical antipsychotics. It is also less sedating than many of the other atypical antipsychotics.

5. *Zyprexa* (olanzapine). The advantage of Zyprexa is that it can be taken once a day; it is also fairly easy to get started on. It has very few EPS, even at higher doses. The main disadvantage of Zyprexa is that

weight gain seems to be more of a problem with this medicine than with many of the other new medications. One advantage of Zyprexa is that it may help women whose menstrual periods have stopped on other medications resume their periods.

> *The new medications have side effects too.*

How Do You Choose One Atypical Antipsychotic Over the Others?

Work closely with your doctor. Discuss the pros and cons of each of the new medications. You might want to ask your doctor the following questions:

- Which atypical antipsychotic do you prefer to prescribe?
- Which one have you had the best results with?
- What is your experience with the side effects of these medications?
- Which ones do you have the most experience with?
- Which one do you recommend for me—and why?

All other things being equal, your doctor is likely to choose the medication that he or she is most familiar with and most comfortable prescribing.*

In the long run, taking the medication long enough for it to work, taking it the right way every day, and finding a dose that works well for you are at least as important as which new medication you pick.

Are you interested in taking one of the new medications?

If so, which one?

I'm already on one of the atypical antipsychotics. Should I think of switching?

Up to this point, we've been assuming that you're on one of the older medications, but many people these days are being treated with one of the newer medications. The bottom line is that most of the issues are pretty much the same no matter what medication you're on right now.

When thinking about switching, you will have to figure out the pros and cons. Remember, the new medications aren't all the same, and no one can tell ahead of time which medication will work best for you.

---

* This may be a problem if your doctor has only had experience prescribing the older antipsychotics. Your doctor may not be comfortable with prescribing any atypical. If this is true, you might want to get a second opinion from a doctor who is more familiar with at least one of the atypical antipsychotics.

If you are already on an atypical antipsychotic and decide to switch, the next medication should probably be another atypical antipsychotic rather than one of the older conventional antipsychotics. Clozaril (clozapine) is somewhat of a special case. If you are on Clozaril, please read chapter 8 carefully!

If you are on one of the other atypical antipsychotics, you might also have to consider differences in side effects between them, including differences in weight gain, sedation, and amenorrhea. These differences have already been covered in this chapter, and are covered in greater detail in the Technical Information section.

7 The Six Steps in Making the Switch

The six steps in making the switch are listed below. You should read through the description of all six steps in this chapter *before* you start changing your medication.

1. Talk to your doctor about the pros and cons of switching.
2. If you switch, make it your top priority.
3. Make a switching plan.
4. Adjust your medication doses as scheduled.
5. Cope with symptoms and side effects.
6. Stay in touch with your treatment team.

**Step 1.
Talk to Your Doctor
about the Pros and
Cons of Switching**

The idea of switching to one of the new antipsychotics may come from your doctor. Or you or someone in your family may have brought up the idea. If you are interested in switching to a new antipsychotic medication, the first step is to talk to your doctor.

Many people get nervous talking to their doctor about medication. Since the doctor is the expert, they don't feel comfortable raising the issue of switching to another medicine. A good way to start the discussion may be to ask a question. You also want to let the doctor know about the problem that has made you think about a medication change.

You might say something like:

"I'm having a lot of side effects on the medication I'm taking now. Do you think I might have less trouble with one of the new atypical antipsychotics?"

or

"I've been taking this medication for 6 months and I'm still having a lot of symptoms. I'm wondering if it might be time to try a different medicine. What do you think?"

It is important for you and your doctor to reach a decision together. Be sure to give your doctor all the information you can about what is going on with your illness and your life at the moment (for example, if you are planning any big changes soon). Listen carefully to what the doctor has to say, too. He or she may have information you have not thought about or concerns you have not considered.

If the doctor says it is not the right time for you to switch medications, be sure you understand why. One option might be that you and your doctor can postpone switching to some later time. For example, if you are in the middle of a big change in your life, such as moving, you and your doctor may decide it would be better to wait for a while before switching. Or if you have just recovered from a relapse or have only been on your current medication for a short time, your doctor may suggest waiting a little longer on your current medication to see how things work out.

Step 2.
If You Switch,
Make It Your
Top Priority

Let's assume that you and your family have already met with your doctor and decided that it's time to change your medication. You've discussed the pros and cons of each new medication and picked the one you're going to switch to. Now it's time to make a switching plan and make the switch!

It's impossible to know ahead of time exactly how your body and brain will react to going off your old medication and starting the new one. While you're going through this switch, you need to make it *the* most important thing in your life—your top priority. Remember, it only has to be a top priority for now. You can usually get back to your other priorities in a few months. So, we're talking about *postponing* other goals, not *canceling* them altogether. Avoid letting other things get in the way of making a successful switch.

How could you handle each problem listed below while making switching your TOP priority?

A. *John skipped a couple of doses of the new medication because he had a job interview and he was afraid the new medication might mess him up.*

What was John's top priority?

What could he have done differently?

What would you have done?

B. *Chris decided to quit taking the new medicine because she got so nervous it was hard to ride the bus.*

What was Chris's top priority?

What could she have done differently?

What would you have done?

C. *Carter was trying to study for his driver's license test and was having trouble concentrating, so he cut back on his new medication.*

What was Carter's top priority?

What could he have done differently?

What would you have done?

> *If you switch, make it your #1 priority.*

Before you start switching, you need to make a very important commitment. You need to make a commitment *to yourself and to your recovery.* Make recovery your number 1 priority while you're switching medications.

**Step 3.
Make a
Switching Plan**

Most of the time, you'll start switching by taking the new medication along with your old medication. Your doctor will probably recommend staying on your old medication for a while, instead of going off it "cold turkey." He or she will probably have you slowly raise the dose of new medication, while gradually lowering the dose of old medication. After several weeks, your doctor will probably tell you to stop taking the old medication. This process of overlapping medications is called a *medication crossover.*

What is a medication crossover?

Some people have terrible memories of their last psychotic episode (relapse or "nervous breakdown") and have discovered the hard way that their medication keeps this from happening. You may feel anxious about the idea of changing your medication.

Fortunately, the doctor can start you on a new medication while keeping you on your old medication. The doctor can add the newer medication while you continue taking the old one. This means you'll take two antipsychotic medications at once, your old one and the new one. The new medication can "sink in" while the old one is still working for you.

Later on, the doctor can decrease your old medication a little at a time. Eventually, the hope is that you'll go off your old medication and take the new one without having an increase in symptoms.

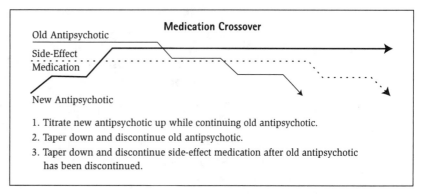

Medication Crossover

Old Antipsychotic

Side-Effect Medication

New Antipsychotic

1. Titrate new antipsychotic up while continuing old antipsychotic.
2. Taper down and discontinue old antipsychotic.
3. Taper down and discontinue side-effect medication after old antipsychotic has been discontinued.

Will I still need a side-effect medication after I switch?

Probably not. The side-effect medications such as Cogentin, Symmetryl, Benadryl, or Artane that are commonly given with antipsychotics are for extrapyramidal or muscle-related side effects (see p. 31). Most of the new antipsychotics don't cause muscle-related side effects, or at least do not cause them nearly as much as the older medications. In general, the atypical antipsychotics have only a very small effect on the part of the brain that causes muscle-related side effects. So, if you take one of the newer antipsychotics, you probably won't need to take a side-effect medication. But you'll need to stay on the side-effect medication for a while before trying to go off (see next question).

Should I stop the side-effect medication as soon as I start the new antipsychotic?

Usually not. Your doctor will probably tell you to keep taking the side effect medicine while you're switching. Then, after you've been off the old antipsychotic for about a month, the doctor will probably start cutting your side-effect medication a little at a time. For example, if you're taking a 2 mg tablet of the side-effect medication Cogentin twice a day, you might follow a schedule something like this:

1. Take 1 tablet in the morning & ½ tablet at bedtime for 7 days.
2. Take ½ tablet in the morning & ½ tablet at bedtime for 7 days.
3. Take ½ tablet in the morning for 7 days.
4. Stop taking the side-effect medication.

It's more of a hassle to do it this way, but it protects you from "rebound" EPS and it is a lot safer.

If you have been taking long-acting Haldol or Prolixin, you will probably need to stay on side-effect medications for a longer period of time.

> There's a good chance you won't need a side-effect medication after you've been on the new antipsychotic medication for a while.

What about other psychiatric medications, such as mood stabilizers or antidepressants?

Many people take other psychiatric medications along with their antipsychotics. These medicines can be mood stabilizers, such as lithium, Depakote, or Tegretol, or antidepressants, such as Prozac, Zoloft, or Paxil. Usually, doctors recommend that you just keep taking those medicines the same way.

What's my role in making the switching plan?

Work with your doctor or treatment team to come up with a plan that is likely to work well for you. If someone in your family is available, it is probably a good idea to work with them too. They might be able to help you with some of the hassles that come with switching. Here are some tips that might help:

1. Listen, ask questions, and state your opinion. Take an active part in making this plan. It's your recovery!
2. Ask your doctor to write down your medication switching plan. Be sure to take the plan home with you and put it in a place where you won't lose it.
3. Make sure you understand and agree with the plan. You're the person who has to follow it. You need to make the plan work. If you don't understand it, you can't make it work. If you disagree with the plan, you probably won't follow it. If you don't understand, ask questions. If you don't agree, speak up, listen, and negotiate—but be willing to compromise, too.

4. Take notes. Write down key parts of the plan. This will help you avoid making mistakes later. You can read your notes to jog your memory and make certain you're on track. What important parts of the plan would you write down?

5. Don't wait until problems happen. Plan ahead. Talk with your family and treatment team about what you can do if you start having problems. Work out the answers to these questions before you switch:

- How long should you wait before you call someone about problems?
- Whom should you call?
- How long will it take someone to talk to the doctor and get back to you?
- If you run into problems, should you quit taking the new medication until your next appointment?

**Step 4.
Change Medication
Doses as Scheduled**

Your doctor will tell you when to increase the dose of the new medication and when to decrease the dose of the old one. The doses might change every few days or every few weeks, depending on which medications you are taking. In some cases, it may take a month or more to complete the switching plan. Here are some tips to help you remember and change medication doses as scheduled.

Make a "switching calendar."

Use a calendar to show important steps in the switching process, such as

- The first day you'll take the new medication ("Start new medication today!")
- The days you'll be making each dose change ("Start taking 1 pill of the new medication and 2 Haldol today")
- Appointments with your doctor, therapist, and case manager ("Case Manager to visit at 3 PM today")
- The day you'll take the last dose of your old medication ("Last dose of Haldol today")
- The day your doctor says you can expect the new medication to be working as well as can be expected. ("The new medication should be working by now. How am I doing?")
- Mark off the days as you go along so it's easy to see what "today" is.

A sample switching calendar is provided in Part VI of this book along with a blank calendar (see pages 203, 204) that you and your treatment team can use to show *your* switching schedule.

Use a 7-day pill box.

A 7-day pill box is probably *the* best way to avoid skipping doses. The kind that has a box for one dose a day usually costs around $2. If you take medication twice a day, you could get two of these pill boxes and use one for morning and the other for evening. Or, you could get a larger box. The kind that has boxes for 4 doses a day costs $8–$10. If you take medication more than once a day, get the larger pill box if you can afford it. Here are some tips for using a pill box:

- Refill your pill box on the same day every week.
- Reread your notes about the switching plan to refresh your memory before you refill your pill box.
- Look at your "switching calendar" before you refill your pill box to make sure you're making dose changes on the right days.
- You might want to have a friend, a family member, or someone on your treatment team help you fill the pill box and double-check the medication adjustments.
- Bring your pill boxes with you to your appointments, especially if you didn't take everything as scheduled.

Even if you don't like the idea of using a pill box, look at it as a short-term solution. It makes sense to use a pill box while your medications and doses are being adjusted. Most of the time, the switch won't take longer than a month or two. After that, you probably won't need to keep using a pill box if you're good at taking your medication the right way every day.

> *Doing a medication crossover can be tricky.*
> *Using a 7-day pill box and bringing your medication with you can help make it easier.*

Tell your doctor or treatment team what's really happening with your medications, not what you think they want to hear.

It's normal to feel embarrassed if you didn't do everything the doctor recommended. The truth is very few people actually do everything *exactly* as the doctor recommends. It's better for your doctor or treatment team to know what's really going on with you. Be honest. Tell them if you skipped doses, quit taking a medication, cut back on your medication, or took more pills than you were supposed to. This will help them know how the switch is really going.

**Step 5.
Cope with Symptoms
and Side Effects**

While switching from your current antipsychotic to one of the new atypical antipsychotics, you may have one of the following problems:

- A temporary increase in your psychiatric symptoms

- Side effects caused by withdrawal from the old antipsychotic
- Early side effects from the new antipsychotic

In the following sections, we describe each of these problems. Remember that these problems *are usually temporary and go away with time and treatment.* If you're not sure how to tell the three kinds of problems apart, that's OK. It can be very hard to tell them apart.

A temporary increase in symptoms

The most common problem people have when switching to a new antipsychotic medication is a temporary increase in symptoms. This can happen when the old medication is stopped before the new medication has had time to really start working.

Sometimes switching medicine is like doing road work. Have you ever noticed that when the highway department starts widening or repairing a road, things usually get worse before they get better? Traffic gets all backed up, detours have to be taken, and it takes a lot longer to get where you're going. But after the road work is finished, traffic moves along much better than it did before. The inconvenience ends up being worth it, because the end result is such a big improvement. For many people, that's how it is with switching medication. Things sometimes get worse before they get better. But in the end, the inconvenience is often worth it because they feel so much better after the switch is over.

Your chances of avoiding an increase in symptoms are better if your old medication is continued for a while as you are starting the new medication. When your medication is switched this way, you'll be taking two antipsychotics for while. If all goes well, your old medication will eventually be stopped and you'll just be taking the new one. We described this overlap process, which is called a medication crossover, on page 53.

What are some things that could warn me that I might be about to relapse?

Before psychotic symptoms develop, people with a psychotic illness may have other problems with ordinary activities. For example, they may have trouble sleeping, find it difficult to concentrate, or have a hard time going to work or visiting friends. Such problems are often called "early warning signs" of relapse. Early warning signs are different for each person.

It's always a good idea to know *your* early warning signs of relapse. Early warning signs can happen for many other reasons besides switching medications. But your chances of getting early warning signs are greater during switching than at other times. Therefore, if you don't know your early warning signs, or are just a bit rusty about them, it makes sense to review them before switching.

When you became ill in the past, what did you notice even before symptoms became worse?

Talk with your friends and family. What things did they notice before they realized your symptoms were getting worse?

What early warning signs should you be aware of in the future?

What should I do if my symptoms start getting worse?

If you start having more positive (psychotic) symptoms, call someone on your treatment team. The doctor may need to change your switching plan. Don't wait until your next appointment. You might be relapsing, and the longer you wait, the harder it will be to stop the relapse. Don't ignore it and hope it will go away. Call and tell someone on your treatment team what's going on.

> *Don't ignore a symptom flare-up. Call your treatment team.*

What might my doctor do to keep my symptoms from getting worse?

If you get a flare-up of psychotic (positive) symptoms, the doctor might decrease your old medication more slowly. If you're already off the old medication, the doctor might start you back on it. The doctor might also raise the dose of new medication. Most people need more than just the starting dose of the new medication to control their symptoms. So don't be surprised if your dose needs to be increased several times.

If you get early warning signs or a symptom flare-up during the crossover, your doctor might

- Raise the dose of your new antipsychotic medication
- Raise the dose of your old antipsychotic medication
- Add a medication for anxiety or insomnia such as lorazepam (Ativan) or clonazepam (Klonopin)
- Not do anything right away, but wait and watch to see how you do

Are there things that can help besides medication changes?

In some cases, your doctor, therapist, or case manager might make suggestions that have nothing to do with medication. They might suggest things you can do to help yourself recover like cutting back on caffeine, practicing relaxation skills, or staying busy with a hobby. Many people already know some things that help when symptoms get worse, as well as things that make their symptoms worse. For one person, being alone might help. For another person, being with other people might help. With all these choices, chances are good that you'll find something to help you feel better quickly without stopping your new medication.

When you are having more symptoms or feeling bad, what kinds of things help you to feel better?

What kinds of things make you feel even worse?

What advice would you give yourself if you start to have more symptoms?

Withdrawal side effects

You can get side effects if you stop taking a medication too quickly. These are called *withdrawal side effects.* You are less likely to have withdrawal side effects if you do a slow medication crossover. This means slowly decreasing your old medication while gradually increasing the new medication. Because of withdrawal side effects, it is generally not a good idea to stop antipsychotics and side-effect medications suddenly.

Withdrawal side effects usually last for a few days after you take the last dose of your medicine. Some examples of the kinds of side effects you could get when you stop your old antipsychotic are listed below.

- Nausea, diarrhea, or low energy
- Restlessness or jitteriness
- Stiff muscles or shakey hands

> *What feels like side effects from the new medication may actually be a withdrawal reaction from the old medication. You're less likely to have withdrawal reactions if you do a slow medication crossover.*

I was told that I have tardive dyskinesia. Will the new medications help?

The new medications may help in the long run, although no one is really sure whether the new medications help treat tardive dyskinesia (TD) that's already there. However, we do know that symptoms of TD often get worse for a while after the old medications are stopped or lowered. This happens because the TD was there in the first place. The older medication blocked some of the TD symptoms, and when the older medication is stopped, the TD becomes unblocked. These symptoms usually show up between 1 to 4 weeks after lowering or stopping the old medication. That means that they appear right at the time the new medication has taken over the job of the old medication. You'll blame the new medication if you don't know that the increase in dyskinesia is an expectable, and normal, withdrawal reaction. In fact, this problem is so common that it has its own name, "withdrawal dyskinesia."

The most important thing to remember about withdrawal dyskinesia is not to panic. Don't forget that the problem is really from the old medication, not the new one.

Are withdrawal problems caused by the new medication?

No. Withdrawal reactions are caused by going off the old medications. The most important thing to remember is that these withdrawal reactions are *not* caused by the new medication, and they *will* go away. Don't panic if you get one of them. They can be treated and they go away.

If you think your new medication is causing the problems, you'll probably stop taking it. In most cases, that would be a mistake. Most withdrawal reactions usually disappear after you've been off your old medication for a few weeks. The balance of chemicals in your brain is changing. It takes time to get the old medication out of your system. Give your brain time to get used to the changes.

> It's usually a bad idea
> to "cold turkey" your old antipsychotic or side-effect medications.

What are "early" side effects?

Early side effects are caused by the new medication you are taking. These side effects can be bothersome and annoying, but they aren't dangerous and they *usually* go away in a few weeks. They're caused by the chemical changes going on in your brain. The medication is balancing your brain chemistry. As your body and brain get used to the new medication, the early side effects will go away on their own. Don't stop taking the medication. Give your brain a chance to get the chemicals in balance.

Some early side effects you might notice include changes in sleep and alertness, including tiredness and/or insomnia. Other early side effects are more physical and include nausea, dizziness, and orthostatic hypotension (a sudden drop in blood pressure when you stand up suddenly that can make you feel temporarily dizzy).

> *Early side effects usually go away in a few weeks.*
> *Keep taking your medication.*

What should I do if I get early side effects?

Early side effects can be frustrating because they often happen before the new medication starts working. Keep taking the new medicine. Talk with your treatment team and find out when you can expect the side effects to go away. If you're thinking about stopping your medication, ask the doctor if changing the switching plan might help. Tell your team if the side effects are getting to be too much for you to deal with.

How can I tell if I'm having a withdrawal reaction or side effects from the new medication?

Most likely you can't tell by yourself. That's the sort of thing you need to ask your treatment team. If you have problems, call for help. If you can't call your doctor directly, call your therapist or case manager. They can pass on your message to the doctor and call you back.

Your treatment team may tell you that you're having early side effects. They might tell you not to worry and to stick with the switching plan. If so, remind yourself that your body is just getting used to the new medication. Don't stop taking it. Give your brain time to adjust to the changes.

> *You're changing the balance of chemicals in your brain.*
> *Give your body time to get used to the changes.*

Step 6.
Stay in Touch with
Your Treatment Team

Your doctor may need to change the switching plan if your symptoms get worse or if side effects bother you a lot. To know when the plan needs to be changed, the doctor will have to count on you (and your therapist, case manager, and family) for updates on how the plan is working. Remember, only you know what's happening in your body and your brain!

1. *Keep your appointments.* Write them on your "switching calendar" so you'll remember to go.

2. *Talk honestly and openly.* Tell your team about

   - How you're doing
   - How the medication is working
   - Problems you're having
   - Side effects that are bothering you
   - Symptoms you're having
   - Whether you're taking your medication as prescribed

3. *Call someone on your team if problems come up between visits.* If something bothers you about the medication—call. If you can't reach the doctor, call your therapist or case manager and tell him or her what the problem is. Your case manager can explain the problem to your doctor.

4. *Don't change the plan on your own.* Don't cut the medicine, raise the dose, skip dose changes, or stop taking any of the medications unless the doctor tells you to. Switching can be very tricky. Making changes in the plan by yourself could make things *much* worse. Call for help. Don't change the plan on your own.

> *Don't change the plan on your own.*
> *Call for help.*

8 What Will Happen After I Switch?

After you've gone through the "six steps to switching," give the new medication time to work. This is the last part of the medication trial. During this time, you'll probably be taking the new medicine *without* the old one. Your new medication will be working on balancing your brain chemistry. The atypical antipsychotic has three important jobs:

1. Allowing EPS from the older medication to wash out of your system
2. Blocking some of your dopamine to improve your positive (psychotic) symptoms
3. Blocking some of your serotonin to reduce your negative symptoms

Give the new medication plenty of time to do a good job!

How Long Does it Take for an Atypical Antipsychotic to Work?

One of the hardest parts of switching is waiting for the new medication to work. It can be very frustrating, especially if you're bothered by side effects or symptoms. Research has shown that it can take *up to 3 months* for an atypical antipsychotic medication to be fully effective.* The medication will start working in a week or two. But it will take up to 3 months to know how well it's going to work for you. And some of the changes might happen so slowly that you won't really notice them.

> *It takes up to 3 months to know how much an atypical antipsychotic medication will help you.*

Exactly how long you'll need to wait depends on the goals of the new medication, how quickly the dose of your medication is raised, and your

---

* The 3-month medication trial is a compromise between giving the medication enough time to work and the realities of cost and suffering while waiting for it to work. There is still some disagreement over how long you should wait. The 3-month medication trial is for people in the community. If you're in the hospital, a medication trial can usually be started there and continued in the community.

own individual brain chemistry. Here are some general rules about how long you can expect to wait before you can tell if the medication is working for you.

- If you changed medications because of EPS, you should start feeling better one month after your old medication has been *completely* discontinued.

- If you changed medications because of ongoing positive symptoms, you should feel better in about 2 months on *adequate* doses of the new medication.

- If you changed medication because of negative symptoms, you, your treatment team, or your family should notice at least *a little* improvement after about 3 months on *adequate* doses.

- If you are starting a new medication to treat an acute relapse, most doctors recommend waiting about 4 weeks to see if the medication works for you.

When does the waiting period start?

Don't forget that the waiting period starts the first day you take a therapeutic dose, not the first day you actually take the first pill of the new medication. You should ask your doctor about your therapeutic dose.

How Can I Tell If the New Medication Is Working for Me?

No two people are alike. People don't respond exactly the same way to new medications. Still, after about 3 months on a high enough dose of the new medication, you'll probably be able to tell how well it's working for you. You might notice that the medication works better, you might feel about the same, or you might feel like it doesn't work as well as the medication you used to take.

How does your new medication compare to the one you took before?

__ The new medication works better.

__ There is not much difference.

__ The old medication worked better.

__ Some things are better and some things are worse.

__ I don't feel better, but I can do things I couldn't do before.

If I Have a Lot of Problems during the First Month of Switching, Does It Mean the New Medication Won't Help Me?

No. Many people who have problems during a medication crossover, eventually do better on the atypical medicine. Having a rough time for the first few weeks doesn't tell you whether or not the new medication will work for you. Your brain needs time to adjust to the effects the new medication has on your dopamine and serotonin. You don't know how well a medication will stop or block your symptoms until you take it every day, at a therapeutic dose, for *up to 3 months*. A symptom flare-up before then doesn't mean the new medicine won't work. Keep taking it. Give it time to do its job.

Do everything you can to stick with the plan. Make it a priority to get through the medication trial and stay on the new medication, even if you're having a tough time. If you have problems, talk with your treatment team. There may be things your doctor can do to help you get through the waiting period. For example, sometimes antianxiety medication can be added if you're feeling anxious or having trouble sleeping.

Will the doctor need to increase the dose of my new antipsychotic?

Most people need more than the starting dose to control their symptoms. The doctor will probably have to raise the dose several times to balance your brain chemicals. For most of the new medications you can't just start on a higher dose. The medication has to be increased slowly while your brain corrects the chemical imbalance a little at a time. Raising the dose slowly cuts down on side effects. Once you've gotten up to the right dose, then the medication needs plenty of time to do its job.

> *Most people need more than their starting dose of the new medication to control their symptoms.*

What If I Get on a New Medication that Doesn't Work Very Well?

If you switch to a medicine that doesn't do a good job of controlling your symptoms, don't give up. Tell someone on your treatment team about your symptoms. Talk about what can be done to help you get better. The next step will probably be one of the following:

- Wait a while longer to give the medication plenty of time to work.
- Take a higher dose of the new medication.
- Go back to your older medication.
- Switch to one of the other new antipsychotics. If one doesn't work, you can still try another. The new antipsychotics don't all work in the same way, so one of the other new medications might do a better job for you.

What are the advantages of going back to my old medication?

Your old medication has the advantage of being familiar to you. You know what to expect. The good news is that your older medication will probably work as well as it did before. Another advantage is that your doctor already knows the proper dose of the medication for you, and (except for Clozaril) it is easy to quickly get back on your old medication. These advantages can be very reassuring, especially if you were frightened because your symptoms got worse during the crossover.

What are the disadvantages of going back on my old medication?

Although your older medication will probably work as well as it did before, the bad news is that, by going back to the old medication, you won't get the kind of relief you were hoping for. Therefore, even though it feels safe to go back to your old medication, you should also consider going on to another newer medication.

> *If the new medication doesn't work out,*
> *you and your doctor need to decide whether to go back*
> *to your old medication or try another new medication.*

How do I know a different medication will work?

At this point, no one can predict which of the new medications is most likely to work for you. The good news here is that people *do respond* to some of these medications even if they don't respond to *all* of them. It's not a guarantee, but it may be worth trying several of the new medications if the first one you try doesn't work.

I've tried several of the new medications, and *none* of them have helped. What do I do next?

Have you tried Clozaril (clozapine)? Clozaril seems to help when all other medications don't work. Doctors may not recommend it at first because it has many difficult side effects. But if nothing has helped and you haven't yet been on Clozaril, you should think about trying it. Finally, there are other treatments that doctors can try when Clozaril doesn't work.

If Clozaril is so great, why didn't I try it first?

Clozaril has significant risks. Approximately 1 person out of 100 who starts Clozaril will stop making white blood cells, which is a very serious medical problem. To check for this, everyone taking Clozaril must get blood tests regularly. Also, while Clozaril does not cause EPS, it has other side effects that can be troublesome.

I've Tried Several Medications and None Have Worked Well. I Feel Like Giving Up. Can Clozaril Really Help?

Anyone considering Clozaril should think of trying one of the other new atypical antipsychotic medications first. Some people might even want to try all of the new medications before starting Clozaril. These other medications are safer than Clozaril and have far fewer side effects. For many people, these other new medications work very well and are much easier to live with than Clozaril.

Those who do very well on other atypical antipsychotics are lucky. Others haven't been so lucky. They tried other medications hoping for the best but were disappointed. After a few such tries, it's no surprise that they are skeptical about trying yet another medication—this time Clozaril. But many people feel much better and function much better on Clozaril than on any other medication.

> *Clozaril may work better*
> *even when none of the other new medications*
> *have worked well for you.*

How do I know if it might be worth trying Clozaril?

There are several good reasons for switching to Clozaril. If one or more of them fit your situation, you should definitely consider trying Clozaril. Do any of these apply to you?

__ My symptoms are so severe that I've had to stay in the hospital a long time even though I've tried several other medicines.

__ My symptoms are so severe that I think of killing myself all the time, or I have come close to suicide on several occasions, and the medications don't seem to help much with these suicidal urges.

__ My symptoms are so severe that I've ended up in the hospital a lot, even though I take my medications as prescribed and I haven't used drugs or alcohol.

__ I've tried several other antipsychotics and I still have a lot of symptoms that bother me or keep me from reaching my goals.

How long will it take to know if Clozaril is working?

If you decide to start Clozaril, plan to give it at least 4 months before deciding whether it works for you. Clozaril needs to be started at a low dose and increased over time. Once it is at full dose, it takes many weeks before it is really effective. It takes 6 months to get maximum benefit from Clozaril. There is no point in starting a Clozaril trial if you are not willing to give it enough time to work.

> *It can take up to 6 months*
> *to get maximum benefit from Clozaril.*

When to Consider Switching Again

Even though my medication works for some symptoms, I'm frustrated that I'm not fully recovered. What's going on?

Even when medication helps improve your symptoms, they may not go away entirely. Many people continue to have some symptoms, even when they take their medication. These are called "residual" symptoms.

Residual symptoms may not be very obvious. For example, if your concentration isn't 100% back to normal, it would be very difficult to train for a job. Or if you still have some anxiety and feel nervous, you might find it very difficult to be around other people, drive a car, or do your work. You might have these symptoms even if your new medicine has helped you more than any of the others.

What residual symptoms are you experiencing?

What problems are they causing for you?

If I'm doing better after switching medications, but I still have symptoms, should I switch medications again?

Good question! Because there are several new medications to choose from, it is unlikely you have tried them all. There hasn't been enough research yet to know whether it might be worth switching again if you've already switched and are doing better, but still have bothersome symptoms or side effects. Many times it becomes a personal decision in which you must balance the hope of improving things even more and the concern that you would have to go through another crossover period, or that the new medication won't work as well.

Still, consider yourself lucky! At least you know that the medication you're on is better than the one you were on before.

How do I know if it might be a good idea to switch again?

The things to think about in this situation are very similar to those you considered the last time you thought about switching medications (see p. 35). There is nothing "magic" about the newer medications in terms of helping you know whether to switch again.* But, before you switch again, be sure you've given yourself enough time to really benefit from your improvement. It would be a shame to lose any of the gains you've made from finding a better medication. You probably should wait *at least* a year before switching again—and you might even think of waiting 2–3 years to really reinforce and build up your gains from switching.

> *If you're doing better after switching, you should probably wait* at least *a year before trying to switch again.*

---

* Except Clozaril (clozapine). If you are on Clozaril, please review pp. 69–71, which tell you why Clozaril is different.

Would you want to switch medications again?

__ Yes, because

__ No, because

Should I Switch to Another Medication If I Am Taking Clozaril?

Many people who are taking Clozaril are doing much better than they ever did before trying Clozaril. At the same time, many people on Clozaril have to live with irritating side effects and have to get blood tests every week or two to be sure their body is still making white blood cells. Common side effects from Clozaril include sleepiness, weight gain, drooling, and, occasionally, nausea, to name only a few. Despite these side effects, many people on Clozaril believe that the medication has been so helpful that they never want to try anything else.

Other people on Clozaril wonder whether they would be better off switching to something with fewer side effects, especially with new medications becoming available. For them, the problems with taking Clozaril almost feel worse than the symptoms they had when they were taking other antipsychotics. It is important to consider all of the reasons to switch and all of the reasons not to switch, and to work with your psychiatrist and other clinicians to come up with a joint decision. As part of this decision, there are a number of things to consider.

__ *Are you doing better on Clozaril?* Many people do better on Clozaril than on other medications. People who have done very well on Clozaril often do not do as well when they switch, even when they switch to one of the new atypical antipsychotic medications.

__ *Have you given Clozaril enough time to work?* Clozaril takes a while to work. This means that if you switch off Clozaril and then decide to go back on it, it might take weeks or even months to regain its full effectiveness. It also takes a while to build up to a full dose of Clozaril.

__ *What might happen if you relapse?* While you are switching from one medication to another, consider what could happen in your life if things did get worse. *The chances of relapse are higher when you switch from Clozaril to another antipsychotic than when you switch from other medications.*

> *There is a higher risk of relapse when switching from Clozaril to another antipsychotic medication.*

What is the best way to switch from Clozaril to another medication?

Let's assume you've considered the pros and cons. You've talked things over with your family, your doctor, and your treatment team. Everyone agrees it's time to switch from Clozaril to one of the other new antipsychotics. There are some things you can do to decrease the risk involved in the switch.

1. Pick the time for the switch carefully. It is important to pick a time when your life is stable and there are no big changes around the corner (see p. 38).

2. Make sure that people around you know about the switch, so that they can help out if things get worse temporarily.

3. Make the change slowly. If you've done well on Clozaril, it will be safest to start the new medication while you're still taking Clozaril. After the new medication has been increased to an effective dose, it's usually a good idea to keep taking it with your regular dose of Clozaril for a week or two. Then the Clozaril will probably be slowly tapered off over 2–4 months. This slow "crossover" is important for a number of reasons:

   • It keeps the person from going through the withdrawal that comes from stopping Clozaril too suddenly.

   • It helps ensure that the new medication is at an effective dose before Clozaril is withdrawn.

   • If the new medication is not as effective as Clozaril, the gradual withdrawal allows symptoms to emerge slowly so that the person has time to adjust. If symptoms emerge during this very gradual transition, the person can either find ways to cope with them, or may decide to remain on Clozaril.

The main issue is to make the transition cautiously, minimize risk, and be sure you and your treatment team have time to monitor changes and make decisions accordingly. The following example illustrates some of the problems that can occur when switching from Clozaril to another antipsychotic.

Jamie had spent years in a state hospital. Nothing seemed to control his symptoms well enough for him to be discharged—until he took Clozaril. He improved a lot on 400 mg of Clozaril a day and was eventually able to live outside the hospital. He attended day treatment, visited his family, and enjoyed life for the first time since high school.

About a year after discharge, he and his family talked with the doctor about switching to one of the other new antipsychotic medications. Jamie said he was tired of having blood tests done every week. The psychiatrist wrote a prescription for an atypical antipsychotic and told Jamie to stop taking Clozaril as soon as he started the new medication.

Jamie's symptoms returned about a month later. Increasing the new medication didn't help. Jamie ended up back in the hospital again and was started back on Clozaril. He improved and was discharged again.

Jamie's been back on Clozaril for about 6 months now, but, even at 600 mg a day, he's still having a lot more symptoms than he did before the switch.

What might have triggered Jamie's relapse?

What could have been done differently to reduce the chances of relapse?

What would you do if your psychiatrist told you to stop taking Clozaril as soon as you started taking a new antipsychotic medication?

Is It Realistic To Expect One of the New Medications to Cure Me?

If you are dissatisfied with how you're doing, even though your symptoms are *much* better, make sure that you're not expecting too much from your medications. It doesn't make sense to switch medications if your expectations are out of line with the possible benefits. It *is* unrealistic to expect medication to *cure* schizophrenia. If you expect a cure, you're going to be disappointed. It's important to talk with the doctor about what you hope to get from switching medications and to listen to your doctor's experience about whether or not your hopes are realistic.

Don't Give Up: The Keys to Recovery

Imagine you're locked in a room with no windows and only one door. You have a ring of keys. What would you do? Of course, you'd use the keys to try to unlock the door. If the first key didn't work, would you give up? No, of course not. You'd try another key. Would you keep trying the same key over and over again if it didn't work? No, you'd give it a good try, then try the next key. Would you try only two or three keys and give up? Not if you were locked in a room and wanted to get out— you'd try every key on the ring, wouldn't you?

Medications Are the Keys to Recovery

That's how it is with mental illness. The illness locks you in. It keeps you from going places, doing things, and achieving goals. Antipsychotic medications are the keys. You don't know which medication might be the key that unlocks the door. The only way out is to try every key. Don't give up if the first medication doesn't work. Don't keep taking the same medication for years if it doesn't work. There are other medications to try. Medications are the keys to recovery.

Shelly was switched to an atypical antipsychotic and took it for 6 months. She didn't skip any doses and wasn't using drugs or drinking alcohol, but she was still having a lot of symptoms. She talked with her family and treatment team about how she was feeling. Since she was already on a pretty high dose of medicine, they talked about switching to one of the other atypical antipsychotics. Everyone agreed—it was time to try another medication.

The crossover switch was done slowly. Shelly took the new medication for several months to give it plenty of time to work. Unfortunately, even at a high dose, the new medication didn't seem to do a very good job of controlling Shelly's symptoms either. She was really disappointed, but she was also determined. Instead of giving up, she talked with her family and treatment team about trying another new antipsychotic.

Shelly changed medications again. They did the crossover switch slowly but she started having side effects and was feeling worse instead of better. Shelly kept taking the medication anyway because she knew how important it was to give it a chance to work. The new medication was gradually increased and, 3 months later, Shelly could really tell the difference. Now, for the first time in years, she's able to think clearly, sing in the church choir, go shopping, and enjoy life again.

What was Shelly's top priority?

What might have happened if Shelly had just kept taking the first new medication?

Why do you think Shelly kept switching medication instead of giving up?

What would you have done if you were Shelly?

9 Getting Better

If you switch to a medicine that works a lot better than the ones you have taken in the past, you'll probably experience a kind of lifting of symptoms that you have not felt since before you became ill. You may also find that your life changes quite a bit. In this chapter, we talk about some of the experiences people have when they switch to an antipsychotic medication that works better for them. In the next chapter, we will give you some suggestions for dealing with these changes in your life.

> *If the new medication works well for you,
> your life might change quite a bit.*

What Can I Expect If I Switch to a Medication That Works Really Well?

Let's hear what some people say about how switching medications has helped them. These comments come from people who have done better after switching medications. Remember, their good experiences don't mean that the atypical medications will work as well for you.

Fewer positive symptoms

Many people find that their persistent positive symptoms, such as hallucinations, delusions, or confused thinking, improve after they switch to a newer antipsychotic.

"There are many differences in the way I think on the newer medication. Before, my thinking was really slowed down. During an interview, it took me about 5 minutes to come up with dates and information. My counselor said, 'This girl is not ready for work.' Now I can answer questions as fast as she asks them. My thinking isn't slowed down anymore. I really am ready for work."

Fewer negative symptoms

Many people also have fewer problems with persistent negative symptoms after they switch to a newer antipsychotic. Some people have more energy. They may feel like taking a shower, brushing their teeth, and wearing clean clothes more often. They may enjoy spending time with other people again.

"On the older medication, I didn't look like myself. I would look in the mirror and see a face that wasn't my own. This wasn't just my reaction. Something happened that really bothered me. I had just gotten my hair done and thought I looked really pretty. But then a man on the street stopped me and said to me, 'I feel as bored as you look.' I was so embarrassed because I didn't feel bored and hadn't intended to look bored. Now, on the new medication, I look more like myself than I have in years."

Fewer side effects

Many people who switch to one of the newer antipsychotics have fewer side effects. They have fewer problems with restlessness (akathisia), feeling slowed down (akinesia), shaky hands (tremors), dry mouth and blurry vision (anticholinergic problems), and, for women, problems with menstrual periods (amenorrhea).

"On the old medication I felt tense, stiff . . . my muscles were always tight . . . and it really slowed me down. It was bad. I feel lots better since I changed medicine. This new medication doesn't make me stiff or slowed down."

"I hated that restless, jumpy feeling I had on my old meds. I couldn't sit still. It was like my motor was running all the time. I was really antsy. I was constantly getting into trouble in classes, you know, in and out, up and down all the time. People thought I was just cutting up, or worse— sometimes they thought I was agitated. Wow, what a difference this new medication makes. I can sit still and concentrate again."

"My hands used to shake so bad that I held my own hands, crossed my arms, or kept my hands in my pockets all the time. It was the only way to keep them still. I was afraid people would think I was an alcoholic or drug addict—you know—going through withdrawal. It was embarrassing. Now I hardly even notice it anymore. My hands still shake sometimes, but not nearly so much. This new medication has really made a difference."

"Have you ever had a bad case of cotton mouth and constipation? I did. I was always drinking something. I carried a cup around with me wherever I went. And constipation was miserable. I was taking stuff every day to deal with that problem. Not anymore. I finally talked with my treatment team about it. They switched me to one of the new medications. It controls my symptoms without drying me out."

"I didn't have a period for a long time—seemed like years maybe. When I was really sick I used to think I was pregnant. But when I got better I realized it was just a medicine side effect—it messed up my system. You might think, 'Gee, I'd love not having a period, no more hassle'—but I didn't feel

that way. It was like I wasn't a woman. You know, it really bugged me. Now I'm taking one of those new medicines. My period's back again. I'm glad."

Greater stability and freedom from relapse

Many people find that their illness is more stable and that they have fewer relapses after switching to one of the newer antipsychotics.

"I just couldn't keep taking that other medicine. Those pills made me feel worse. They kept me down. I just wasn't myself. So, most of the time, I just didn't take it. Then my doctor tried me on some new kind of pills. I don't mind taking them so much. I feel better than I have in a long time. I think I can handle this medicine. Seems like it works with me instead of against me."

"Every time I started a job, the symptoms just took over again. It was so frustrating!! I'd be doing pretty good and decide "OK, maybe I can make it this time." But when I got a job, it all came apart again. I hated not working. I felt like a failure. This new medicine has made a big difference. Sometimes, when I'm under a lot of pressure on the job, some of my symptoms act up. But I can handle it. I'm in better control. I can keep a job now—success!"

Can I Expect Improvements Like These If I Switch Medications?

Unfortunately, no one can tell you for sure. You need to talk with your doctor about what it is realistic to hope for. You also might want to review some of the information we discussed in the earlier chapters of this book (see pp. 35, 38). In those sections, we discuss some of the things that tell us if someone might be helped by switching medications.

What If the New Medication Works Better than the Previous Medication in Some Ways But Not As Well in Others?

Sometimes switching medication is a "good news/bad news" kind of situation. The medication works better in some ways, but worse in other ways. If that happens to you while you're doing a medication crossover, be patient. During a crossover, it's really hard to know if the new medication isn't working well or if it just hasn't had enough time to "sink in."

However, some people will get a "good news/bad news" kind of response even after waiting it out. Let's hear what people have experienced.

Trading old side effects for new ones

"It's been a trade-off for me. I still had a lot of symptoms on the old medication. And I was restless. This new medication works lots better. Most of my symptoms are gone and now I can even sit still. But I'm really putting on weight. I just seem to gain more and more every week. I guess it was a good decision. I am better, but I hate being so fat."

Some side effects get better but some get worse.

"One good thing about this new medication, I'm having periods again. I feel more normal. But even taking my pills at night, I feel tired all day. I

just drag through the day. It controls my symptoms, but I don't feel like waking up. I don't know, maybe one of the other ones wouldn't make me feel like this and would still let me have periods. I hope so."

The first step here is to see if you and your doctor can figure out a way to fix the problem while still getting the extra benefits of the new medication. Often, the new problem can be solved by a dose adjustment (for example, if the problem is sedation), by adding a new medication (for example, if you have obsessions), or by adjusting your lifestyle (exercising and changing eating habits to prevent more weight gain). If the side effects of the new medication remain troublesome, you can always try another one of the newer medications or go back to your old medication. Remember, there are more options these days than ever before!

10 Getting On with Life

For many people, life gets a lot better after switching medications. When symptoms improve, or side effects aren't such a big problem, it can feel like a fog or dark cloud has been lifted. Almost everyone wants to get back to having the kind of life they had before they became ill. They wonder what their life would have been like if they hadn't gotten sick. More and more people are discovering that switching to a new medication opens doors to building a new life, to achieving goals, and to getting life back on track.

Of course, if you do well on one of the new medications, there will also be new challenges to face. Instead of dealing with symptoms and side effects so much of the time, you'll be able to put more energy into getting on with the rest of your life.

Does Doing Better Sometimes Lead to New Problems?

For many people, having fewer symptoms opens up a whole new world. You may be able to do more than you could before. Your concentration may be better. You may feel more comfortable being around people. If any of these things have happened to you because you tried a new medication, that's wonderful news!

However, doing better can also give you some new problems to handle. When you finally get some relief after suffering for a long time, it's hard to hear about any problems. Still, it's better to learn about the problems that *could* come up, so they won't catch you too much by surprise if they happen to you.

Some of the stages people may experience as they recover include:

- Wanting to leave the illness behind
- Feeling overwhelmed by new emotions
- Wanting to make up for lost time
- Coping with feelings of loss
- Trying to do too much at once
- Feeling disconnected from other people
- Dealing with depression

- Wanting to drink or get high
- Trying to fulfill intimacy and sexuality needs

Wanting to Leave the Illness Behind

If you suddenly feel much better, you may enter a "honeymoon" period. You may feel so elated that your terrible symptoms or miserable side effects are gone that you almost forget that you still have an illness. You might think you don't need any more treatment. You might forget that you still need to watch out for symptoms. People can overdo it here, either by taking on too many things all at once or by trying to go out on their own without continued support from their treatment team. These desires are normal and understandable, but they can fool a person into putting their new level of recovery at risk.

Feeling Overwhelmed by New Emotions

Sometimes people experience new kinds of emotions. You might experience emotions you've never felt before or re-experience old feelings you'd forgotten you ever had. Sometimes it can feel good to have these emotions return, but many people find they have trouble dealing with new emotions at first. They've forgotten the feelings of joy and sadness or what it feels like to be lonely or to miss family. When feelings like this come back, it can be very frightening and overwhelming. It is rather like starting to hurt from surgery when anesthesia wears off too quickly.

While you're getting used to having emotions again, it's important to remind yourself that it's OK to have emotions. Also, it's not a good idea to make major changes in your emotional or spiritual life shortly after switching medication. Give yourself time to simply grow and enjoy the new feelings. Don't rush into major changes.

Andy is 26 years old. He started having psychotic symptoms while he was in high school. He had been treated on and off with older antipsychotic medications since he was 18. Off medication, Andy is preoccupied by voices and very suspicious of others. He does much better with these problems when he is on medication, but he still has trouble concentrating and thinking clearly.

Andy started a newer medication and was much, much better. Everyone around him realized the difference. He sounded better, looked better, and could think more clearly. For the first time in his life, he wanted to reconnect with his father, whom he hadn't seen in many years. He traveled to the city where his father lived and tracked him down. Unfortunately, when he found his dad, he didn't get a very warm welcome. Andy felt very rejected, stopped taking his medication, and his symptoms returned. Later on, when he got back on medication and got better again, Andy realized that he had tried to make a very big change too quickly.

What could Andy have done differently?

Why do you think Andy quit taking his medication?

What would you have done?

Wanting to Make Up for Lost Time

It's natural to want to make up for lost time. It's very hard to take things slowly when you're finally feeling better—especially after what may have been years of frustration from having to live with limitations and not being able to do the things other people do.

A severe psychiatric illness can take up so much of your time and energy that it interferes with normal parts of growing up, like finishing high school or getting a job, dating, or getting married. When you are having a lot of symptoms, you may not have the energy to pay much attention to these things. If the new medication really works, you might find yourself feeling and thinking much more normally, but you may also feel way behind in doing the things that other people are likely to have done by your age.

When the symptoms finally decrease or go away, it seems like you have to make up for lost time. It's only natural to want to experience all the things you've missed. It might feel like being released from prison or finally getting something to eat after you've been starving.

What have you missed out on while you've been ill?

Coping with Feelings of Loss

It is easy to get discouraged because you have lost so much. You might feel frustrated by how much work it will take to put your life back on track. Although you are feeling much better, it has been a long time since you have done normal activities such as reading a book, taking a class, having a date, or holding a job. It may be hard to know where to start.

What if I am behind my brothers, sisters, or friends in accomplishing things? If I have lost years of living because of my illness, does that mean it will always seem like I'm behind in life?

You may wonder how long it will take to "catch up." We are *all* in the process of growing and learning throughout our lives. Once your symptoms are controlled by medication and start to fade away, you might still react in some of the same ways that you did before you became ill. For example, if you first got sick as a teenager and have finally gotten better in your 20s, you may feel and act in some ways like a teenager.

What kinds of growing up issues do people commonly deal with during recovery?

Teenagers normally go through a process of pushing their parents away. They are learning to think of themselves as individuals separate from their families. After going through this phase, teenagers then usually join back with their families. People who have had this process interrupted by their illness might act in some ways like a teenager, pushing their families away as they explore who they are as individuals. People who first became ill in their teens may not have been able to fully mature, at least in certain ways. If that's true for you, you might sometimes behave like someone younger than your actual age. If you are getting better and just acting like yourself for the first time in ages, your family may wonder if you're getting sick.

It is important to give yourself time to grow. To do that, there is no substitute for the passage of time and experiencing life—one step at a time. You *can* become a mature adult with time—just don't rush it. Remember that, although you have missed some things because of your illness, you have also learned to cope with many things and deal with frustration, depression, and disappointment. You will have your own kind of maturity and wisdom based on the experiences you've had.

Barbara was 24 and lived in a group home for people with schizophrenia. She wasn't doing much of anything. She always kept to herself, didn't have friends, and was never any trouble. She started taking one of the atypical antipsychotics and had a remarkable response. She was more energetic and assertive than she had been in years!

The problem was that Barbara didn't know how to deal with all the changes. She knew she'd outgrown some of the strict house rules but she didn't know how to talk about the problem. She didn't have the skills she needed to negotiate. She was ready for changes now that she was better, but she didn't know how to help change her situation for the better. She started acting like a brat. She refused to do her laundry at the residence, and was arguing a lot.

Why do you think Barbara started refusing to do things around the house?

What could she have done differently?

What would you have done?

Trying to Do Too Much at Once

Can trying to do too much at once cause problems?

Yes, you can quickly run into problems if you make too many changes at once. It's easy to get overwhelmed. It may sound strange, but getting better can be very stressful. You may need some time and support to get used to having fewer symptoms or side effects.

Let yourself get used to your new level of recovery. It's hard to stay stable if you change your routine, start a new job, go to school full time, move into an apartment, or tackle extra responsibilities right away.

> *Getting better can be very stressful.*

What would you want to change about your life?

How could you be sure you didn't make those changes too soon?

How might getting better be stressful for you?

I've been ill for 10 years—will it take me that long to catch up?

There aren't really any definite answers to that question. But we do know it is important to be patient and avoid doing too many things at once. Time is on your side: You have years ahead of you to have the experiences you want and to reach your goals. There are many other conditions that can also cause people to lose years, such as a major substance abuse problem. Figure out what you want to experience. Make a list of your goals. Work out a realistic time line for all the experiences and goals you want to reach. Then work toward them one at a time.

Sam had been ill since he was 17. When he was 27, an atypical antipsychotic totally changed his life. For the first time in 10 years, he didn't have to spend all his time and energy struggling with his illness. Over the next 2 months, he was gradually discharged from the partial hospitalization program he'd attended for over a year. The problem was that Sam no longer had anything to do with his time. He decided it was too soon to get a job, and there wasn't a clubhouse program near by. He started taking GED classes twice a week, but he still felt bored and lonely.

What could Sam do?

What would you do?

Feeling Disconnected from Other People

Many people who have recovered enough to go to work, return to school, or begin dating find it hard to "get back into life." They have a lot of goals and dreams but are held back by feeling disconnected from other people. Here's what some people have said about their struggle to get reconnected with life.

"At first, it was really hard to talk to people at work. I didn't know what to say. I didn't seem to have anything in common with anyone. Most of them talked about other jobs they'd had, their children, and their marriages. What did I have to talk about? I didn't want to tell them about my medication, being in the hospital, going to day treatment, or what it's like to have symptoms—but those things have been a big part of my life for a long, long time. Someone told me once that most people like talking about themselves. So I just listened and asked questions to keep the discussion focused on the other people. That helped a lot and gave me time to think of other things to say."

"After I got a lot better, I had some hard decisions to make. In some ways, it would have been easier to just keep the same friends. They had a mental illness, too. We'd been through a lot together and they accepted me for who I was. I didn't want to cut them out of my life. But I really wanted to get into things on campus. I started hanging out with people from school—people who didn't have psychiatric problems. It was hard at first. I felt OK in classes but I was nervous around the other students outside class. Being in school, though, gave me things to talk about. We had something in common. I made up my mind to relax and fit in. It wasn't easy, and it took time, but I'm not so out of it now. I've made a couple of friends."

Dealing with Depression

Do some people feel discouraged and hopeless after getting better?

Just like everyone else, people with schizophrenia can experience times of depression. Sometimes, depression comes shortly after the other symptoms of schizophrenia improve. Doctors don't know exactly why people get depressed at this time. It may be related to brain chemistry, psychological reactions to symptoms getting better, or a grief reaction from realizing that many years, goals, and dreams have been swallowed up by illness. If these feelings get really bad, it is called *postpsychotic depression*. Often, postpsychotic depression comes like a big crash, right after the person starts to feel better.

What are some of the feelings I might have during a postpsychotic depression?

Here is what some people have said when they were in a postpsychotic depression.

"I feel so far behind. I have so much to accomplish. I don't have a car, a job, a wife, children, a college degree—how will I ever catch up?"

"I feel like such a failure. I still can't work!"

"I thought that, when the voices finally went away, I'd be cured. But then, the voices came back. It's hopeless!"

If you start to have these sorts of feelings, it is very important to know that postpsychotic depression is a phase. When it happens, it is a part of the healing and recovery process, and it gets better with time and treatment. The most dangerous part of this depression is that it sometimes puts people at risk for suicide.

Have you ever had these kinds of feelings?

What did you do?

How did you cope?

What should I do if I feel hopeless?

If you have been getting better on the new medication and then start to feel very depressed or suicidal, get help immediately. Keep telling yourself that these horrible feelings are temporary and will get better. Tell your doctor or your treatment team about any new suicidal thoughts. Alert your family and friends to how bad you feel. They may not know how you feel because they are focusing on all the other ways in which you've gotten better.

Remember, postpsychotic depression is a phase and people feel better with time and treatment. Get help for suicidal urges. *Do not give up—the terrible feelings will pass and then you can move on with your recovery.*

Are people more likely to become depressed at certain points of recovery?

Because the newer medications work better for some people, they may suddenly realize what a hole the illness has put in their lives. The first few months after switching are a high-risk time for depression. However, it's important to realize that the new medication *isn't* causing the depression.

> *Depression isn't caused by the new medication—
> it's part of the process of recovery.*

Ralph is a 26-year-old graduate student in chemistry who could only take a part-time course load because of persistent psychotic symptoms. He changed medications during a summer break. By fall semester, his symptoms were much better and he could finally take a full course load. He seemed to be able to handle the demands of his schedule.

However, Ralph became more and more discouraged about his past academic difficulties. Even though he was doing better, he felt he couldn't make up for his past "failings." By Christmas, Ralph was feeling hopeless and suicidal. Fortunately, he was able to tell his doctor and family.

His doctor diagnosed postpsychotic depression and gave Ralph antidepressant medications and more sessions. His family was able to be more supportive and saw him through this period. Ralph's depression slowly resolved, and he has been much happier. His symptoms remain in much better control, and the postpsychotic depression hasn't come back.

Why do you think Ralph started feeling depressed?

What might have happened if Ralph hadn't told anyone about how he was feeling?

What would you have done?

Wanting to Drink or Get High

If you feel a lot better on the new medication, you may be tempted to experiment with drinking or getting high. Now that you're feeling better, you may socialize more. Many people socialize by drinking or getting high with friends. While this is understandable, it's really risky for you. It's important to ask yourself if it's worth it to drink or use street drugs right when you're doing better on a new medication. Drugs and alcohol can keep your medicine from working and make your symptoms worse.

Think about it. Which is most important to you: getting high or getting better?

Fulfilling Intimacy and Sexuality Needs

What about dating, falling in love, and being sexually active?

You may find your sexual and romantic interests improve after switching medication. If so, good! But, there are new challenges and responsibilities to deal with when a reawakened sense of sexuality comes into your life. You may need to relearn how to socialize, make friends, flirt, and date. Making friends and dating are good ways to start developing relationships that might grow into love or marriage. Dating can be fun and exciting, but it can also be disappointing. You might meet someone you really like, but that person doesn't feel the same way about you. Or it might work the other way around. That's a natural, normal part of dating. You'll probably meet and date a lot of different people before you're ready to commit to a long-term relationship. As you know, it could take months or years to find someone you really connect with. It takes time and patience to find a good relationship in which you love each other enough to want to spend the rest of your lives together.

When should I tell people about my mental illness?

That's a very important question. Many people wait to see whether or not the relationship is going to last. A lot of people who have a mental illness don't want to risk being rejected or "scaring" people away. They don't want to wade through all those issues with people they aren't serious about. They don't tell everyone they date. They wait until they know the other person well, and they're thinking about committing to a long-term relationship. They only discuss their illness when they're starting to fall in love, or when they're thinking about being sexually intimate, living together, or getting married.

If you decide to become sexually active, you'll need to cope with the same fears of intimacy and sexual concerns that everyone does. You'll also need to consider your responsibilities in birth control and preventing sexually transmitted diseases. One suggestion is to be slow and cautious about restarting intimate or sexual relationships. (Note to women: with many of the newer medications, your menstrual cycle will return to normal, so it is more important than ever to use birth control when having sex.)

You may want to think about the following questions and then discuss them with your family or someone on your treatment team.

- When was the last time you went out on a date?
- Would you like to date?
- Fall in love?
- Be sexually active?
- What method of birth control would you use?
- When will you talk with people about your mental illness?
- What will you tell them?

How Can I Start to Put My Life Back on Track?

It is important to develop realistic goals for yourself. Figure out which goals you can accomplish in the next few months and which may take the next few years. Some goals may have to be achieved first, before you have much of a chance to achieve others. For example, it is almost impossible to succeed in school or keep a job if your substance use is out of control. Develop goals that are specific and practical, and then work with your friends, family, doctor, and treatment team to make a plan to help you accomplish them.

11 Final Thoughts

A Teacher Describes the Changes in Her Life

Martha is a 50-year-old divorced mother who had to quit working because of her illness. Two years after she switched from Thorazine to one of the newer medications, she was able to return to teaching full-time. Now she's studying for a Master's degree in education while she does what she loves best—working as a teacher. In the following sections, Martha explains the ways switching to one of the new medications has changed her life.

On the difference between new and old medications:

"Shortly after switching, I realized my mind was clear for the first time in years. The older medication slowed me down so much I couldn't get on with my life."

On reaching for goals:

"I can do so much more now. Just the fact that I can go for my Master's degree is a miracle to me. Each semester I seem to do better and better at school—which makes me feel really proud of myself."

On self-esteem before and after switching medications:

"Before I switched medications, I felt like a dope because I was always sick. When I was sick, I couldn't count on tomorrow. Now I can count on tomorrow. Now I can get dressed. It wasn't possible to live a normal life on the older medications. I was always fighting the medication."

On the fear of switching medications:

"At first, I didn't want to switch medications. I was afraid of getting sick—getting more psychotic episodes. Then, when I was sick, I didn't have a choice and my doctor gave me a new medication." (Although Martha refused to switch when she was stable, Martha's doctor was able to switch her medications during one of her relapses.)

On taking antipsychotic medications:

"Before, I was always fighting the Thorazine. I would excuse myself to go to the bathroom and flush it down the toilet. I would always fight with my doctor, trying to get him to lower the dose, while he was telling me to increase it. I knew the doctor was right, but I didn't do what he said. Now,

on the new medication, I don't fight it anymore. No one needs to watch me take my medication anymore."

Other Ways to Help with the Recovery Process

In this book, we focus on antipsychotic medications—especially the newer ones. Medications are a necessary part of recovery. But medications alone are not enough. We would also like to tell you about some things—besides medications—that people can do to help themselves recover. Of course, no two people are alike, and what might help one person might not work for someone else. We suggest you look over the list that follows and think about what has helped you in the past or what might make sense for you to try as you are moving toward recovery.

Faith

Mental health professionals don't often mention using faith, or religious beliefs, in helping someone recover. Perhaps this is because religious ideas can sometimes be a symptom of mental illness. But we are not talking about faith or religion as a symptom here. We're talking about people using their own faith or religious beliefs as a way to help them make sense of what's happened to them and as a way to heal. Many people who have recovered have said that their faith, or their belief in God, made all the difference.

"I read the Book of Job over and over again. It gave me a lot of comfort during my setbacks. I think it helped me stay on course."

"I don't know why God gave me this illness, but there must be a reason. I put my trust in Him and He has helped me recover."

"I talked to my minister. He was so understanding, and said that God will always love me, even though I'm so embarrassed about what I did when I was sick."

Hope

People can get through the most terrible experiences when they have hope. When hope goes away, people give up. Many people who recover from mental illness have been able to hold on by continuing to hope that their illness will get better. Remember, though, there can be a fine line between maintaining hope and expecting too much, too soon.

"I always thought I could do better than putting up with all those side effects. Wanting to lead a normal life means I have to be very picky about my medications. This means there are certain side effects I will argue about with my doctor, even if he doesn't think the side effects are so bad."

Patience

You probably know the children's story about the turtle and the rabbit. The rabbit challenged the turtle to a race and everyone was sure the rabbit would win. But in the end it was the turtle who won. The rabbit got off to a fast start but had to stop, exhausted, before the finish line. The turtle, slow and steady, finished the race and won.

People who recover from schizophrenia need to be more like the turtle than the rabbit. Recovery comes very, very slowly. Months might go by during which it will seem like there has been little progress. But people learn that slow, steady progress is actually the *fastest* way to recovery. If you try to go too fast, it is hard to continue in the long haul. Here's what some people have said about the road to recovery:

"It took me forever to finish college . . . 7 years instead of 4! At first, I wanted to finish at the same time as everybody else and I took a full course load. But I would get sick around exam time and have to take the classes over again. I learned the hard way that, for me, the way to graduate was to take half the number of courses and that's what I did!"

"I hate this psychiatric day program. I want a real job where I make real money. But, until I switched medications, I never had enough energy to go to work. I guess I'll stick around this day program until I know I can show up on time, every day."

"Since I switched medications, I've been really lonely. On the old medication, I was too out of it to get lonely. Now I want a girlfriend . . . but I haven't dated in years. Maybe I should just get back with some of my old friends and learn how to hang out with them before I ask anyone out."

Perseverance

People who recover are persevering—they don't give up. They use the new medications to help improve their lives. But there can be long delays between feeling better and doing better in life. A person has to adjust to a new level of symptoms and figure out what's now possible and what's still out of reach. Often, there are no obvious improvements in someone's social life or work life for a year. It is easier to stick with things and work toward recovery if you are persevering.

"I have been able recover because I have a determination not to let my handicap interfere with having a life . . . being handed a mental illness is a bad deal and bad luck. I just want to lead a normal life apart from mental illness and that's why I've kept trying when I got better with these new medications."

Sense of purpose

Many people find it helps them if they can develop a sense of purpose, of having a mission in life. That sense of purpose helps people get up in the morning and deal with all of life's little hassles as well as any big setbacks they may encounter.

"I need to be well so I can continue to volunteer teaching English as a second language to the people in my community."

"My grandfather always believed in me. He said I was strong. He's gone now, and never saw me being sick. I need to be strong for him."

"I need to get better so I can take care of my children."

"My mother has diabetes and needs help getting around. She needs me now, so I need to be able to take care of her."

As you can see, these goals are not very fancy or grand. These goals are very human and very normal—wanting to help others and wanting to be recognized and appreciated.

Connecting with others

Mental illness is isolating. The symptoms of mental illness make it harder to connect with other people. But then being alone often makes the symptoms worse. After a while, you may find yourself disconnected from others. It might seem like you don't know how to relate to other people anymore. Or you may feel embarrassed about your illness, which makes it harder still to reach out to others.

However, many people who recover find that connecting to other people even a little bit goes a long way to help with the healing process. These people say that having a group of people—or even just one person—whom they could connect with regularly helped them through setbacks and disappointments.

Some people have found that kind of relationship with someone in their family; others with people in the community; and still others, with a mental health professional.

"I went to a self-help group at the clinic. Knowing it was there helped me through the rough times."

"I couldn't have recovered without my mother. She believed in me even when no one else did, not even myself!"

> We wish you the best of luck
> on your road to recovery.

Part II
Technical Information

This part of the book is meant to be used as a reference guide rather than being read from start to finish. It assumes you are familiar with at least some of the terms that are used to describe properties of medications and their benefits and risks. If you come across terms you are not familiar with, chances are you can find them explained in "plain English" in the Glossary (p. 161). If most of the terminology is unfamiliar to you, you might first want to read other educational material that can give you basic information about schizophrenia and its treatments. You will find some helpful books and pamphlets listed in the Resources section (p. 183).

Part II is divided into five chapters:

12. Antipsychotic Medications
13. Common Side Effects
14. Switching Medications
15. Assessing the Response to Switching
16. Long-Term Issues After Switching

A cautionary note. The information in this section is based on a variety of sources, including published studies, treatment guidelines, and the authors' clinical experience. Some of the findings described in this section—especially that the newer medications are usually better for persistent negative symptoms—have not been fully demonstrated in long-term clinical trials. Finally, research on the switching process itself is virtually nonexistent. Most of the recommendations here are based on the authors' clinical experience.

12 Antipsychotic Medications

In this chapter, we discuss both the older (so-called "conventional") and newer (so-called "atypical") antipsychotic medications. We also give information about some other medications that may be used in the treatment of schizophrenia. A medication fact sheet is included for each of the newer antipsychotic medications that gives information on the drug's pharmacology, efficacy, and side effects.

The older antipsychotic medications are known as "conventional" antipsychotics (they are also called "neuroleptics" or "typical" antipsychotics). The conventional antipsychotics are usually very helpful in reducing or eliminating the positive symptoms of psychosis. They also reduce the chances of relapse. When someone stays on a conventional antipsychotic after recovering from a relapse, the chances of that person having a second relapse within 1 year go down from about 75% to about 30%.

But conventional antipsychotics also have many serious limitations. Many people continue to have positive symptoms. Many still have relapses despite taking medication regularly. Perhaps even more serious, these medications are rarely effective in treating the long-term negative symptoms of schizophrenia.

Conventional antipsychotics also have serious neurological side effects known as extrapyramidal symptoms (EPS), and can cause a serious, potentially permanent side effect called tardive dyskinesia (TD).

The major differences among the conventional antipsychotics are the dose ranges prescribed and their side-effect profiles, as shown in the table below. Conventional antipsy-

chotics are classified by their *potency*, depending on how many milligrams (mg) of the drug are usually prescribed. For example, it takes a larger amount (more mg/day) for a low-*potency* antipsychotic than a high-*potency* antipsychotic. High-potency antipsychotics also have more EPS (when given without an anticholinergic medication). On the other hand, low-potency antipsychotics have less EPS than high-potency medications but are more sedating and have more anticholinergic side effects. All of the conventional antipsychotics have the same likelihood of causing TD.

The conventional antipsychotics have the following *advantages* over the newer medications:

- Many people are already on these medications and know their own response to them.
- Many clinicians are familiar with the older medications, but have less experience with the newer ones.
- The older medications are much less expensive.
- Some of the conventional antipsychotics can be given by long-acting injection as well as by mouth. None of the newer drugs is available in long-acting forms and must be given orally.

Overview of Conventional Antipsychotics

This table lists the most common conventional antipsychotics and gives information about their doses and side effects.

Medication	Usual Dosage Range in Adults (mg/day)	Potential for Acute EPS	Potential for Anticholinergic Side Effects	Potential to Cause Sedation
High-potency				
Haloperidol (Haldol)[1]	2–20	Very high	Very low	Very low
Fluphenazine (Prolixin)[1]	2–20	Very high	Very low	Very low
Pimozide (Orap)	2–6	Very high	Very low	Very low
Medium Potency				
Thiothixene (Navane)	5–30	High	Low	Low
Trifluoperazine (Stelazine)	5–30	High	Low	Low
Perphenazine (Trilafon)	8–64	High	Low	Low
Molindone (Moban)	50–225	Moderate	Moderate	Moderate
Loxapine (Loxitane)	25–100	Moderate	Moderate	Moderate
Low-potency				
Chlorpromazine (Thorazine)	200–800	Low	High	High
Thioridazine (Mellaril)	150–600	Low	High	High
Mesoridazine (Serentil)	75–300	Low	High	High

[1] Haloperidol and fluphenazine are available in long-acting injections known as depot forms. Patients who take depot medication can receive all their antipsychotic medication in injections that are given every 2 weeks or monthly.

This fact sheet from *Breakthroughs in Antipsychotic Medications* (W. W. Norton & Company, 800-233-4830) may be reproduced.

Summary of the Newer Antipsychotic Medications

The table below lists the atypical antipsychotics that are, or soon will be, available and describes some of their characteristics.

Medication	Usual Doses (mg/day)[1]	Available Strengths	Comments
Clozapine (Clozaril)	300–700	25 and 100 mg scored tabs	First available atypical antipsychotic Only atypical specifically indicated for refractory psychosis Virtually no EPS but many other side effects (see p. 97) Weekly or biweekly CBC monitoring needed to check for low white cell count Routine switching of clozapine patients to newer atypical antipsychotics not recommended.
Risperidone (Risperdal)	3–6	1 mg scored tabs; 2, 3, & 4 mg unscored tabs	Low EPS rates when prescribed in the 3–4 mg/day range Orthostatic hypotension may occur during first few weeks Can be prescribed once a day Liquid form available
Olanzapine (Zyprexa)	10–20	2.5, 5, 7.5, & 10 mg unscored tabs	10 mg/day recommended therapeutic dose; 15 mg/day may be more effective for persistent negative symptoms Can start at 10 mg/day without problems No problem with once-a-day dosing Sedation common at first; usually improves within 4 weeks
Quetiapine (Seroquel)	300–750	25, 100, & 200 mg unscored tabs	Orthostatic hypotension may occur during first few weeks Therapeutic dose 300–400 mg/day Some patients may need higher doses Excellent EPS tolerability profile Sedation common at first; usually improves within 4 weeks Short half-life: usually needs to be given twice a day Eye exams sometimes recommended
Ziprasidone (Zeldox)	80–160	20, 40, & 80 mg caps	As of January 1999, still in testing Only antipsychotic for which a short-acting injectable form will be available May cause less weight gain than the other newer medications Short half-life: may need to be given twice a day

[1] The doses here are the usual target doses for medically healthy adults with a diagnosis of schizophrenia. Doses will often be much lower when starting the medication. Doses are also usually lower for very young or very old individuals, or when there is a coexisting medical problem.

Comparing Conventional and Atypical Antipsychotics

Psychosis is due to excessive dopamine in the limbic system in the brain. Conventional antipsychotics block dopamine in the limbic system—but they also reduce dopamine in other brain areas, which causes serious extrapyramidal side effects (EPS). The newer atypical antipsychotics block dopamine *and* serotonin receptors. This effect on serotonin may boost the medications's antipsychotic effect while reducing effects on the parts of the brain that cause EPS. Or the new medications may be more selective in the parts of the brain they affect.

The table below summarizes differences between older conventional antipsychotics and newer atypical antipsychotics. This table is only a generalization and should therefore not be used as a guide for treatment selection.

Feature	How They Compare	Comments
Efficacy issues		
Positive symptoms	Atypicals equal or better	Clozapine is the only atypical antipsychotic proven to have positive symptom efficacy > conventional antipsychotics.
Negative symptoms	Atypicals better	Many experienced clinicians believe that the newer medications are even better for negative symptoms than controlled trials have shown.
Relapse prevention	Atypicals much better (for patients who are compliant with medication)	Studies have convincingly shown fewer rehospitalizations among patients assigned to a newer antipsychotic than in a comparison group of patients treated with a conventional antipsychotic.
Side effect issues		
Relief from acute EPS	Atypicals much better	Very strong evidence for better EPS control even at the high end of therapeutic dosage.
Prevention of tardive dyskinesia (TD)	Atypicals possibly better	Although not conclusive, evidence suggests that the risk of TD from the newer drugs is about half that of the conventional antipsychotics.
Subjective preference	Much better with atypicals	Patient preference strongly favors the newer antipsychotics.
Relief from amenorrhea	Much better with atypicals	Unlike conventional antipsychotics, most newer antipsychotics do not raise prolactin levels.
Weight gain	Worse or much worse with atypicals	Both conventional and atypical antipsychotics are associated with weight gain, but in general weight gain is more of a problem with atypicals.
Other issues		
Complexity of medication regimen	Mixed effects	Some atypical antipsychotics need to be given twice a day.
Route of administration	Much better with conventionals	Short-acting IM forms are not available for any of the atypical antipsychotics. (Ziprasidone will have one when approved.)
		None of the atypical antipsychotics has a long-acting or depot form available.
Ease of prescribing	Mixed effects	Atypical antipsychotics are easier in terms of side effects and patient acceptance; however, many clinicians are unfamiliar with these drugs and/or unsure of how to do a crossover to a newer drug.
Cost of medication	Atypicals much more costly	Direct cost of atypicals (at pharmacy) is much higher.

Clozapine was the first of the atypical medications. First tested in the 1970s, it was discontinued because of serious blood reactions. It was reintroduced in the United States in 1989. It is different from other atypicals in the following ways:

- *Clozapine is the only atypical conclusively proven superior to conventionals for refractory positive symptoms.*
- There is almost no risk of extrapyramidal side effects (EPS) or tardive dyskinesia (TD).
- Despite advantages, clozapine has a range of potentially dangerous side effects: white blood cell reactions, cardiovascular problems, and seizures.
- Many side effects are not usually dangerous but can be very uncomfortable (e.g., sedation, dry mouth, constipation, blurred vision, urinary retention, orthostatic hypotension, nausea, hypersalivation, weight gain).

Although clozapine has unique benefits for many patients, most doctors try other medications first because of clozapine's problematic side effects. However, clozapine should be strongly considered for people whose symptoms don't respond adequately to other medications, *including those who do not respond to other atypicals.* Experts on schizophrenia have reached the following conclusions:

1. It is important to try clozapine when all other medications fail, including the other atypical antipsychotics.
2. Because of side effects, most people should try one or more of the other atypicals before trying clozapine.

Pharmacology

- Receptor profile: Clozapine binds to many different receptors, including serotonin, dopamine, muscarinic, histaminic, and alpha receptors. Broad receptor binding may partly explain both why clozapine is so effective and why it has so many side effects.

Dosing and forms available

- Usual effective dose: 300–700 mg/day.
- Full-dose trial considered ≥ 600 mg per day (may sometimes be precluded by side effects at lower doses).
- Although lower doses can be given once a day, the daily dose usually needs to be split to minimize side effects.
- Because clozapine is very sedating, a larger dose is usually given at night and a smaller dose in the morning.

- Blood levels can be helpful in determining medication absorption and optimal dosing when the response is not as good as hoped for. Target blood level: ≥ 350 ng/mL.
- Available in scored 25 and 100 mg tablets

Efficacy

- Multicenter inpatient trials showed that refractory patients on clozapine had significantly better improvement in positive and negative symptoms and EPS than those on conventionals.
- Other outpatient studies found lower relapse and rehospitalization rates on clozapine than on conventionals.
- A large-scale epidemiologic study showed lower suicide rates among patients on clozapine.

Side-effect and adverse-event profile

Despite its very favorable efficacy profile, clozapine has numerous side effects that prevent its use as a first-line antipsychotic medication:

- 1% incidence of a white blood cell problem called agranulocytosis (this problem is the reason for the baseline and ongoing blood tests required with clozapine).
- Clozapine can cause seizures, especially at higher doses. No more than 450 mg should be given in a single dose to minimize risk of seizures. *Patients with histories of seizures can still go on clozapine, but the risk is higher and often patients are simultaneously treated with an antiseizure medication.*
- Significant problems with orthostatic hypotension and sedation can occur early in treatment (need to start at very low doses and titrate upward very slowly).
- Very high rates of non-EPS side effects. Common side effects from clozapine include sedation, hypersalivation, weight gain, stomach distress, and sexual problems.
- Risk of heat stroke. During summertime or in hot climates, patients taking clozapine should use fans or air conditioners and drink plenty of fluids.

Considerations when switching *to* clozapine

- A baseline blood test is needed before starting clozapine. Weekly blood monitoring is required for the first 6 months; if there are no blood count problems after 6 months, blood monitoring is reduced to every 2 weeks.

- If patients are reluctant to try clozapine because of having to get blood tests indefinitely, it may help to agree on a predetermined trial period (e.g., ask the person to make a commitment to 16 blood draws over 4 months). Then, leave it up to the patient to decide, *at that time,* whether or not it is worth it to continue with clozapine.
- Some other medications may need to be discontinued or adjusted before starting clozapine because of risk of blood problems (e.g., carbamazepine [Tegretol]), respiratory problems (e.g., sedatives such as benzodiazepines), or drug interactions (e.g., fluvoxamine [Luvox]).
- Many early side effects (e.g., sedation, orthostatic hypotension) are dose-related. It may take several weeks to reach minimum therapeutic dose of 300 mg/day.
- Because of the sedation and orthostatic hypotension, the clozapine dose cannot be raised too rapidly. It can take up to a few months after starting clozapine to actually arrive at therapeutic doses.
- Because of the frequency and complexity of dose adjustments early in treatment, doctor and patient should carefully review instructions and pills. Medication monitoring and/or the use of a pill box may be needed to ensure the titration schedule is followed correctly.
- Expect daytime sedation and increased need for sleep. Patients (or their treatment programs) may need to readjust their schedules when they start clozapine.
- The patient should immediately report to the doctor any fainting or loss of consciousness after starting clozapine.
- If the patient experiences sudden jerky arm movements ("myoclonic jerks"), the patient may be at greater risk of having a seizure.

Considerations when switching *from* clozapine to another medication

Because of its side effects, many patients on clozapine are interested in switching to another medication. However, switching from clozapine to any other medication, including one of the newer medications, carries a significant risk of relapse. Patients who have done better on clozapine than with any other antipsychotic should not switch unless their side effects on clozapine are truly intolerable or they are prepared to accept a high risk of relapse to find a more tolerable medication.

Should the person decide to switch from clozapine, the crossover should be done very slowly, with clozapine lowered by very small amounts (e.g., decreasing the clozapine dose by only 25 mg per week) and the next medication started before the clozapine is reduced. If possible, the dose of the new medication should be raised to the high end of the recommended therapeutic range.

Other options besides switching when side effects are a problem

It can be a dilemma when clozapine seems to be the single most helpful antipsychotic but its side effects become intolerable at therapeutic doses. For dose-sensitive side effects (e.g., severe sedation, nausea, and vomiting), another option is to use a lower dose of clozapine (e.g., 300–600 mg/day) and also add another atypical antipsychotic.

Switching for agranulocytosis

Do not confuse agranulocytosis with a more "normal" drop in white count. A patient's WBC will often decrease with clozapine, but not so severely that it would be dangerous. This is not agranulocytosis. Clozapine should usually be continued in these situations with closer WBC monitoring and regular reevaluation.

Agranulocytosis is *not* dose-related. If it develops, clozapine must be stopped immediately and completely. Agranulocytosis is one of the rare occasions when one needs to stop clozapine suddenly rather than slowly tapering. Another antipsychotic at high therapeutic doses should then be given immediately. Anticholinergic withdrawal from stopping clozapine can be treated with an anticholinergic medication (e.g., benztropine).

Risperidone was the second atypical antipsychotic introduced. It was the first atypical antipsychotic that could be used as a first-line medication.

Pharmacology

- Receptor profile: Risperidone binds strongly to serotonin and dopamine receptors; has affinity for alpha receptors.

Dosing

- Optimal dose for schizophrenia: usually 3–6 mg/day.
- When EPS is a primary concern, most doctors use 3–4 mg/day.
- Outpatients taking risperidone for long-term maintenance treatment may do well on even lower doses (in the 2–3 mg/day range).
- When persistent positive symptoms are of most concern, doses up to 16 mg/day have been found safe and have been tried for patients with persistent symptoms that have not responded to lower doses.
- Usually prescribed twice a day, or once at bedtime, but it can be given any time of day, or in split doses if desired.

Forms available

- 1 mg scored tablets; unscored 2, 3, and 4 mg tablets
- Liquid form available
- Long-acting and short-acting IM forms not available

Metabolism

- Metabolized to another active antipsychotic (9OH-risperidone) with a half-life of over 24 hours, allowing once-a-day dosing after initial dose titration period.

Efficacy

- Clinical trials showed risperidone to be more effective than haloperidol for the inpatient treatment of positive and negative symptoms of schizophrenia.
- Studies suggest that risperidone is better than conventional antipsychotics for relapse prevention.
- Inpatient study comparing risperidone to haloperidol

found 6 mg/day (3 mg b.i.d.) to be optimal. 6 mg/day was the usual dose when risperidone first came out. Since then, research has shown that 4 mg/day is as effective as 6 mg/day and causes fewer EPS.

Side-effect and adverse-event profile

- Very few EPS at doses ≤ 4 mg/day.
- EPS rates increase at doses > 6 mg/day.
- Most common side effects: sedation and weight gain.
- Causes more weight gain than most conventional antipsychotics, but less weight gain than olanzapine or clozapine.
- Raises prolactin levels (like the conventional antipsychotics) and can cause amenorrhea in women.

Switching considerations

- No baseline laboratory tests are needed.
- When first available, the recommended switching titration was to start with 1 mg twice a day and increase dose every day up to 6 mg/day. Doctors have since found this titration schedule too fast for most patients.
- Many doctors now increase the dose much more slowly (e.g., by 1 mg every few days). Target dose for outpatients is often about 4 mg/day.
- Because of the frequency of dose adjustments during early treatment, doctor and patient should carefully review instructions and pills. Medication monitoring and/or the use of a pill box may be needed to ensure the titration schedule is followed correctly. Patient should call with any questions about dose or dosing schedule.
- Can cause orthostatic hypotension (dizziness on standing) early in treatment, which usually abates within a few weeks.
- Usually started as a twice-a-day medication; it can easily be consolidated to once a day after a few weeks.
- Early (usually mild) sedation and/or early insomnia is possible.
- Patients being switched to risperidone may enroll in the Person-to-Person program sponsored by Janssen (800-376-8282). This program is designed to assist patients and clinicians in maintaining continuity of care.

Olanzapine (Zyprexa)

Olanzapine was the third atypical antipsychotic introduced. It can be used as a first-line antipsychotic medication.

Pharmacology

- Chemical structure: similar to clozapine.
- Receptor profile: similar to clozapine, binds to serotonin and dopamine receptors; also has affinity for muscarinic, histaminic, and alpha receptors.

Dosing

- Recommended starting dose for schizophrenia: 10 mg/day.
- Recommended dose range: 5–20 mg/day.
- Up to 20 mg/day shown to be safe and effective.
- Many clinicians have found doses of 15–20 mg/day to be more effective for persistently ill patients whose positive or negative symptoms do not fully respond to a trial of 10 mg.
- Very few published data on effectiveness of doses > 20 mg/day. Clinical experience seems to indicate doses up to 40 mg/day can be safely prescribed, but there is no consensus or evidence for effectiveness of doses > 20 mg/day.
- Olanzapine is usually prescribed at bedtime because of sedating properties, but can be given any time of day, or in split doses if desired.

Forms available

- Unscored 2.5, 5, 7.5, and 10 mg tablets
- Liquid and long-acting and short-acting IM preparations not available

Metabolism

- Half-life is > 24 hours, allowing for once-a-day dosing.
- Can be taken with food or on an empty stomach.
- No known active metabolites; antipsychotic effects come directly from parent compound.

Efficacy

- Clinical trials found olanzapine as effective as haloperidol in acute treatment of positive symptoms and better than haloperidol in acute treatment of negative symptoms.
- Patients responding to and maintained on olanzapine are less likely to be rehospitalized at 1-year follow-up than comparison group of haloperidol responders.

Side-effect and adverse-event profile

- Most common side effects: sedation and weight gain.
- Sedation: usually worst when starting olanzapine or when dose is raised; usually improves after a few weeks. Often worst in the morning, gets better as day goes on.
- Significant weight gain occurs in about one-third of patients (probably less than with clozapine but more than with risperidone or quetiapine). Weight gain can occur within 6 weeks of starting olanzapine, so patients concerned about weight gain should be alerted early on. If present, weight gain often persists over time during continued olanzapine treatment.
- Several clinical trials show EPS rates on olanzapine are no different than on placebo. There may be some EPS in sensitive patients at doses ≥ 20 mg/day.
- Less prolactin elevation than with conventional antipsychotics or risperidone. Women usually resume normal menstrual cycles about 3 months after switching to olanzapine.

Switching considerations

- No baseline laboratory tests are needed.
- Because olanzapine does not cause orthostatic hypotension, it can be started at the recommended therapeutic dose of 10 mg/day.
- Because of sedation, olanzapine is usually started as a single dose at bedtime. Expect increased need for sleep early on; watch for sedation. Sedation usually (about 80% of the time) abates in several weeks.
- Occasional subjective sense of dizziness not related to orthostatic hypotension.
- Occasional constipation and dry mouth.
- Watch for increased appetite and weight gain. Rapid weight gain (> 20 lbs) in the first six weeks often signifies that weight gain will continue during the first six months of treatment.
- After switching to olanzapine, blood tests may reveal an increase in liver function tests (LFTs). These lab abnormalities are not by themselves clinically significant and values return to normal after several months.

This fact sheet from *Breakthroughs in Antipsychotic Medications* (W. W. Norton & Company, 800-233-4830) may be reproduced.

Quetiapine is the fourth atypical antipsychotic introduced. It can be used as a first-line antipsychotic medication.

Pharmacology

- Chemical structure: related to clozapine and olanzapine.
- Receptor profile: binds to serotonin and, less strongly, dopamine receptors; also has affinity for histaminic and alpha receptors, but virtually no muscarinic activity.

Dosing

- Low-potency antipsychotic (i.e., potency and dosing roughly equivalent to chlorpromazine).
- Recommended dose range for patients with schizophrenia: 300–800 mg/day.[1]
- Up to 750 mg/day shown to be safe and effective; very few data on doses > 800 mg/day.
- Prescribed twice a day (b.i.d.); effectiveness of once daily dosing is not yet established.

Forms available

- Unscored 25, 100, and 200 mg tablets. Other dose strengths may become available.
- Liquid and IM preparations not available.

Metabolism

- Half-life approximately 7 hours
- Can be taken by itself or with food

Efficacy

- Clinical trials showed antipsychotic effects at 150–700 mg/day.
- At least 300 mg/day is needed for full antipsychotic efficacy in schizophrenia.
- Many experienced clinicians raise dose to 700–800 mg/day if patients do not fully respond to 300 mg/day. Higher doses are generally well tolerated.
- Clinical trials of quetiapine found that quetiapine at doses ≥ 300 mg/day was as effective as haloperidol in the short-term acute treatment of positive and negative symptoms. There are no published long-term data.

Side-effect and adverse-event profile

- Common side effects: sedation, orthostatic hypotension, and weight gain. Sedation and orthostatic hypotension usually resolve after first few weeks of treatment; weight gain may persist beyond initial titration period.
- Very favorable acute EPS profile.[2]
- Prolactin levels are basically normal; quetiapine should not cause amenorrhea or galactorrhea in women.
- In animal testing, cataracts were associated with high-dose quetiapine treatment in dogs. This problem was not found in monkey studies or human clinical trials. Baseline and follow-up eye examinations are recommended by the manufacturer. However, some researchers feel this is not needed except to protect against medical/legal risk.

Switching considerations

- No baseline laboratory tests are required.
- Many, but not all, doctors refer patients for a baseline eye examination before starting quetiapine.[3] Exact recommendations will vary among doctors.
- Because of orthostatic hypotension, starting dose is usually much lower than the final target dose. The dose titration period can be as short as a few days, but usually it is longer for crossovers for outpatients when quetiapine is added to the ongoing medication regimen.
- Because of frequency of dose adjustments during early titration, doctor and patient should carefully review instructions and pills. Medication monitoring and/or the use of a pill box may be needed to ensure titration schedule is followed correctly.
- Needs to be taken twice a day (b.i.d.). Sometimes taking more of the medication before bedtime is helpful. If symptoms recur between doses, dosing schedule should be increased.
- Watch for increased appetite and weight gain.

---

[1] Recommended dose on package insert is 300 mg/day. However, many clinical investigators have preferred to use the higher end of the therapeutic dose range for quetiapine (i.e., in the 600 mg range).

[2] Several clinical trials found EPS rates on quetiapine no different than on placebo across all dosage ranges of quetiapine. Keep in mind, however, that these results are group averages; some vulnerable patients may still develop EPS on quetiapine.

[3] This is not a requirement.

Ziprasidone (Zeldox)

Ziprasidone is a new antipsychotic in late stages of FDA evaluation. Approval was initially expected in 1998 but it has been delayed pending further testing. The current FDA approval date is hoped to be late 1999 or early 2000. It probably will be used as a first-line antipsychotic when it becomes available. One difference between ziprasidone and the other atypical antipsychotics is that ziprasidone appears to cause fewer problems with weight gain. Also, a short-acting intramuscular form will probably be available shortly after the oral form is released.

Pharmacology

- Receptor profile: Ziprasidone binds strongly to serotonin and moderately to dopamine receptors. It is also a $5HT_{1A}$ agonist. At higher doses, it also is a serotonin and norepinephrine reuptake inhibitor, similar to certain antidepressants. Ziprasidone has little affinity for muscarinic, histaminic, and alpha receptors.

Dosing

- 80–160 mg/day, given in divided doses, found as effective as haloperidol for positive and negative symptoms of schizophrenia in several dose-finding studies in inpatients with schizophrenia.
- Ziprasidone should be taken with meals.
- Doses of $\geq$ 40 mg found more effective than placebo in relapse prevention in an inpatient maintenance study.

Forms available

- Expected to come in 20, 40, 60, and 80 mg capsules.
- A short-acting injectable form will probably be available shortly after the oral form is released.

Metabolism

- Ziprasidone has a short half-life and has mostly been studied as a twice-a-day medication. Ongoing studies are looking at whether ziprasidone can be given once a day.
- No active metabolites; antipsychotic activity from parent compound.

- Has been tested against a wide variety of drugs that commonly cause drug-drug interactions. So far it does not appear to cause any significant interactions.

Efficacy

- Ziprasidone has been found to be as effective as haloperidol for the short-term treatment of positive and negative symptoms in doses ranging from 40–120 mg/day.
- Higher doses of ziprasidone may have some antidepressant effects.
- Ziprasidone has been found to be better than placebo in a relapse prevention study, but there are no studies comparing relapse prevention with ziprasidone and other antipsychotics.
- The same study showed that ziprasidone patients had continued improvements in negative symptoms over the course of one year.

Side-effect and adverse-event profile

- Favorable EPS profile compared to haloperidol.
- Prolactin levels basically normal; ziprasidone should not cause amenorrhea in women.
- Some reports of nausea early in treatment.
- Some reports of insomnia and activation early in treatment.

Switching considerations

- So far, no baseline laboratory tests are required.
- Recommended starting dose will be 40 mg twice a day (80 mg/day).
- Some investigators have noted early nausea and vomiting soon after starting ziprasidone that abate within a few weeks of continued treatment.
- Some investigators have noted problems with early-onset insomnia and activation during the first few weeks of treatment, especially with doses > 80 mg/day; these problems seem to resolve within 6 weeks. Lorazepam or other benzodiazepines may be useful during the first few weeks of ziprasidone treatment to help with agitation and insomnia.

Medications for Extrapyramidal Side Effects

Side effect medications are commonly used to treat the neurologic (EPS) side effects of antipsychotic medications. The most commonly used side-effect medications are listed below. Most of them work through their anticholinergic properties, so they are also known as anticholinergics. Anticholinergics work best for parkinsonian symptoms such as tremor, muscle rigidity, and slowness of movement (akathisia). Dopamine agonists may also help with these symptoms if the patient cannot tolerate anticholinergics. These anticholinergic side-effect medications can cause side effects themselves, which are discussed in more detail on page 110. Akathisia (restlessness) is a type of EPS that often requires other medications, such as beta-blockers, benzodiazepines, or antihistamines.

Most patients who switch to a newer antipsychotic drug will not need these side-effect medications and will eventually be able to stop taking them. However, some patients may continue to need side-effect medications even when taking the newer medications.

Anticholinergics

Benztropine (Cogentin)

Biperiden (Akineton)

Trihexyphenidyl (Artane)

- Most useful for treatment of parkinsonism (tremor, rigidity, and akinesia) and prevention of dystonia; may also be helpful for akathisia.
- Can often be discontinued after switching to an atypical antipsychotic medication, but should usually be continued during the crossover period to avoid withdrawal reactions.
- Whenever possible, anticholinergics should be tapered slowly rather than stopped abruptly.
- Might be required for several months in patients switching from long-acting haloperidol or fluphenazine decanoate.
- Common side effects of anticholinergics include dry mouth, blurry vision, and constipation.
- Can interfere with memory. While this is a particular problem in older patients, some memory impairment occurs in most patients taking these medications

Anti-akathisia

Propranolol (Inderal) and other beta-blockers

- Probably the single most effective treatment for akathisia.
- Only certain beta-blockers are helpful for akathisia; consult with doctor for appropriate choice.
- Should be avoided with asthma, diabetes, and certain heart conditions.

Benzodiazepines

Clonazepam (Klonopin)

Lorazepam (Ativan)

- Can be used during the switching process to treat symptoms of anxiety or insomnia that emerge during the crossover period.
- Should be used cautiously in patients who have substance abuse problems.
- Should be used cautiously with clozapine because of possible risk for respiratory depression.
- Patients taking benzodiazepines for more than a month need to stop them slowly to avoid withdrawal problems.

Antihistamine

Diphenhydramine (Benadryl)

- Often used for rapid relief of acute dystonic reactions.
- May be useful for treatment of akathisia, especially when sedation is needed.

Dopamine Agonists

Amantadine (Symmetrel)

- Offers similar antiparkinsonian benefits without anticholinergic problems.
- Not effective for akathisia.
- May be less effective for parkinsonian side effects than anticholinergic agents.
- May take several weeks to take effect.
- May occasionally cause increased psychotic symptoms.
- Can often be discontinued after the switch to the newer medication is completed.

Other medications are commonly prescribed along with the antipsychotics, including:

- Mood stabilizers such as lithium (Eskalith; Lithobid), valproic acid (Depakote), and carbamazepine (Tegretol)
- Antidepressants such as tricyclic antidepressants (Tofranil, Elavil, and others) and SSRIs (Prozac, Zoloft, Paxil, and others)
- Anti-obsessive medications (Anafranil, Luvox, and the SSRI antidepressants)
- Medications for anxiety and insomnia such as lorazepam (Ativan) or clonazepam (Klonopin)

These medications are most often used as a *primary* treatment for other psychiatric disorders. For example, mood stabilizers are the primary treatment for bipolar (manic-depressive) disorder, and anti-obsessive medications are the *primary* treatment for obsessive-compulsive disorder.

However, many patients with a *primary* diagnosis of schizophrenia or schizoaffective disorder may be given one of these medications as adjunctive treatment (to treat so-called "ancillary" symptoms). In those situations, the medication is prescribed to augment the effects of the antipsychotic medication or to treat a symptom that does not respond to the antipsychotic. For example, an antidepressant might be prescribed to treat a postpsychotic depression that does not get better with antipsychotic medication alone.

Mood stabilizers

Lithium

Valproic acid or divalproex (Depakote)

Carbamazepine (Tegretol)

General considerations: Adding a mood stabilizer to an antipsychotic is a second-line treatment approach for persistent positive or negative symptoms. However, using adjunctive medications in schizophrenia is usually not as effective as switching to an atypical antipsychotic.

Mood stabilizers are often prescribed along with antipsychotics for patients with schizoaffective disorder to treat the mood symptoms of this condition. Some people with schizophrenia also have mood symptoms and may benefit from taking a mood stabilizer along with an antipsychotic. While mood stabilizers alone are effective for the treatment of bipolar disorder, *mood stabilizers alone are not effective for the treatment of schizophrenia or schizoaffective disorder. Continued treatment with an antipsychotic medication is needed.*

Issues related to switching antipsychotics while taking mood stabilizers:

- Carbamazepine (Tegretol) has major effects on the metabolism of almost all antipsychotics. Blood levels of the antipsychotics will often decrease over days to weeks after carbamazepine is added (while blood levels of antipsychotics will increase soon after carbamazepine is stopped).
- Because carbamazepine (Tegretol) and clozapine both can cause low white blood cell counts, they should not be prescribed together. Patients should usually have their carbamazepine discontinued prior to starting clozapine.
- If someone taking a mood stabilizer and a conventional antipsychotic has successfully switched to a new antipsychotic medication and done better on the newer medication for at least 6 months, it may then be possible to gradually lower and discontinue the mood stabilizer. However, most patients with bipolar or schizoaffective disorder are likely to need to continue taking a mood stabilizer regardless of which antipsychotic medication is prescribed.
- Evidence suggests that abruptly stopping a mood stabilizer is riskier than slowly tapering and discontinuing the medication. It seems advisable—whenever possible—to use a slow taper approach over several months when discontinuing a mood stabilizer.
- Valproic acid or divalproex (Depakote) is sometimes used with clozapine to decrease seizure risk, especially when clozapine is given in a relatively high dose.

Antidepressants

Tricyclic antidepressants (e.g., Tofranil, Norpramin, Elavil)

Selective serotonin reuptake inhibitors (SSRIs) (e.g., Prozac, Zoloft, Paxil)

Monoamine oxidase inhibitors (MAOIs) (e.g., Parnate, Nardil)

Other antidepressants (e.g., Wellbutrin, Effexor, Remeron, Desyrel)

General Considerations: Antidepressants are most helpful when the person's positive (or psychotic) symptoms are stabilized and at their baseline level. Depressive symptoms that worsen along with increased psychotic symptoms should be treated with antipsychotics alone.

Issues related to switching antipsychotics:

- When someone already taking an antidepressant is switching from one antipsychotic to another, most doctors continue the antidepressant throughout the crossover.

- If a person shows new symptoms of mania or hyperactivity while switching, the doctor may recommend lowering or discontinuing the antidepressant.
- Some people who respond to a newer antipsychotic medication may later suffer from a postpsychotic depression. If depressive symptoms worsen within 6 months of responding to a new medication, the doctor may recommend adding an antidepressant to the new antipsychotic.
- Antidepressants generally raise the blood levels of antipsychotics, and vice versa. The extent of this effect varies somewhat depending on the specific medications involved. The doctor may need to make dosage adjustments during switching based on these drug interactions. Of the newer antipsychotics, clozapine is more likely to cause significant drug interactions with antidepressants. Of the antidepressants/anti-obsessives, fluvoxamine (Luvox) is the most likely to cause drug interactions.
- MAOIs are not frequently used because of problems with hypertensive crises and the need for a special diet. However, they can be safely combined with antipsychotic medications.
- Bupropion (Wellbutrin) is now also being used to help people stop smoking. When used for smoking, it is called Zyban.
- Trazadone (Desyrel) is a sedating antidepressant that is commonly used as a treatment for insomnia.

Anti-obsessive medications

Clomipramine (Anafranil)

Fluvoxamine (Luvox)

General Considerations: The approach to prescribing adjuvant anti-obsessives is generally similar to that used for adjuvant antidepressants, except that obsessive rather than depressive symptoms are the major treatment target.

Issues related to switching antipsychotics:

- After switching to a newer antipsychotic medication, some patients may experience an improvement in positive or negative symptoms but a worsening of obsessive symptoms. If the obsessive symptoms persist, it can sometimes be helpful to add an anti-obsessive medication.
- Anafranil is the most effective for obsessive symptoms, but is often a second-line choice for obsessions because of its many side effects. Most doctors will suggest trying an SSRI anti-obsessive first before going to Anafranil.
- Luvox is an SSRI that is effective in treating obsessive symptoms. There are more drug interactions with Luvox than other SSRIs, especially when it is used along with clozapine.

Anti-anxiety agents

Benzodiazepines:

  Clonazepam (Klonopin)[1]

  Lorazepam (Ativan)

People with schizophrenia are often extremely anxious. If substance abuse is not a concern, the ongoing use of benzodiazepines may be helpful for certain patients.

Issues related to switching antipsychotics:

- Benzodiazepines are commonly added to the medication regimen during the crossover period to help with anxiety, insomnia, or other uncomfortable symptoms that may occur during the medication transition period.
- Although benzodiazepines have some potential for abuse, persons with schizophrenia generally do not abuse this class of medications. The very short-acting benzodiazepines (e.g., alprazolam [Xanax]) have more abuse and withdrawal problems than others, and probably should not be used.

Notes

Adjuvant medications used to be one of the most common ways doctors tried to boost antipsychotics when there were persistent positive and negative symptoms of schizophrenia. However, the newer medications have now largely replaced the adjuvant medications for the first-line treatment of these persistent symptoms. Adjuvant medications are still used for other common symptoms seen in patients with schizophrenia—in particular, the persistent depressive, obsessive, and anxiety symptoms many patients continue to have despite the newer medications.

Most of the time, the patient's adjuvant medications are left alone during the crossover process. Then, well after the crossover is done, the role of the adjuvant is reassessed. However, there are some exceptions. For example, carbamazepine needs to be stopped before starting clozapine; antidepressants may need to be stopped if the patient develops grandiose or psychotic symptoms during the crossover period. Adjuvant medications can also be helpful during the switching period, especially benzodiazepines for any early anxiety symptoms and the antidepressants in case a postpsychotic depression happens after the crossover is completed.

[1] Clonazepam (Klonopin) is actually indicated for seizure disorders, but is often prescribed for the treatment of psychiatric conditions involving anxiety and related symptoms.

13 Common Side Effects

In this chapter, we discuss some of the more common side effects that can occur with the older and the newer antipsychotic medications. We focus on side effects that might be a reason to consider switching medications. We also cover side effects that are frequently seen with the newer medications.

Different people experience different side effects; we therefore include a number of fact sheets, each of which focuses in detail on a specific type of side effect. When you read the fact sheets, remember that other things besides side effects can cause some of the problems listed. For example, antipsychotic medications can cause women to stop having their menstrual periods—but so can being pregnant. The side effect akathisia can cause restlessness, but so do positive symptoms. It is not a good idea to change medications because of a problem that is thought to be a side effect but that turns out to be caused by something else. For this reason, the fact sheets also include discussions of other possible causes of the problem besides side effects.

Before switching medications because of a side effect, the doctor and patient should consider other possible causes of the problem. Also, there may be easier ways to treat the side effect than switching medications. The fact sheets review other treatment options to consider.

Definition and description

The neurological side effects of the antipsychotics are known as "extrapyramidal" symptoms, or EPS for short. They have this name because they disrupt a part of the brain known as the extrapyramidal system.

These syndromes result in disorders that affect normal movement. In this fact sheet, we discuss certain common types of EPS that patients taking antipsychotics frequently experience.[1] These are: akathisia, dystonia, tremors, muscle rigidity, and akinesia. Because tremors, muscle rigidity, and akinesia are often seen in Parkinson's disease, they are grouped together and called parkinsonian symptoms.

Akathisia refers to a kind of restlessness. The person may have a constant need to stand up, pace around, or move his or her legs and fidget. The person often also has a subjective feeling of restlessness that can be very distressing. The akathisia can come and go, and usually worsens when the person is alone. The distress can be bad enough to cause people to become suicidal. The restless feelings are often localized in the thighs or trunk area. People experiencing akathisia often describe it as "feeling like I'm going to jump out of my skin."

Dystonia is a kind of muscle spasm that comes on suddenly and unexpectedly. The muscle will stay in spasm for a brief period, and then relax on its own. This kind of spasm can happen with one muscle at a time or several muscles together. The most common muscles affected are those in the face, neck, mouth, eyes, or arms and hands. Writer's cramp is an example of a common dystonia. Dystonic reactions tend to come and go, and can be triggered by anxiety or stress.

Tremors are shaking to-and-fro movements. Hand tremors are the most common, but tremors can also occur in other parts of the body. Tremors from EPS may come and go, and may worsen with anxiety, specific positions of the limb, or when the muscle is resting. Tremor can be caused by a variety of medications, and the type of tremor caused by antipsychotics is usually distinct from other causes.

Muscle rigidity is an increase in the general tenseness of muscles that is not caused by anxiety or exercise. This rigidity causes the muscles to tire more easily. It can also make it difficult to perform repetitive movements precisely. A reli-

able sign of muscle rigidity from EPS is a decreased arm-swing while walking.

Akinesia is a generalized loss of energy and spontaneity. The person may be listless or slow when initiating body movements or conversation. People with akinesia will often look "wooden" and have a decrease in spontaneous facial movements. Akinesia can be primarily behavioral—that is, the person describes feeling slowed down ("like a zombie"), even when other physical signs are absent. It can be very difficult to tell the difference between akinesia from medication and negative symptoms from schizophrenia. Fortunately, from a practical point of view, both akinesia and negative symptoms may improve on atypical antipsychotics.

Dyskinesia is also technically an EPS. However, to avoid confusion, we discuss dyskinesia in the next fact sheet, which covers tardive and withdrawal dyskinesia.

Causes and risk factors

The antipsychotics cause EPS by interrupting the normal flow of the neurotransmitter dopamine in the part of the brain that controls movements. Aside from the risk factors associated with taking antipsychotic medications, other risk factors include individual vulnerability (especially the person's past history of EPS), chronicity of illness (with patients who have recently become ill more vulnerable to EPS), and age (older people are more vulnerable).

Medication risk factors include medication dose (higher doses are more likely to cause EPS than lower doses), how quickly the dose is raised, and whether or not anticholinergics are prescribed. Among the conventional antipsychotics, high-potency agents are more likely to cause EPS than low-potency agents. All the newer agents are less likely to cause EPS than the high-potency conventional antipsychotics. Among the newer antipsychotics, clozapine is least likely to cause EPS.

EPS can come and go in the same person, even when the medications stay the same. For example, EPS are sensitive to the person's anxiety level; as anxiety goes up, so do EPS. This situational change in severity can cause other people to feel that the side effects are not real. It also means that caffeine can sometimes make some EPS worse.

Differences between newer and older medications

Risk of EPS: The risk of getting acute EPS is much lower with the newer medications. There had been some controversy about whether the EPS benefits were more apparent than real, because high doses of the older conventional antipsychotics were used as the basis for comparison in most studies. However, recent studies have resolved the debate in favor

[1] These EPS can happen shortly after the antipsychotic medication is started or develop over the course of antipsychotic treatment. The EPS mentioned here all resolve within weeks or months from when the antipsychotic medication is stopped. There are other neurologic side effects that develop after years of therapy and may not go away after the medication is stopped. These kinds of problems are categorized as "dyskinesia" or "tardive dyskinesia." Although dyskinesia is technically an EPS, to avoid confusion it is covered in a separate fact sheet.

of the newer drugs, since some of the newer drugs were found to cause fewer EPS than even low doses of haloperidol.

However, please keep in mind that a *lower* risk for EPS is not the same as *no risk.* Although the newer medications represent a major advance in the EPS problem, they can still cause EPS, especially akathisia, in certain individuals.

Possible treatments other than switching antipsychotics

Akathisia. The first treatment that is usually tried is adding an anti-akathisia medication, such as the beta-blocker propranolol (Inderal), a benzodiazepine (e.g., Ativan), an anticholinergic (e.g., Cogentin), or an antihistamine (e.g., Benadryl). Clinicians usually try one or two of these treatments before switching antipsychotics. The good news is that, when anti-akathisia medications work, they usually take effect quickly. The bad news is that response rates to any particular anti-akathisia medication are no better than 50%.

Acute dystonic reactions. Adding an anticholinergic such as benztropine or an antihistamine such as Benadryl is very effective for acute dystonic reactions. *Because dystonic reactions often go away on their own after a few weeks, switching to a newer medication is not usually necessary after an acute dystonic reaction has been successfully treated.*

Parkinsonian symptoms (tremor, rigidity, or akinesia). The first step is usually to add an anticholinergic medication. Other options include lowering the dose of the antipsychotic medication or switching to a low-potency conventional antipsychotic such as chlorpromazine.

Switching issues

Continuing anticholinergics during the crossover period: If someone is already on anticholinergics but still has EPS, he or she might switch medications for this reason alone. However, even though the new medications are much better for EPS, anticholinergic medications should be continued well after the older medication has been completely stopped. This is because the old medication has residual effects in the brain that may continue to cause EPS even after it is out of the bloodstream.

Although the newer medications represent a major advance in the EPS problem, they can still cause EPS in certain individuals. Therefore, switching medications is not a guarantee that EPS will be completely eliminated.

If the *only* reason for switching is because of persistent EPS, olanzapine, quetiapine, or ziprasidone should be considered first, before risperidone or clozapine At higher doses, risperidone has more EPS than the other atypicals. While clozapine has almost no EPS, it has too many other side effects to be the *first* atypical chosen for problems due to EPS. However, other reasons for switching and non-EPS side effects should also be considered in choosing a medication.

Clozapine or quetiapine may be less likely to cause EPS for patients who are *very* vulnerable to EPS (the elderly or people with coexisting psychosis and Parkinson's disease). Clozapine and quetiapine should be considered for patients who continue to have persistent EPS *as their major problem* on the other atypical antipsychotics.

Tardive Dyskinesia and Withdrawal Dyskinesia

Definition and Description

Dyskinesia is an abnormal writhing-like movement that can occur in the face, mouth, tongue, hands, and feet. Dyskinesias tend to wax and wane, and are usually painless. Often the person does not notice the movements, although other people do. There are many different types of dyskinesia and many different causes. While certain neurological conditions can cause dyskinesia, the dyskinesias discussed here are all caused by antipsychotic medications.

Unlike almost any other side effect, the medication that *causes* the dyskinesia also *suppresses* it. This means that many diskinesias worsen rather than improve when the medication is stopped.

- *Tardive dyskinesia (TD)*: persistent abnormal movements caused by antipsychotic medication. Unlike other EPS, TD doesn't necessarily happen soon after starting medication. Usually, it takes years of medication treatment before a person gets TD.

- *Withdrawal dyskinesia:* a dyskinesia that happens shortly after antipsychotic medication is discontinued or lowered. It is usually temporary and goes away within 3 months. If it persists longer, it is termed TD.

There is no way to tell right away whether a dyskinesia that happens shortly after lowering or discontinuing an antipsychotic is a withdrawal dyskinesia or a tardive dyskinesia. The only way to tell is to wait it out.

Causes and risk factors

TD is caused by long-term exposure to medications that block dopamine. Patients on conventional antipsychotics have approximately a 4% risk of developing TD each year of treatment. Other risk factors for TD are increasing age, repeatedly going on and off antipsychotic medications, or having a mood disorder or a history of alcohol abuse, diabetes, a neurological disorder, or brain damage.

Differences between newer and older medications

- Although not conclusive, evidence suggests the newer medications have at most half the risk of causing TD as the older medications (a risk of approximately 2%/year). The risk with clozapine seems to be even lower. *The risk of TD can never be 0% because anyone can develop dyskinesia, even without being on antipsychotics.*

- Clozapine is the most widely accepted choice for reversing severe tardive dyskinesia in patients who need antipsychotic medication.[1] It is unclear whether the newer medications are helpful treatments for TD. The frequent occurrence of withdrawal dyskinesia when medications are changed makes it harder to assess TD after switching.

Possible treatments other than switching antipsychotics

- No intervention if the TD is mild and not bothersome.
- Take vitamin E (1200 to 1500 IU per day).[2]
- If possible, try to discontinue antipsychotic medication.[3]
- Slowly lower the dose of the current medication.[4]
- Change time of day when antipsychotic is taken.
- Lower or discontinue any anticholinergic medication.[5]
- Improve mouth and dental condition for mouth TD.
- Botox (botulinum toxin) injections for localized forms of tardive dystonia.[6]

Switching issues

When switching antipsychotics, it is very important to distinguish withdrawal dyskinesia from TD. Withdrawal dyskinesia, a reaction from going off the older medication, may happen in the first weeks to months of switching. There is no clear consensus among doctors whether patients doing well on conventional antipsychotics should switch to an atypical antipsychotic solely to reduce the risk of future TD.

---

[1] Severe forms of TD: abnormal movements affecting the person's ability to breath or swallow; dystonic movements "called tardive dystonia"; or movements that are disfiguring or embarrassing. Fortunately, these severe forms are relatively rare.

[2] Research studies on adding vitamin E have shown mixed results; however, there are virtually no risks in adding vitamin E at these doses.

[3] Unfortunately, studies in schizophrenia in which the medication was discontinued found a paradoxical long-term increase in dyskinesia because of the increased likelihood of relapse resulting in the need to go back on higher doses of medication.

[4] This dose lowering should be done very slowly and in small step-wise reductions over a period of 3–6 months. During this time, the dyskinesia may get worse (see withdrawal dyskinesia) before it gets better.

[5] Anticholinergics tend to make dyskinetic movements worse, but are often needed to treat the other EPS caused by the antipsychotic, which may worsen when the anticholinergic is discontinued.

[6] Botox (botulinum toxin) is injected into affected muscles to weaken them and reduce spasms and contractions for several months. This therapy is safe and effective for persistent dystonic syndromes but should be done only by someone experienced in this kind of therapy.

Definition and Description

Anticholinergic effects happen when the cholinergic receptor is blocked (choline is a neurotransmitter found in nerve cells in the brain and all over the rest of the body). Anticholinergic effects that occur in the brain are called *central anticholinergic effects*. The major benefit of central anticholinergic effects is that they can *reverse some EPS*. The most common problems from central anticholinergic effects are *memory problems*.

Anticholinergic effects that happen in other parts of the body are called *peripheral anticholinergic effects*. Peripheral effects include *dry mouth, blurry vision, constipation, and difficulty urinating*.

Many medications have anticholinergic properties. Some of these medications are given specifically *because* they have anticholinergic properties and are effective in countering the common neurological (EPS) side effects of antipsychotics. They decrease the stiffness, restlessness, and tremor caused by the antipsychotics.

The anticholinergic medications that are most commonly used to treat the side effects of antipsychotics include: benztropine (Cogentin), trihexyphenidyl (Artane), and biperiden (Akineton).

Some antipsychotics also have significant anticholinergic properties. The antipsychotics with the greatest anticholinergic properties are thioridazine (Mellaril), chlorpromazine (Thorazine), mesoridazine (Serentil), and clozapine (Clozaril).

Risk factors

- *Central anticholinergic effects.* The memory problems caused by anticholinergics can be subtle and very difficult to distinguish from psychiatric symptoms. Severe memory problems can lead to delirium (symptoms of confusion and disorientation). Elderly and medically ill people are at higher risk of delirium.
- *Peripheral anticholinergic effects* usually start shortly after the anticholinergic is added or the dose is increased. They often diminish after the first few weeks of treatment. For medically healthy adults, anticholinergic side effects can be uncomfortable but are usually not medically dangerous. However, for older people, anticholinergic side effects, especially urinary problems (which can block urinary functioning) and constipation, can be dangerous.

Differences between newer and older medications

- Anticholinergic medications for side effects are less likely to be needed with the newer antipsychotic medications because the newer antipsychotics are less likely to cause EPS.
- The newer medications also vary in the strength of their anticholinergic effects. Among the newer medications, clozapine has the most anticholinergic effects and olanzapine has some anticholinergic effects.

Possible treatments other than switching antipsychotics

- Slowly lower the dose of or discontinue the anticholinergic medication used to treat the EPS.
- Try treating the EPS side effects with a medication without anticholinergic side effects such as amantadine (Symmetrel) for tremor or muscle stiffness or propranolol (Inderal) for restlessness.

Switching issues

One of the potential benefits of switching from a conventional to an atypical antipsychotic is eventually being able to go off the anticholinergic side effect medication. In doing so, the medication regimen is simplified and the person does not have to contend with the anticholinergic side effects mentioned above. However, there are some technical considerations that caution against discontinuing anticholinergics too early in the switching process.

When anticholinergic medications—or antipsychotics with anticholinergic properties—are lowered or discontinued, some potentially serious withdrawal and rebound reactions can occur:

- Rebound EPS, including tremor, stiffness, akathisia, and dystonia; rebound EPS can be even worse than the initial EPS that led to the addition of the anticholinergic.
- Anticholinergic withdrawal, the symptoms of which include nausea or vomiting and feelings of malaise.

To avoid rebound reactions, the anticholinergic side effect medication is often continued during the crossover from an older to a newer antipsychotic medication. Once the crossover period is over and some time has gone by, the doctor can try to lower and discontinue the anticholinergic medication.

Sedation and Insomnia

Definition and Description

The newer antipsychotics may cause sedation or insomnia. Although these effects are sometimes desired, in this section we discuss situations in which they are unwanted. *Sedation* means that the medication causes an increased need for sleep, makes it more difficult to wake up in the morning, or causes daytime sleepiness. *Insomnia* means having problems falling asleep or staying asleep.

Causes and risk factors

Sedation can be caused by all antipsychotics, as well as by other medications, negative symptoms of schizophrenia, and poor sleep habits at night.

There are many causes of insomnia, such as sleeping too much during the day, drinking too much caffeine, feeling anxious, or trying to sleep in a noisy living situation. Insomnia can also be an early warning sign of increased symptoms. Therefore, insomnia should not be automatically attributed to the new medication. The treatment for insomnia depends on the underlying cause.

The effects of antipsychotics on the sleep cycle are probably related to their effects on the histaminic, alpha, and serotonin receptor systems.

Differences between newer and older medications

- Among the older medications, low-potency medications with high anticholinergic activity seem to cause more sedation than the medium or high-potency medications.
- Among the newer antipsychotics, clozapine is the most likely to cause persistent sedation over long periods of time. Olanzapine and quetiapine are more sedating than risperidone or ziprasidone. The sedation caused by olanzapine and quetiapine, unlike that caused by clozapine, usually *occurs during the first few weeks of treatment* and then resolves on its own.
- Risperidone and ziprasidone are more likely to cause insomnia than the other atypicals, most often as an early side effect that tends to go away on its own after several weeks.

Possible treatments for sedation

- Sedation is very sensitive to dose adjustments—slowing the rate of increase or decreasing the dose when appropriate may help.
- It may help to take medication at bedtime or experiment with timing dosages to maximize benefits of sedation at certain times.
- Using caffeine late in the day to counteract sedation is *not* recommended. Caffeine should either be discontinued or taken only in the morning.
- Adding a stimulant medication (either prescribed or over-the-counter) is *not* recommended.

Possible treatments for insomnia

The usual treatment is to add a sleeping medication (e.g., Ativan, Ambien). These sleeping medications are safe to take with all the newer medications, with the possible exception of clozapine, but clozapine almost never causes insomnia.

Switching issues: Sedation

- Patients should be warned about possible sedation when switching medications and told (if taking olanzapine or quetiapine) that the sedation is usually an *early* side effect that goes away.
- Sedation from clozapine may also go away over time, but is generally more likely to persist long-term.
- If sedation occurs during the crossover, the patient should not drive or do other tasks that require alertness until the person adjusts to the medication.
- If the sedation does not go away in a month, possible treatments include lowering the dose or changing the dose schedule (for daytime sedation, move the dose toward bedtime; for morning sedation, give the dose earlier in the day).

Switching issues: Insomnia

- Insomnia can be a symptom of antipsychotic withdrawal, especially when someone goes off clozapine quickly.
- Of the atypical antipsychotics, ziprasidone is the most likely to cause insomnia during the crossover process, with risperidone the next most likely. Clozapine, olanzapine, and quetiapine rarely cause insomnia.

The major problem with insomnia during the crossover process is that it tends to happen at a bad time, when the person is already feeling anxious and vulnerable due to the stress of switching medications. The added stress from insomnia can be quite uncomfortable and can lead to exacerbation of other symptoms if it is not dealt with quickly. Therefore, unlike sedation, early insomnia should be treated right away.

Definition and description

Antipsychotics may cause people to *gain weight* or *make it harder to lose weight*. Unless the person is underweight to begin with, this is an unwanted side effect.

Causes and risk factors

Weight gain is associated with all antipsychotic medications. The mechanism is not totally understood, but may be related to effects on the cholinergic, histaminic, and serotonergic pathways in the part of the hypothalamus that controls feelings of hunger and fullness. The effects on weight are probably caused by changes in appetite rather than metabolism or level of activity. However, keep in mind that there are other causes of obesity unrelated to antipsychotic medications (e.g., many psychiatric patients have inactive lifestyles and/or poor diets).

Differences between newer and older medications

- Among the older medications, the low-potency medications seem to cause more weight problems than the medium or high-potency medications.
- Of the older medications, molindone (Moban) seems to cause the least weight gain.
- With one exception, all the newer antipsychotics can cause more weight gain than the older antipsychotics.
- Among the newer antipsychotics, clozapine and olanzapine seem the most likely to cause weight gain.
- Risperidone and quetiapine seem to cause more weight gain than conventional antipsychotics, but less than clozapine or olanzapine.
- Ziprasidone seems to be the only new antipsychotic under development that does not cause weight gain over and above that of the conventional antipsychotics.

Possible treatments other than switching antipsychotics

- Diet and exercise are sensible approaches for dealing with weight problems, regardless of the cause of the weight gain.
- Adding a weight-reduction medication (either prescribed or over-the-counter) is *not* recommended.
- After someone is switched to a newer medication, it is sometimes possible to try lowering and discontinuing other adjuvant medications (e.g., mood stabilizers, antidepressants, and anticholinergic medications) that can also cause weight gain. Cautiously lowering and then discontinuing these adjuvant agents 3–6 months after successfully switching to an atypical antipsychotic may be helpful.
- Although the new medications tend to cause weight gain, the increased activity and better sense of well-being they bring can actually help some patients lose weight. There may be a lag time of about a year before these secondary health benefits become apparent.
- Preliminary observations suggest that switching to ziprasidone may help some patients lose weight.

Switching issues

- Patients should be warned about possible weight gain when switching from an older to a newer medication. For patients concerned about weight gain or for whom it may cause medical problems, monitor weight and dietary intake before, during, and after switching.
- Possible weight gain from switching antipsychotics needs to be factored into the risk/benefit assessment for patients at high risk for medical problems (e.g., a person already overweight from diabetes). Options include not switching or choosing risperidone or quetiapine, which cause relatively less weight gain than olanzapine or clozapine.
- Not everyone gains weight. It is not possible to predict ahead of time who will gain the most weight on a new atypical antipsychotic.
- It is a good idea to get a baseline weight prior to switching, otherwise it may be impossible to assess the effect of the new medication vs. other factors in managing weight-related concerns.
- Weight gain related to switching seems to start right away, and can continue for up to 6 months after switching. Weight gain usually plateaus after 6 months.
- Rapidly progressive weight gain right after switching (e.g., > 20 pounds in 6 weeks) usually means the weight gain is likely to continue, and continuation of the new medication should be carefully reconsidered.
- Unlike other side effects, like EPS or sedation, the degree of weight gain seems unrelated to the dose of the newer medication. Therefore, weight issues might influence *whether* to switch or *choice* of medication, but probably should not influence the *dose* of medication after switching.
- Although it is important to stop smoking, smokers who switch to a newer antipsychotic should probably delay trying to quit smoking until well after the switch.

Sexual dysfunction is a complicated issue. It is hard to separate medication effects from those of the illness because sexual dysfunction and loss of interest in sex are common symptoms of schizophrenia. Recreational drugs (most notably marijuana and cocaine) can also cause sexual dysfunction. Patients using these substances must quit before one can make any causal connection between medication(s) and sexual difficulties. To make the matter even more complicated, doctors often do not obtain a thorough sexual history, making it still more difficult to identify the cause of sexual problems. As part of their evaluation, doctors should assess whether sexual difficulties are present. The following questions should then be considered before attributing sexual difficulties to medications:

1. What is the specific nature of the problem?
2. Is it a social problem (e.g., finding a partner), a problem of sexual desire (loss of libido), or a performance problem (e.g., inability to achieve orgasm or erection)?
3. Did the problem begin with the psychiatric illness or develop when the medication was added or changed?

Definition and description

Antipsychotics have been reported to cause almost every kind of sexual problem, including loss of sexual desire (libido) and difficulty achieving orgasm in both men and women, and difficulty with erection and ejaculation in men. People with schizophrenia can also have many sexual difficulties besides those caused by medications. *It is usually very hard to know for sure the underlying cause of the sexual problem.* It is very important for the person to give a complete history of sexual functioning *before and during* medication treatment, and to be psychologically ready to deal with a trial and error process to solving the problem that takes time and patience!

Causes

Medications cause changes in the serotonin, dopamine, and anticholinergic systems that can result in loss of sexual desire and problems with sexual functioning.

Differences between newer and older medications

Both conventional and atypical antipsychotics can cause sexual dysfunction. It is not known whether the atypical antipsychotics cause a lower rate of sexual dysfunction than the conventional antipsychotics or whether there is any dif-

ference among the atypical antipsychotics. The atypicals can have clear benefits for sexual functioning when the sexual problems are related to negative symptoms, especially poor socialization, poor grooming, and low energy. The atypical antipsychotics (other than risperidone) also do not raise prolactin levels as much as conventional antipsychotics and can be helpful when the sexual difficulties are due to high prolactin levels. Unfortunately, there has been very little research on how to tell which sexual difficulties are related to prolactin levels. Among the conventional drugs, thioridazine (Mellaril) is most likely to cause erection and ejaculation problems.

Possible treatments other than switching antipsychotics

- When possible, simply lower the antipsychotic dose to see if the sexual difficulties improve.
- The SSRI antidepressants (Prozac, Zoloft, Paxil, and Luvox) frequently cause sexual side effects. When possible, try discontinuing an adjuvant SSRI.
- Anticholinergic agents may cause problems with erections and orgasm. When possible, try lowering or discontinuing the anticholinergic medication.
- Medical consultation should be considered when the problem is intractable or when there are coexisting medical problems (e.g., diabetes).
- Viagra (sildenafil) is a pill used to treat erectile dysfunction and may be effective for erectile difficulties caused by psychiatric medications. Viagra should not be taken with certain cardiac medications.
- Many other medications (e.g., Periactin [cyproheptadine]) and herbal remedies have been used, which have their own side effects and risks. It is very important for the patient to discuss any nonprescription treatment for sexual difficulties.

Switching issues

We do not have much research data about the chances of improvement in sexual functioning when switching from a conventional to an atypical antipsychotic. Clinical experience suggests that sexual dysfunction *directly* caused by medication does not always get better from switching to an atypical antipsychotic. Chances are better when the sexual problems seem to be due to persistent negative symptoms. When someone is regaining sexual functioning after switching medications, it is important to offer psychological support and information on birth control and safe sex.

This fact sheet from *Breakthroughs in Antipsychotic Medications* (W. W. Norton & Company, 800-233-4830) may be reproduced.

Amenorrhea and Galactorrhea

Definition and Description

Amenorrhea means loss of normal menstrual periods. *Galactorrhea* refers to a leakage of milk from the breasts that is unrelated to childbirth. These problems can happen because of the increased prolactin level caused by conventional antipsychotics and risperidone.

Causes and risk factors

The amenorrhea and galactorrhea that can occur with antipsychotic medications are due to prolactin elevation. Although amenorrhea and galactorrhea can in rare cases be caused by tumors of the pituitary gland, there is usually no cause for alarm if the amenorrhea or galactorrhea occur while taking antipsychotics that are known to raise prolactin levels.

However, there are other common causes of amenorrhea—such as pregnancy and menopause. One should also consider pregnancy as a possible cause of new-onset amenorrhea in sexually active women.

Differences between newer and older medications

All the conventional antipsychotics cause amenorrhea and galactorrhea. The atypical antipsychotics, with the exception of risperidone, do not cause these side effects. Switching to one of these medications should lead to a resumption of normal menstrual functioning and/or stop the galactorrhea.

Possible treatments other than switching antipsychotics

- Amenorrhea is not a medically dangerous side effect; therefore, switching medications is not necessary for women who are not concerned about this side effect.
- Sometimes amenorrhea can be a temporary side effect after starting an antipsychotic. It is possible that menses will eventually return without any medication changes.
- Lowering the dose of the antipsychotic medication may be effective in helping menses return and should be considered before switching.
- It is possible to add another medication (bromocriptene) that counteracts the antipsychotic's effects on prolactin and may help amenorrhea or galactorrhea if lowering the dose or switching medications is not an option.

Switching issues

- Among the atypical antipsychotics, olanzapine, quetiapine, and ziprasidone are the best choices to avoid amenorrhea and galactorrhea. Although clozapine is effective in lowering prolactin, it has too many other side effects to be used only for this reason.
- It usually takes about 3 months after going off a conventional antipsychotic before normal menses return. The time may be longer when the conventional antipsychotic was given in a depot formulation.
- Pregnancy should always be considered when there is a new onset of amenorrhea. Women are at higher risk for pregnancy once normal menses return and should use appropriate birth control if they are sexually active.

14 Switching Medications

In this chapter, we discuss technical issues related to the switching process. The organization of this chapter follows the actual sequence of steps in changing antipsychotics:

- Reasons to consider switching medications (indications)
- Reasons to stay on the current medication and not to switch (risks and contraindications)
- Timing issues if and when the decision to switch is made
- Choice of new antipsychotics
- Switching techniques during the crossover period

In order to simplify the section, we have assumed that the person who is considering switching medication:

- Is a stable outpatient in the community
- Has a diagnosis of schizophrenia or another psychiatric disorder requiring long-term antipsychotic therapy
- Is currently taking a conventional antipsychotic that is only partly effective and/or causes side-effect problems
- Is an adult and does not have any major medical or neurological problems

Outpatient status: We assume that the person is stable and receiving medications as an outpatient. The decision about switching is *elective.*

Diagnosis of schizophrenia or a related disorder: We assume that the person needs long-term antipsychotic medications. This assumption is appropriate when the medication is being given for schizophrenia or schizoaffective disorder. The situation may be quite different when the antipsychotics are being given to treat other psychiatric disorders such as depression or bipolar disorder. The discussions about long-term antipsychotic medications may not apply to patients with a primary mood disorder. If there is uncertainty about the diagnosis, or the diagnosis has recently changed back and forth between schizophrenia and a mood disorder, the doctor and patient should first clarify the situation.

Currently taking a conventional antipsychotic: We assume that the person is *currently* taking one of the older conventional antipsychotics and is considering a switch to one of the newer atypical antipsychotics. However, each day there are fewer patients on conventional antipsychotics, while more and more patients are taking atypical antipsychotics. Patients on the newer atypical antipsychotics will still have to contend with persistent positive and negative symptoms and, to some extent, persistent side effects from the atypical antipsychotics. The issues involved in switching among the newer atypical antipsychotics are almost the same as switching from a conventional antipsychotic to an atypical antipsychotic. Therefore, the information in this chapter also applies to a patient who is currently taking one of the newer medications and has never taken one of the older conventional antipsychotics.

Medically healthy adult: We assume that the person taking the medication is a medically healthy adult. The recommendations will be different for elderly patients or patients who have medical or neurological conditions. In general, medication doses will be much lower for elderly patients (typically a quarter to half of the usual dose). Patients with neurological conditions, such as Alzheimer's or Parkinson's disease, are also much more sensitive to medication toxicity, so that the risks of combining antipsychotic medications or continuing anticholinergic medications during the crossover are much higher.

It is usually much easier and more straightforward to try to optimize the current medication regimen than to change medication. The first step in the switching process is to make sure that the person is getting the most out of the current medication regimen (this is called *optimizing* the regimen). Most of the time, there is little to be lost by delaying the switching plan and first trying to optimize the current medications. The medication switch can be started if the optimizing response is unsatisfactory.

The table below lists some factors that can make someone's current medication less effective. It is beyond the scope of this book to review all the details of how to optimize medications, but the doctor and patient can review what steps have been taken to optimize the current medication regimen.

Possible Ways to Optimize the Current Medication Regimen

Factor	Comments
Dosage	Is the dosage adequate? Before switching because of persistent positive symptoms, make sure that doses were given at the upper end of the recommended dose range.[1] Before switching for persistent EPS, was lowering the dosage considered?
Duration	Has the medication been given for long enough? Some people take a while to respond to antipsychotic medications. Ideally, a medication trial for acute psychosis should last 4–6 weeks. When medications are changed because of chronic symptoms, the trial should last about 3 months.
Compliance	Is the medication being taken daily as prescribed? It is not unusual for patients to inadvertently or unknowingly skip doses or take medications incorrectly. Many people think they're taking medication as prescribed when they aren't. Using a weekly pill box for a short period of time can help accurately assess medication compliance.
Drugs	Is the person using any street drugs or alcohol that are interfering with the antipsychotic medication? If so, the drug or alcohol use needs to be curtailed before it is possible to assess how well the antipsychotic medication is working.
Depot route	Is the person actually taking the medication? When the person has a hard time taking oral medications, another option is to try one of the long-acting depot medications.

[1] Assuming the person was able to tolerate the higher doses.

The decision to change medications can be complicated. There is no single "correct" reason to change medications. One has to weigh the potential benefits of switching (known as "indications") against the potential risks. A variety of factors come into play. It is easiest when all the considerations point in the same direction—then there are no hard choices to make. More often, however, the reasons point in opposite directions, with some reasons suggesting it would be worth trying a new medication while other reasons suggest staying on the current medication. Here we review common reasons physicians recommend switching medications, as well as reasons patients and families may request a change.

Physicians switch antipsychotic medications when the current antipsychotic medication is not working well enough or when the person has unacceptable side effects. If an antipsychotic is "not working," the person may have relapses or persistent positive or negative symptoms despite taking the medication as prescribed. Common examples of unacceptable side effects are persistent extrapyramidal symptoms (EPS) or tardive dyskinesia (TD).

While this list sounds relatively straightforward on paper, in practice there are many gray areas. For example, it is not always clear how severe a problem should be before a doctor considers it unacceptable for his or her patient and recommends switching medications. Another factor is the doctor's impression that the newer medications might be better for the person.

Of course, it's the patient who takes the medication and the patient who finally decides. Switching issues need to be looked at from the patient's perspective. Patients and doctors often have different treatment priorities. The doctor tends to consider symptoms and side effects in terms of their severity on a psychiatric rating scale. The patient, however, is concerned about the distress from symptoms and side effects or impairment or loss of functioning. Some patients who are doing very "well" (from the doctor's point of view) may want to switch medications because of high levels of distress from persistent symptoms of schizophrenia, frustration over being unable to meet life goals or function independently, or being embarrassed from having a "medicated" look. Other patients who are doing "terribly" (from a functional perspective) have adjusted to their life situation and from their perspective are doing just fine.

Family members and loved ones may have yet another point of view! Family members experience the burden of being caretakers for the patient. They may be grieving the loss of emotional contact with their loved one because of akinesia.

If there are different perspectives, it makes sense to discuss them when weighing whether or not to switch medications. Patient, physician, and possibly family members, should:

• Discuss current problems and concerns.
• Review potential gains from switching medications.
• Review potential risks from switching medications.
• Attempt to gain consensus or, failing that, an understanding of the nature of the disagreement.

Going through this process before switching medications takes more time and effort, but it greatly increases the likelihood of success in the event of a switch.

In the table on the next page, we present reasons to switch medications from the perspectives of the major "stakeholders" in a switching decision. In the righthand column, we give an estimate of how likely a person is to achieve a clinically meaningful improvement by switching from a conventional antipsychotic to one of the newer medications in the circumstances described.

Reasons to Switch Medications

Doctor's Perspective	Patient's Perspective	Family's Perspective	Chances of Improvement
Relapse despite compliance	Inability to function independently in the community	Dealing with multiple crises and setbacks	Very high[1]
Persistent positive symptoms	Anxiety and depression from having positive symptoms	Disruptiveness and agitation	Moderate
Persistent negative symptoms	Inability to meet life goals	Emotional and financial burden	Moderate
Persistent EPS	Dysphoria or distress from EPS	Heartbreak of seeing their relative or partner burdened by akinesia, akathisia, rigidity, or tremor	Very High
Persistent anticholinergic symptoms (from anticholinergic medications that counter EPS)	Dry mouth, blurry vision, constipation, problems urinating	Increased symptoms of forgetfulness or confusion	Very high[2]
Galactorrhea and amenorrhea in women	Disruption of sexual identity because of disturbance in reproductive functioning	Disappointment or frustration on the part of the sexual partner	Very High
Prevention of tardive dyskinesia	Fear of getting tardive dyskinesia in the future	Fear of tardive dyskinesia in the future	Possible
Treatment of persistent tardive dyskinesia	Distress from tardive dyskinesia	Distress from tardive dyskinesia	Possible
Medication-induced sexual dysfunction	Embarrassment and frustration over problems with sexual functioning.	Disappointment or frustration on the part of the sexual partner	Unknown[3]

[1] Assumes that the person has been taking the older medications regularly. Even though the newer medications are generally better tolerated, many individuals who were noncompliant with the older medications remain noncompliant with newer medications.

[2] Anticholinergic problems often improve because side effect medications can often be eliminated from the medication regimen after switching to a newer antipsychotic.

[3] There are two issues to consider here. First, there are different underlying mechanisms for medication-induced sexual problems. Although the newer medications are better at keeping prolactin levels normal, the newer medications may still cause sexual difficulties for other reasons. Second, there are many causes of sexual problems that are unrelated to medication. It can be very difficult to figure out whether the problem is due to medications or another reason.

Many of the concerns about switching medications have to do with the risk of a symptom exacerbation or a relapse in someone who was previously stable. This concern is especially worrying for patients who have trouble stabilizing, whose relapses are associated with dangerous behavior, or who need a long-acting depot medication to remain on medication. The following table lists some of these concerns from the perspective of the doctor, the patient, and the family member.

Reasons to Avoid or Postpone Switching

Issue	Doctor's Concern	Patient's Concern	Family's Concern	Comments
Doing well enough with current medication	Satisfied with benefits and side effects of current medication or does not know or believe that newer antipsychotics are better than older ones	Person has adjusted to his or her symptoms and life functioning Fear because of an unsuccessful attempt to switch medications in the past Skepticism about claims that medications are better "this time"		Expectations of what constitutes a "good" or a "bad" response to medication vary
Risk of symptom exacerbation while switching	Risk of symptom exacerbation or relapse	Fear of emotional turmoil, disruption, or danger of a relapse		One of the most common reasons to avoid or postpone changing medications
The person is on a long-acting (depot) antipsychotic medication	Concern that the patient will stop taking medication if not given by long-acting injections	Inconvenience of having to take pills every day	Possibility of relative stopping pills or getting into conflicts and arguments over medication	Willingness and ability to stick with a daily pill routine need to be assessed before switching from a depot medication
Expense of newer medication	Medication will not be covered by the formulary or insurance plan	Unable to pay for the new medication	Cost burden of new medication for family	See section on "Paying for Medications" (p. 151)
Current drug or alcohol use complicating treatment	Concern that further progress is unlikely while abusing drugs or alcohol regardless of antipsychotic prescribed; substance abuse issues need to be a priority	May want to continue to "party" regardless of medications; may not want medications to interfere with the "highs"	Concern about risk of combining medications with drugs or alcohol	Greatest risk of mixing drugs and/or alcohol with antipsychotic medication is usually inadequate response to treatment and increased risk of relapse; the relative risk of dangerous adverse interactions is low
Already on clozapine	Risk that other medications cannot substitute for clozapine; difficulty restarting clozapine once it has been stopped	Troubled by the many side effects of clozapine and wants to change to another medication	Worry that other medications won't work as well; danger of disruption and relapse	Risks are greater when switching from clozapine than when switching from other medications; none of the other atypical antipsychotics has been proven to be as effective as clozapine

In deciding whether or not to change medications, there is often no right or wrong answer. We have already discussed some of the more technical aspects of what to expect from the new medications. In this section, we deal with some of the emotional aspects of making a decision to switch medications.

- Patients who have had discouraging experiences during past attempts to switch from one conventional antipsychotic to another conventional antipsychotic may be understandably leery of trying an atypical antipsychotic. While there are no guarantees, the atypical antipsychotics have helped many people with schizophrenia do better than they ever thought possible.

- After switching, some problems are more likely to improve than others. For example, persistent EPS symptoms of muscle rigidity and tremor almost always get better on a newer medication. It is less likely that a new medication will be better for persistent positive symptoms.

- Remember that all medication comparisons are statistical—they reflect the results of clinical trials of many individuals and compare the averages. *The statistical findings about a medication's effectiveness are no guarantee of how effective a medication will be for any one person.* For example, the statistics show that, on average, clozapine is better than conventional antipsychotics for positive symptoms. However, some individuals' positive symptoms may respond better to conventional antipsychotics than clozapine.

- What are the risks if the new medication doesn't work out? While there is a lot that can be done to minimize the risks of switching medications, there is always the possibility of a symptom exacerbation. Therefore, in deciding to switch, it is important to consider the possible consequences of having symptom flare-ups during the medication crossover.

Other questions to consider

- *What is the person's risk tolerance?* Is the person willing to take chances in order to improve his or her situation? People have different risk tolerances. For example, when faced with the decision to move to another group home that may or may not be better, some people would take a chance and move, while others would stay where they are.

- *Can the person accept and tolerate the current symptoms?* Switching antipsychotics is less urgent if the patient has come to accept his or her symptoms or does not feel distressed by them. The more bothered the person is by the symptoms, the more it may be worth considering switch-

ing (however, patient and family need to keep their hopes realistic or they will be disappointed no matter what).

- *Is the timing favorable?* Some times are better than others to switch. If the timing doesn't favor a switch right now, it may be better to postpone the decision.

When the patient can't seem to decide

If the person is stuck and can't decide whether or not to switch, it is possible that his or her symptoms may be interfering with the ability to make decisions. Apathy and indifference are common negative symptoms that can make it hard to be motivated to do anything. "Psychotic ambivalence" and severe obsessions can also interfere with the ability to make decisions. Patients with these symptoms may feel almost totally unable to make any decision, no matter how trivial. This kind of situation can feel like a "catch-22" in which the patients who most need to switch are too impaired to want to switch.

Sometimes family members get frustrated when doctors aren't more active in making the person switch. However, there is a fine line between persuasion and coercion. Doctors cannot be coercive unless there is imminent danger. However, there are ways to help the person come to a decision to switch. The main thing is to be patient. Someone who has negative symptoms or psychotic ambivalence may need to take longer to review the reasons to switch. It may take a lot longer for the person to make a final decision. Yet patients who are stuck because of severe negative symptoms, psychotic ambivalence, or obsessions sometimes benefit greatly from a switch.

Complicating situations

The decision to try a new medication is affected by many factors that are unique to the person's own circumstances. However, there are two complicating situations that are quite common and affect the decision-making process: (1) when the person is also using illicit drugs or alcohol, and (2) when the person opposes taking *any* antipsychotic medication (e.g., when there is denial of illness). These situations are discussed next.

After the decision has been made to try a new medication

After the decision to change medications has been made, several important steps need to be taken. These include timing the switch properly, choosing a new medication, and following the safest procedure during the switch. These topics are discussed later in this chapter.

Is it safe to switch antipsychotic medications when a person is actively using drugs or alcohol? This combination of severe mental illness and drug abuse is often called "dual diagnosis." Before discussing the switch, let's clarify the general role of antipsychotics when there is an active substance abuse problem in addition to schizophrenia. Many patients with schizophrenia are advised that it can be dangerous to mix drugs or alcohol with their antipsychotic medication. Unfortunately, many patients (and some mental health clinicians) misinterpret this recommendation to mean that antipsychotics need to be stopped before the person uses drugs or alcohol. Stopping medication before getting high or drunk is just the wrong thing to do. While it is, of course, best to avoid illicit drugs or alcohol in the first place, in reality, many people with schizophrenia continue to use drugs or alcohol despite the warnings.

If a person with schizophrenia is going to use illicit drugs or alcohol anyway, it is crucial that he or she continue taking antipsychotic medications.

There are several issues to consider in deciding whether to switch antipsychotics when the person has active substance abuse problems. One issue is whether any of the atypical antipsychotics are less safe than the conventional antipsychotics for someone who abuses drugs or alcohol. Although no good studies have been done on this question, the atypical antipsychotics are probably not very different from the conventional antipsychotics in terms of medical risks. In theory, clozapine might be riskier when substance abuse complicates the picture because clozapine has a greater risk of seizures, which may be increased by alcohol, and a greater risk of cardiac problems, which may be increased by cocaine. Another issue is that dual diagnosis

patients are unlikely to recover as long as they are actively abusing drugs or alcohol.

Unfortunately, very little research has been done on the psychopharmacology of antipsychotic medications when substance abuse problems are present. However, we can give some clinical impressions based on switching patients who had active substance abuse problems.

- The chances that switching to a new medication will be successful or will lead to meaningful and sustained improvements in symptoms are much poorer when there is a coexisting substance abuse problem.
- Switching to atypical antipsychotics does not routinely solve substance abuse problems. Other psychosocial treatments that directly address the substance abuse or a program specializing in the needs of dual diagnosis patients are necessary.
- If there is a pattern of stopping antipsychotic medications during episodes of substance abuse, switching to a long-acting depot injection may be a better strategy than switching to an atypical antipsychotic. With the depot injections, therapeutic levels of antipsychotic medications remain in the bloodstream when the person is getting "high."
- If a person with active substance abuse problems is switched, he or she should be encouraged to refrain from drug use for at least 6 weeks to avoid complicating the switching period by a substance abuse episode. If the trial of the new medication is "unsuccessful," a substance abuse evaluation should be done. If the person was "getting high" during the switch, it is impossible to compare the effectiveness of the older and the newer medications.

Switching When the Person Denies Having an Illness

Many patients with schizophrenia have a hard time acknowledging that they suffer from a mental illness. They may not believe they need to take antipsychotic medications. Patients *deny* their symptoms or illness for many reasons, and there are many different consequences of this denial. If a person is reluctant to take medication because he or she does not believe medications are necessary, this denial can throw a monkey wrench into the whole discussion about the pros and cons of switching medications. It makes it much harder for the person taking (or being asked to take) antipsychotic medication to properly assess the situation. It also makes it much more difficult for clinicians and family members to discuss the newer medications with the person.

Denial of need for medication during acute episodes. Sometimes the person denies the need for medication *only* during an acute psychotic episode. When the acute episode resolves, the denial also resolves. For example, if someone who is usually OK about taking medication becomes acutely ill, he or she may refuse medication out of a fear that everything has been poisoned. When the fear of poisoning goes away, the person's willingness to take medication should return. When the medication refusal fits this kind of pattern, the main goal is to find the most effective medication to help reduce the acute symptoms. The focus in these situations is on stabilizing the acute episode. In this situation, long-term issues that favor the atypical antipsychotics often become secondary. Under these circumstances, clinicians often choose a conventional antipsychotic such as haloperidol, especially if the conventional antipsychotic has helped the person in the past. In the long run, however, there is no problem switching the person to an atypical antipsychotic. In fact, if the atypical antipsychotic does a better job preventing relapse, it is more likely to stop the downward spiral of symptoms that can cause denial.

Ongoing denial of the need for medication. Another common situation is when a person consistently does not believe in taking antipsychotic medication. The belief is a longstanding one and is often at odds with the recommendations made by the doctor. It is usually contrary to the opinions of family members or friends as well. The person might be taking medication anyway, but does so for reasons other than a personal belief that medication is needed. People may continue to take medication even when they don't think it is needed because of the influence of others in their social or treatment network. The person may stop medication because he or she does not believe medication is necessary and/or denies he or she has a mental illness. Or the person may acknowledge that antipsychotics were once needed, but believes the psychiatric problems are a thing of the past and medication is no longer needed. Unfortunately, switching to an atypical antipsychotic medication is unlikely to change a patient's opinion about the need for medication.

Notes

- Denial of illness is a very common issue among patients with schizophrenia. Many, but not all, patients who deny their illness are noncompliant with their medications.

- In the short run, the newer medications do not seem to change denial of illness for outpatients who have consistently denied their illness.

- For patients who show lack of insight into needing medication *only* when they are psychotic, their short-term recovery depends on their getting on a medication that is effective for acute symptoms. Conventional and first-line atypical antipsychotics are roughly equal in their effectiveness under those circumstances, and clozapine is usually not an option because of problems with cooperation.

- *Compliant* outpatients who take their medication despite denying their illness are likely to benefit from a medication switch in terms of symptom response and side-effect improvement.

- Switching to a newer medication for *noncompliant* patients who deny their illness is unlikely to change compliance in the short run.

- A patient who *persistently* denies the illness should not be swtiched from a long-acting depot antipsychotic to an oral atypical antipsychotic.

After the decision is made to switch medications, the next question is *when* to switch. Sometimes there is no choice, for example, if the current medication is causing a severe or dangerous side effect or is completely ineffective. However, there is usually leeway in deciding when to switch. Choosing the right time can lessen the risks and maximize the chances that the new medication will be successful.

During periods of stability

Whenever possible, it makes sense to switch medications when conditions improve the chances of success:

- If the switch is being made for persistent side effects or persistent negative symptoms, choose a time when the positive (psychotic) symptoms are relatively stable. If psychotic symptoms are worse than usual, focus on stabilizing them back to baseline.
- Pick a relatively low-stress time. For example, students might consider switching medication during a summer break to avoid switching during a time of academic stress; or it might be wise to postpone switching medications if the person is about to change residences.
- Elective switching is best done when the doctor or treatment team has worked with the person for a while and there is an atmosphere of collaboration and trust.
- Allow adequate time to review the pros and cons of switching; be sure the person is emotionally ready to make a commitment to the switching process.
- Everyone directly involved in the person's treatment network should be aware that a significant change in medications will take place. Be sure a line of communication is open between the patient, the family, and the mental health treatment service.
- Be sure the treatment network is ready to respond promptly to any symptom exacerbations during the crossover process.

During periods of instability[1]

- If the person's acute symptoms are responding to the current medication, the current medication should be continued, perhaps with an increase in dose.
- If the person is recovering from an acute psychotic episode that has been successfully controlled by a particular medication, wait 3–6 months before trying to change medications, even if the current medication is not fully

controlling every symptom or is causing EPS.[2] This waiting period is needed to allow time for the medication response to solidify. Although it is possible to switch medications right after an acute psychotic episode resolves, this greatly increases the risk of complications from the switch.

- Consider trying an atypical antipsychotic when the person is hospitalized for a relapse. This is a time when it is much safer to try a new medication with the hopes of finding a better antipsychotic to stay on after discharge from the hospital.

During hospitalization

The indications to switch medications are roughly the same, whether the person is an outpatient or in the hospital. However, the hospital setting is very different and the factors influencing treatment decisions are also very different.

- Switching antipsychotic medications is indicated when the acute psychotic episode does not respond to the first antipsychotic prescribed during the hospitalization. The recommended time for switching medications is somewhere between 3 and 12 weeks of treatment. If the first medication tried during the hospitalization was not an atypical antipsychotic, the second one should be.
- Another reason to switch medications during a hospitalization for an acute psychotic episode is the potential *long-term* benefits of a newer medication. It can be much easier to start and monitor a new medication when it is started in a highly structured setting such as an inpatient psychiatric unit. The hope is that the new medication will help with the acute psychotic episode and will also be a better medication in the long run in terms of side effects or controlling negative symptoms. Prompt input from the outpatient treatment system and/or the family can be a very important factor in persuading the inpatient service to try a new medication.
- Before switching to a newer medication in the hospital, consider whether the new medication can be continued after discharge. Is there adequate insurance coverage to pay for the new medication? Has the outpatient center been informed of the new regimen? Will that outpatient program continue with the new medication?

[1] Instability refers to a worsening of the person's positive symptoms that goes beyond "normal" fluctuations in symptoms.

[2] That is, assuming that the person is able to tolerate the symptoms and side effects during this time. If possible, treat symptoms and/or side effects during this period by adjusting the dosage of the person's current antipsychotic or adding a medication to treat the side effects.

Currently, there are not enough research data or accumulated clinical experience to help us know how to choose among the newer antipsychotics. We can only give rough guidelines, which will need to be revised as our understanding of the newer drugs increases.

- First-episode patients should be started on one of the newer antipsychotic medications.[1]

- Experts disagree on which of the first-line atypical antipsychotics—risperidone, olanzapine, quetiapine or ziprasidone—should be chosen for a first-episode patient or for a patient who hasn't yet tried any of the newer medications.

- Clozapine is not appropriate for a first-episode patient because it is reserved for patients who have failed at least one other medication.

- Whenever a patient is switching antipsychotics, the next antipsychotic should be one of the newer antipsychotics if possible. Exceptions to this general rule are when the patient needs a long-acting depot antipsychotic for compliance reasons[1] or when there are cost barriers to using the newer medications.

[1] Recommendations based on consensus of experts in a recent survey: McEvoy, J.P., Scheifler, P.L., & Frances, A., et al., The expert consensus guidelines series: Treatment of schizophrenia, 1999. *Journal of Clinical Psychiatry* (in press).

- The newer antipsychotics do not all work equally well for all patients. If one doesn't work well, try another! For outpatients, allow up to 3 months at therapeutic doses (minimum 6 weeks) to determine the degree of response.

- None of the atypical antipsychotics except clozapine (Clozaril) have been proven better than the others. The choice should be based on the doctor's personal experiences with the newer medications, the patient's past medication experiences and personal preferences based on what is known about the new medications, and differences in the side-effect profiles of the newer medications.

- Because of its serious toxicity, clozapine is not a first-line atypical antipsychotic. However, clozapine is the only antipsychotic proven to be effective for treatment refractory patients—clozapine remains the "heavy hitter." It is a treatment option even when the patient has not responded to the other newer agents.

- If a new medication is definitely working better than the previous one, but the patient or family is frustrated because there are still symptoms or side effects, another decision about switching may need to be made. Most doctors advise staying on the newer medication for at least 1, if not 2, years before trying to switch medications again.

In this section, we discuss how to switch medications safely—to maximize the chances that the person will ultimately get the most out of the new medication in a way that minimizes the risks of going off the old medication.

There are several switching techniques that seem to help make the switching process much safer. One important technique is a process called a medication "cross-over," which involves a temporary overlap between the new and old medications. To better understand the underlying principles of this technique, you need to know about three problems that can occur during the switching process:

- Antipsychotic and anticholinergic withdrawal syndromes
- Delays in obtaining pharmacologic benefits from antipsychotic medications due to lags in brain chemistry changes
- Medication errors due to misunderstandings about the new medications

Withdrawal syndromes

Some of the problems that can arise early in the course of switching medications are caused by withdrawal reactions from stopping (or lowering) the previous antipsychotic medication. The table below lists some of these withdrawal reactions and describes their symptoms and when they usually happen.

Delayed responses when starting or stopping antipsychotics

All antipsychotic medications—both old and new—block a particular kind of dopamine receptor known as the D_2 receptors. This blockade seems to be needed to produce an antipsychotic effect. When the dopamine receptors are blocked, any signal from the nearby nerve cells that uses dopamine is weakened—just as a radio station's signals become weaker when driving into a mountain range. While the dopamine blocking effects come on immediately (within minutes or hours of taking the first dose of medication), the clinical effects on psychosis can take many days or weeks to happen. This is because the brain cells can compensate for the weakened dopamine signals—for a while, anyway. Going back to the radio analogy, as the radio signal is getting weaker in the mountain range, you might try to adjust or fine-tune the station or turn up the volume. These tricks may work for a time, but eventually the radio signal fades for good. When someone begins taking antipsychotics, there is a delay between the time the medications stick to the brain receptors and the time when the dopamine brain signal actually weakens. This delay is roughly 4 weeks, give or take a few weeks. *This means that it can take weeks after starting a new antipsychotic medication for it to show its benefits.*

The same principle works the other way around. It can also takes weeks for a person to lose the benefits of an

Antipsychotic Withdrawal Syndromes

Category	Symptoms	Usual Timing	Comments
Anticholinergic withdrawal	Malaise, nausea, vomiting, diarrhea	First few days	Occurs with low-potency conventional antipsychotics and clozapine More likely to happen with abrupt anticholinergic withdrawals
Rebound akathisia	Typical symptoms of akathisia but may be indistinguishable from psychosis or anxiety	First few days	Consider akathisia in differential diagnosis of behavioral changes soon after antipsychotic or anticholinergic withdrawal Addition of beta-blocker or benzodiazepines might be helpful
Rebound parkinsonism	Parkinsonian symptoms of tremor, muscle rigidity, akinesia	First week	Commonly occurs when an anticholinergic agent and a high-potency conventional antipsychotic are discontinued at the same time May also occur when discontinuing low-potency antipsychotics
Withdrawal dyskinesia	Choreathetoid (writhing) movements indistinguishable from tardive dyskinesia	1–4 weeks	Dyskinesia is clinically indistinguishable from tardive dyskinesia Most are transient and abate within several months Should dyskinesia last > 3 months, change diagnosis to tardive dyskinesia.

antipsychotic after it is stopped. Even when the blood levels of medication are zero, the dopamine receptors will remain blocked for a while. Even when they are unblocked, it may take time for the nerve cells to get the dopamine signals up and running again.

These time lags are the reason that switching medications can be risky. Because each medication is different, it may take weeks to find out how well a new medication works. The opposite is also true—it may take weeks for the old medication to stop working after it is stopped.

Here's the dilemma: If the old medication stops working before the new medication takes over, the nerve cells in the brain behave as if they are completely off all antipsychotic medications, even though there is medication in the bloodstream. When that happens, the person is (temporarily) at higher risk of relapse until the new medication takes effect. This high-risk period occurs roughly 1 month after stopping the old medication.

Overlapping antipsychotics during the crossover

To avoid withdrawal problems and ensure adequate antipsychotic protection, doctors often recommend that the person take both the old and the new antipsychotic together for a period of time. This transition period is known as a medication "crossover" (see the figure at the end of this section) This method requires taking both the old and the new medication together for some period of time. The overlap usually lasts between 2 weeks and 3 months. That's a fairly wide range of time periods. There is no solid research yet on the exact way to do a crossover, so doctors have to rely on their experience with other patients and their knowledge of the patient's situation. The crossover schedule often needs to be revised based on how the person is doing.

In planning the exact crossover schedule, the doctor will consider a variety of factors, including the reason for the switch, the frequency of follow-up monitoring, the specific characteristics of the old and the new medications, and the method of administration of the current medication (see table below).

Avoiding medication errors

Many people have a hard time following medication instructions during the crossover. The medication regimen is more complicated, and many dosage changes are often made over a relatively short period of time. It is not surprising that many medication errors happen during this period. However, careful medication monitoring can greatly reduce these kinds of problems.

While uncommon, there also is a potential for mishaps because of confusion about the name of the new medication. Some medications sound alike, such as Zyprexa (antipsychotic) and Zyrtec (for allergy).

Some of the following techniques can be helpful:

Factors that May Influence Length of Medication Overlap

Issue	Duration of Overlap
Time from last relapse	Longer for more recent relapse
Severity of symptom exacerbation	Longer when a symptom exacerbation causes injurious behavior or is accompanied by a loss of insight
Current symptoms	Longer when there are persistent positive symptoms
Current side effects	Shorter when there are significant side effects from current medication
	Immediate switching needed for life-threatening side effects
Current medication	Longest for clozapine
	Longer for low-potency conventional antipsychotics
	Shorter for high-potency conventional antipsychotics
	No overlap needed for depot antipsychotics[1]
Outpatient follow-up	Shorter when there is frequent follow-up (e.g., weekly)
	Longer when follow-up is less frequent

[1]Although the crossover from depot is easier from a pharmacological point of view, there may be compliance problems due to changing from a long-acting medication given every few weeks to an oral medication taken daily.

- Have the doctor review the crossover procedure with the patient and the family or caregivers.
- Keep a written copy of the medication instructions, and make extra copies for family members or case managers.
- Work out in advance how to call or communicate should questions arise.
- Speak to the pharmacist to review the name and purpose of the new medication. The pharmacist can also double-check for any drug-drug interactions.
- Increase the frequency of follow-up visits with the doctor. If this is not possible, schedule telephone sessions with the doctor or have the patient and family review the medication schedule with the case manager or pharmacist.
- Review the medication schedule and any new medication adjustments at each visit. Patients should bring in all the medication bottles so that it will be easier to review what was actually taken.
- When there are concerns about forgetfulness or disorganization, consider having others assist with scheduling, reminding, and observing the person taking the medication.
- Use a pill-minder system in which a week's worth of medication is prepackaged into daily compartments.

Coping with new side effects

Chances are there will be some new side effects. The first thing to remember is not to be too disappointed or to panic. New side effects are to be expected and often go away with time. Common side effects of almost all the newer medications are sedation and dizziness (especially when getting up). EPS may also occur—although these could be a result of withdrawal from the old medication, they certainly feel like a side effect of the new medication.

- *EPS*: If new EPS occur during the first few weeks of the crossover, the real problem may be a withdrawal reaction from going off the previous medication(s). If EPS develop after the first few weeks, chances are they are caused by the newer medication.[1]
- *Sedation*: Almost all the newer antipsychotics can cause sedation, with clozapine causing the most and ziprasidone the least. When starting a new antipsychotic medication, patients should allow for a period of increased tiredness. It is a good idea to avoid driving until the sedation is gone. Risk factors for sedation include the choice of medication, how quickly the dose is raised, the dosing schedule, and the final target dose of the new medication.

[1] Treatments for EPS that happen on the newer medications are the same as for EPS from conventional antipsychotics.

- *Dizziness*: Many of the newer medications cause a sense of dizziness. This can be due to orthostatic hypotension, which is often experienced as dizziness. This is one of the reasons that some of the medications are started at low doses and then slowly increased to the target dose. This problem goes away with time. During the crossover, patients should take their time when standing up from a bed or chair.
- *Insomnia*: Risperidone and ziprasidone can cause insomnia during the crossover. The insomnia can resolve over time and, in the meanwhile, can be treated with a sedative medication for sleep such as lorazepam (Ativan). If insomnia occurs with the other newer antipsychotics, it is more likely to be caused by a withdrawal reaction, anxiety from the stress of changing medication, or a symptom flare-up. In any event, new-onset insomnia during the crossover requires an evaluation.
- *Nausea and vomiting*: Nausea and vomiting can be due to anticholinergic withdrawal. They can also be caused by the newer medications, most commonly clozapine and ziprasidone. While the nausea and vomiting are often transient and go away after time, they can be very distressing and even dangerous. Dividing the doses and taking the medication with food can improve this problem.
- *Increased appetite and weight gain:* These are probably the most serious side effects with the atypical antipsychotics. Weight gain can start right away, within the first week of switching. Unlike many of the other side effects mentioned here, weight gain tends to persist over time. Please refer to the side effects fact sheet on weight gain (p. 112) for more information and suggestions.

Fortunately, most of these side effects disappear or decrease after the first month of treatment. The exception is weight gain, which may persist. Sedation may also continue to be a problem, especially with clozapine.

Dealing with symptom flare-ups

It is common to experience some increase in symptoms during the crossover. The most common symptoms are anxiety and/or an increase in positive symptoms. Other symptoms may include depression, irritability, and physical complaints. When patients are closely monitored during crossover, these symptom flare-ups can usually be treated effectively and will resolve safely over time. Without close follow-up during this time, it is more likely that a symptom flare-up will progress to a full relapse. *Therefore, close follow-up and rapid intervention during the 6–12 week crossover is a key factor in safely switching antipsychotic medications.*

Possible medication interventions for a symptom flare-up include:

- Increasing the dose of the newer antipsychotic medication
- Increasing the dose (or restarting) the previous antipsychotic medication
- Adding or increasing the dose of an adjuvant benzodiazepine such as lorazepam (Ativan) or clonazepam (Klonopin)
- Decreasing or stopping any antidepressants (when manic symptoms are prominent during the flare-up)

Possible nonmedication interventions during a symptom flare-up include:

- Increasing contact with mental health clinicians to allow for a rapid response to any questions or concerns about dosage titration, new side effects, or new symptoms
- Providing reassurance that symptom flare-ups are usually transient and do not usually lead to relapse
- Providing reassurance that a symptom flare-up does *not* mean that the new medication should be stopped
- Advising the person to take a break from any ongoing activities that cause stress or symptoms (e.g., work or school)

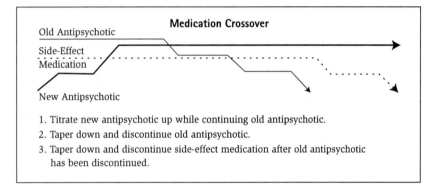

Medication Crossover

Old Antipsychotic

Side-Effect Medication

New Antipsychotic

1. Titrate new antipsychotic up while continuing old antipsychotic.
2. Taper down and discontinue old antipsychotic.
3. Taper down and discontinue side-effect medication after old antipsychotic has been discontinued.

15 Assessing the Response to Switching

It is very important to evaluate (and document) the response to the new medication. Such an evaluation is more important than ever today since we have many more and better medication options available. Many patients and family members assume that it's up to the doctor alone to evaluate medication response. But the doctor is only one part of what needs to be a collaborative effort that includes the patient, case manager, friends, family members, and other members of the treatment team.

What to look for

Assessing whether the new medication is working better than the old one can be tricky. During the first few months, the new medication's benefits are often subtle rather than dramatic. It may be hard to put into words how the person is better; the obvious positive and negative symptoms may be exactly the same, but the patient looks different, often feels and seems more "like his old self," or "there is a twinkle in her eye I haven't seen in years." These "soft" or "intuitive" impressions often prove to be on target and are followed by more obvious improvements in the months that follow.

When assessing medication response during the first few months, there is a huge difference between a *small improvement* and *no improvement*. In general, small improvements call for extending the evaluation period (for about 6–12 months); when there is no improvement, one would consider trying another approach earlier.

The most astute observers of these subtle changes are often family members, the patient's case manager, or therapist—they sometimes notice changes even when the patient says there's no difference! Doctors may not notice changes as readily because they tend to spend less time with the patient. Therefore, family members and other members of the treatment team should communicate their impressions of early response to the doctor, rather than assuming the doctor will be able to recognize these changes alone.

Documenting the response

It's a good idea to document the response to switching medication. Treatment staff can help patients monitor symptoms (e.g., by using a symptom checklist). Symptom monitoring should be started before the crossover and continued throughout the medication trial. Family members can keep a record of medication trials and responses. Such a record should include the name and telephone number of the treatment service, medication names and doses, start and stop dates of all medications, and a brief statement about the benefits and side effects the patient experienced with each medication. If problems with drug or alcohol use or medication compliance occurred, these should also be mentioned. Such a record can help ensure that important information will be available if and when the patient is cared for in different treatment settings by different doctors.

People can show improvements after switching medications in several different ways.

Decrease in side effects

- *Persistent EPS.* EPS (muscle stiffness, slowness of movements, tremor, and restlessness) may get better within the first week of completing the switch, or may take several weeks to improve or clear up.[1] If the EPS get worse right after completing the switch, don't automatically blame the new medication. This could be a withdrawal reaction (see p. 59). When there is an improvement in EPS, it will last! If the atypical antipsychotic is effective, the person can look forward to continuing life with fewer side effects.

- *Amenorrhea.* Premenopausal women do not need to be concerned if their menses do not return right away; it usually takes about 3–6 months for menstrual periods to come back after the old antipsychotic medication has been *completely* stopped.[2] The menses may be irregular at first, and it may take some time for the woman to get back to a normal monthly cycle.

Fewer positive symptoms

Persistent positive symptoms can show several patterns of response. Occasionally, there may be a dramatic improvement within the first few weeks of starting the new medication. In such situations, it is best to take a "wait and see" attitude for at least 6 weeks. During this time period, the old antipsychotic may still be active in the brain—symptoms may come back once the effects of the old medication completely wear off. If the improvement continues for longer than 6 weeks after completing the switch, one can be more certain that the new medication will continue to work better for positive symptoms.

More often, positive symptoms improve slowly and gradually. Like the weather getting warmer as winter moves to spring, there is day-to-day fluctuation in symptoms. A single good or bad day can't tell you which direction the medication response is heading. Like changes in the weather, you have to follow the overall trend for a period of weeks or months.

Finally, positive symptoms do not have to go away entirely. Sometimes positive symptoms, such as delusions or hallucinations, remain unchanged, but they are less bothersome or frightening. The person is better able to fight out-of-control feelings arising from these symptoms, or can ignore them entirely.

Fewer negative symptoms

It is best to keep expectations concerning negative symptoms modest. Improvements in negative symptoms tend to be partial; that is, the negative symptoms get somewhat better but do not go away entirely. Don't expect any new medication to entirely "cure" negative symptoms. Improvements in negative symptoms are usually slow and happen gradually over a period of months. There are also many different kinds of negative symptoms. For example, a person might not have enough energy to work (a negative symptom called anergia) and be socially isolated (a negative symptom called asociality). A new medication might help more with anergia than asociality, or vice versa.

Reduction in other symptoms

The newer medications often help with some of the so-called "secondary" symptoms of schizophrenia. Although these symptoms are not considered an essential part of the diagnosis of schizophrenia, they are not at all secondary in terms of the suffering and havoc they can cause.

- *Depression.* Depressive symptoms are common in schizophrenia. Switching medications can be helpful for depressive symptoms, especially when depression and positive symptoms are intertwined. In those situations, depressive symptoms will lift as the positive symptoms improve.

- *Anxiety.* Anxiety is another common problem in schizophrenia. Anxiety symptoms also tend to get better as other symptoms improve.

- *Dangerous and self-injurious behavior.* Clozapine is known to be helpful for suicidal patients and patients whose psychotic behaviors are dangerous to others. It is not known whether the other atypical antipsychotics are as helpful as clozapine in these situations.

---

[1] It may take longer for EPS to resolve in elderly patients or patients who were previously receiving long-acting depot injections.

[2] It may take longer when the previous antipsychotic medication was given in long-acting depot injections.

"Polypharmacy" literally means use of more than one medication. As used here, polypharmacy refers to combining antipsychotics and does not refer to taking other types of psychiatric medications.

The goal should be a single antipsychotic

Many people take their old and their new antipsychotic medication together during the crossover. Sometimes, especially if the person has a good response during the transition or there is worry about getting off the older medication completely, it can be very appealing to continue *both* medications indefinitely.

The following short-term concerns are *not* good reasons to combine two antipsychotics simultaneously for prolonged periods:

1. The medication crossover is started in one treatment setting, such as an inpatient unit, but is not completely finished. The patient then enters a new treatment setting where, because of inertia or ignorance, both medications are continued indefinitely.
2. The patient shows signs of improvement before the crossover is completely finished, and there is a feeling of "quit while you're ahead."
3. The patient experienced a symptom flare-up during the crossover. The old medication was restarted and the symptoms improved. A feeling of "let's not rock the boat" takes over and the person stays on both antipsychotics indefinitely.
4. The patient or family is nervous about completely stopping the old medication.
5. The doctor is nervous about the same thing and adds the old medication back on to the new one and doesn't want to stop it again.

It is important to complete the crossover and try taking just one antipsychotic medication for important *long-term* reasons:

1. It is much easier to judge the long-term effectiveness of the new medication if the person is taking only one medication. With all the new medications available, it is more important than ever to determine a person's response to *each* medication.
2. It simplifies the medication regimen. It is easy to fall into the trap of continually adding medications to the person's regimen. After a few years, the person may be on multiple medications, making it next to impossible to sort out what's going on.
3. Long-term side effects, especially tardive dyskinesia, are less likely to occur if the person is no longer taking any conventional antipsychotic.

The goals of the crossover should be to finish the transition, get off the old antipsychotic, and take only the new antipsychotic.[1] Generally, a person should be completely off the old antipsychotic within 3 months of starting the crossover.[2] With few exceptions, the goal of switching is to get *completely off* the old medication and *completely on* the new medication.

Long-term combination antipsychotic treatment might be appropriate in the following situations:

- *For clozapine intolerance.* Some clozapine-responsive patients cannot tolerate optimal clozapine doses. Here, a second antipsychotic is added to augment the subtherapeutic clozapine dose.

- *For partial response to clozapine.* There are several factors that support trying combination therapy for patients treated with clozapine who continue to have symptoms. For example, many patients taking clozapine are better than before but are still far from well and further switching options are very limited. Also, there are greater risks from discontinuing clozapine than other antipsychotics.

- *When discontinuing depot therapy is too risky.* Some patients need depot therapy for compliance reasons but are only partially responsive to adequate depot doses. Adding an atypical agent to the depot regimen is a practical way to try to augment the depot response.

- *For patients who refuse to go off their old antipsychotic or refuse to try clozapine.* Sometimes, combination therapy is a second-line alternative when the patient is unwilling or unable to go off of the old antipsychotic medication. Combining antipsychotics is also reasonable when the patient has failed monotherapy with all of the first-line atypical medications and refuses clozapine.

---

[1] This does not mean that the person should get off the other psychiatric medications he or she is taking. These medications will usually continue to be prescribed for some time after the antipsychotic medications have been changed.

[2] Going off clozapine is an exception, since the crossover can take as long as 6 months.

When we use the term *nonresponse* in this section, we mean that the patient's positive or negative symptoms have not gotten better or have even worsened after completing a full medication trial. When we discuss nonresponse, we do not include situations in which the person becomes demoralized or depressed some time after other psychiatric symptoms improve (see p. 136 for a discussion of this problem). The first step is to make sure that the person *really* has not responded. Consider the following issues that can confound the assessment of nonresponse:

- Sometimes new symptoms seem to appear out of nowhere. The person may start describing hallucinations or delusions that seem totally new. Strange as it seems, these verbalizations may actually be a sign of improvement. What can happen is that, although the person had these hallucinations or delusions on the old medication, he or she kept these experiences private because of social withdrawal or paranoid concerns. As the new medication takes effect, the person may become more talkative and begin telling others about these symptoms. From the perspective of the person listening, these naturally seem like new symptoms. *It is very important to distinguish this phenomenon from a real deterioration with exacerbation of positive symptoms.*

- Consider whether the dose and duration of medication are adequate. An inadequate medication trial does not count as a pharmacologic nonresponse. See "Optimizing Current Medications" on page 117.

- Evaluate for problems that may be complicating treatment, such as substance abuse or noncompliance. *If either of these complications was prominent during the switch, the person did not experience a medication failure and the medical record should reflect this fact.*

- After 3 months of treatment, assess whether there is absolutely *no response* or a *slight improvement. Complete nonresponse at 3 months calls for another medication change, whereas a partial (but inadequate) response calls for trying to extend the treatment trial for another 3–9 months.*

- It is normal to be disappointed if the medication has failed. However, it is important to keep up morale and hope during this difficult period. The good news is that a patient may completely fail to respond to one of the atypical antipsychotics but do extremely well on another.

If the new medication has failed, consider the following options:

- *Going back to the previous medication.* This makes sense for patients who are emotionally exhausted from the switching process and would prefer to return to what is, despite any drawbacks, at least a known quantity. After several months back on the old medication, the pros and cons of trying another atypical antipsychotic can be reviewed.

- *Starting another atypical antipsychotic.* If the patient and doctor are willing to continue the search for a better medication, switching to another atypical antipsychotic right away may be best. If one atypical antipsychotic fails, the next one tried could succeed. Clozapine can be particularly helpful for patients who have not responded to other atypical antipsychotics.

- *Changing to a depot medication regimen.* If there is a question of whether the person has actually taken the new medication, going to a long-acting depot medication makes sense. Depot medications can also be a second-line option for patients who seem unresponsive to oral forms of conventional antipsychotics.

The table on the next page outlines the advantages and disadvantages of these treatment options.

Treatment Options after the Patient Has Not Responded to a New Medication

Advantage	Option	Disadvantage
Patient's response to prior medication is known and predictable Helpful when patient cannot tolerate uncertainty of another medication trial Less expensive (when going back to a conventional antipsychotic)	◄ Switching back to the previous antipsychotic ►	Loss of momentum when switch is made for elective reasons Should be avoided when symptom response to prior medication was unacceptable Should be avoided when there were intolerable or dangerous side effects on prior medication
Can be helpful when compliance is a potential problem Can be helpful when substance abuse has complicated the clinical situation Can be helpful when there are metabolic or malabsorption explanations for poor responses	◄ Switching to a long-acting depot conventional antipsychotic ►	Some patients may be reluctant to accept depot medication May take some time to achieve therapeutic levels from depot therapy so oral supplementation is usually needed Depot medications have the EPS profile of high-potency conventional antipsychotics
Continues the attempt to find better treatment There may be differential efficacy between the atypical antipsychotics so patients may respond to another first-line atypical agent despite nonresponse to the first one tried A first-line atypical medication, if successful, will be less burdensome in the long run than switching directly to clozapine	◄ Switching to another first-line atypical antipsychotic (not clozapine) ►	Patient and family have to go through another trial period before response is known Clinician and/or patient may be "burned out" from prior attempt at switching and be reluctant to try again May delay eventual trial of clozapine
Clozapine remains the antipsychotic most likely to be effective for refractory symptoms Clozapine is well established as useful for other difficult treatment situations including violence, psychogenic polydipsia, and severe tardive dyskinesia	◄ Switching to clozapine ►	Although excellent for EPS, clozapine has many burdensome side effects Many patients are reluctant to try clozapine Need for continuous blood count monitoring Once clozapine treatment is begun, it is more difficult to switch from clozapine to another atypical antipsychotic

Postpsychotic depression

Postpsychotic depression is a depression that occurs shortly after a psychotic episode gets better. The period of greatest risk is roughly 3–6 months *after* positive symptoms improve. During a postpsychotic depression, depressive symptoms seem to worsen as the psychotic symptoms improve.[1] Postpsychotic depression can occur after a response to any antipsychotic medication.

Signs of postpsychotic depression include feelings of hopelessness, worthlessness, guilt, and suicidal ideation. A person may become totally preoccupied by feelings of loss from the setback of having schizophrenia and self-loathing from being disabled. While these thoughts are understandable, the intensity of the despair can be overwhelming and the person may lose sight of any gains, personal strengths, current accomplishments, or hope for future recovery. It is essential to be aware of this potentially life-threatening complication. Because postpsychotic depression happens after other symptoms have improved, it can come just when the person's social or treatment network relaxes and is less likely to closely monitor symptoms and provide support.

Suicidal behavior

While there are other times when someone with schizophrenia might become suicidal, we focus here on suicidal symptoms that occur when other symptoms have improved. Generally, suicidal risk is most likely to increase during a postpsychotic depression[2] (i.e., usually a few months after other schizophrenia symptoms have improved). Clinicians and family members can be caught off guard because the person is better in so many other ways.

People usually communicate their suicidal feelings when they are in a suicidal crisis, and one should take any suggestion of new suicidal feelings *very* seriously. The person may tell a family member or a mental health clinician about thoughts of suicide. Unless these reports are part of a long-standing pattern, such a communication needs to be taken at face value, even if the person does not seem very upset or distressed, and should be considered a psychiatric emergency.

Sometimes the person may communicate suicidal thoughts indirectly, verbalizing feelings of hopelessness or despair, often related to a heightened awareness of the losses caused by the illness. While these observations may seem painfully accurate, the extent of the despair is usually distorted. Suicidal urges may arise out of the mistaken belief that things will never get better. Ask the person directly about the presence of any suicidal feelings. Fortunately, once a suicidal crisis passes, the vast majority of people want to stay alive and continue with their recovery despite the hardships.

Most of the time, suicidal episodes following a medication response improve with time and treatment. It is important to recognize the problem and ensure the person's safety. Medication treatment usually consists of adding an antidepressant to the antipsychotic, which should generally be continued. Psychosocial treatment includes increased support, maintaining hope and optimism about the future, and helping the person stay connected with others. With treatment, suicidal feelings usually improve in 4–6 weeks.

Family and friends may find it hard to understand why suicidal feelings escalate just when positive and negative symptoms seem to be getting better. For example, a family member might say, "How can you feel hopeless? Look at how much better you're doing!" Unfortunately, such a response might be misinterpreted and lead to more isolation and hopelessness. Remember that symptom improvements may actually be increasing the suicide risk. Therefore, suicidal thoughts or behavior need to be taken seriously and evaluated even when the person seems better.

Note to patients whose symptoms have improved on antipsychotic medications but who are feeling suicidal. If you have thoughts of suicide now, it's critical to get help *immediately.* Treatment can help relieve suicidal feelings. Speak to the members of your treatment team if you have—or have ever had—these feelings. Then you'll know whom to call if suicidal feelings return.

---

[1] If depressive symptoms increase during an acute psychotic episode, the depressive symptoms are part of the acute episode and should not be treated with antidepressants. One may ask whether the risk of postpsychotic depression nullifies any potential gain from switching to atypical antipsychotics. Fortunately, research shows that, in the long run, atypical antipsychotics are better than the conventionals for depressive symptoms. For example, a very rigorous study on the epidemiology of suicide showed that the risk of suicide was much lower during periods of clozapine treatment.

[2] Note that suicidal feelings are not directly caused by the medication.

16 Long-Term Issues After Switching

Because of the new medications, more people than ever before are showing real progress toward recovery from their illness. The road to recovery is not easy—in this section, we describe many of the pitfalls and hardships that may happen on the way and suggest ways to deal with them.

In this chapter, we discuss how responding to a new medication affects the recovery process We assume that the new medication has worked and the person now has fewer psychiatric symptoms and/or fewer disabling side effects. All the issues we discuss here are part of the recovery process whenever it happens; they do not apply only with new medications. These issues are relevant whenever patients get better— whether they are taking the old or the new medications.

Getting better can be a wonderful and exhilarating experience, not only for the patient but also for friends, family members, and clinicians. However, with improvements come new challenges. This section focuses on some of the difficulties of doing better. We ask that you consider the new challenges in the context of the patient's gains. These responses are covered in the approximate order in which they may appear after responding to a new medication.

Feeling "cured"

When the patient's symptoms disappear, the patient may think that he or she is no longer ill. At first, there is a tremendous sense of relief—but there is also a re-emergence of the hope, or wish, that the schizophrenia is completely cured. The person (or family) might know intellectually that such thoughts are unrealistic. But, in the heart, "hope springs eternal." This kind of hope of cure (also known in psychiatric jargon as the "fantasy of cure") is perfectly normal. It's only natural for patients to interpret a significant symptom reduction as meaning that they are "cured."

However, this (often hidden) hope can cause trouble. The patient may experiment with stopping treatment or reject the notion of having an illness. When positive symptoms return, the hope of cure is defeated, at least for a while. Along with a feeling of defeat, there is a loss of confidence in the new medication. During those times, it is important to remember that the expectation of cure was probably unrealistic in the first place. It is very important to remain optimistic about the *recovery* process, and to emphasize that recovery is possible even without a cure.

Trying to make up for lost time

After getting a good symptom response, there is a natural wish to make up for lost time. Released from years of deprivation and illness, the person often makes a sudden attempt to regain what was lost or left behind. This may mean taking on too many new things at once, such as leaving home, finding a job, and trying to date. There may be a search for psychological meaning or attempts to reunite with lost family members or loved ones. To an outside observer, the sudden shifts in behavior may seem odd, even psychotic. These kinds of responses almost always lead to setbacks. Years of emotional losses simply can't be recovered in months. Unfortunately, people often have to learn these lessons the hard way.

Feeling overwhelmed by emotions

Apathy and psychic indifference are very common and insidious negative symptoms. The behavioral manifestations of EPS also include psychic and physical numbness. This deadening of normal emotional functioning can also be protective. It is hard to feel pain or to know that something is wrong when you can't feel *anything*. Patients are indifferent to their indifference. As they respond to the new medication, the emotional anesthesia lifts, bringing a return of emotions, which can take them by surprise. They may have to deal with painful feelings of loneliness, shame, or sorrow; they may be at a loss about how to handle these difficult feelings and become overwhelmed.

Feeling disconnected from others

Some patients start feeling lonely and disconnected from others shortly after getting better. The underlying cause of this emotional reaction seems to be the interplay among negative symptoms, awareness of those symptoms, and medication response. Patients who have the negative symptom of asociality (no social functioning) may not be bothered by their lack of friendships or the fact that they spend most of their time alone. These patients are *not* lonely. Perhaps it is the indifference to relationships that is the basic problem that subsequently leads to impoverished social functioning.

However, should this symptom improve on a new medication, the person may lose this indifference to being alone and regain a normal need to be with others. When the patient has very little in the way of friendships or social support, he or she has to contend with feeling lonely and disconnected from others.

Recalling painful experiences

After switching medications, people may also begin to relive traumatic memories from psychotic symptoms they had in the past. They may reflect on the psychotic experience in a way that wasn't possible beforehand. They may have a new awareness of just how terrible or frightening the psychotic symptoms were. Or they may feel painfully humiliated remembering what they said or did while they were psychotic. Just as with other posttraumatic experiences of terrible events, the person will need to come to terms with what happened in order to continue in the healing process.

Coping with uncertainty

As functioning improves, patients must face new kinds of stressors. The demands and expectations placed on the person may increase as he or she looks and behaves better. Less monetary or emotional support may be available. Although the symptoms may be better, the person may feel that life has gotten harder. As functioning improves, there is further to fall in case of setbacks. The person may have doubts about the permanence of the medication response and may wonder, "Is this temporary?" or "Can I rely on myself again, now that I'm feeling better?" It may takes several years of continued symptom improvement before the person can feel sure that his or her improvements will actually last.

Disappointment over return of symptoms

Return of symptoms can be very frightening to individuals who already feel on shaky ground from their improvement. The fear is, "Has the medication stopped working? Am I back to square one?" Fortunately, often the return of symptoms has nothing to do with loss of medication response and everything to do with the greater stress from doing better. It is well known that positive symptoms often get worse under stress, and that "good" stress from doing better is just as likely to cause symptoms as is "bad" stress from setbacks. It can be hard to remember that although the symptoms may have come back, they have often come back when the person is at an entirely different level of functioning, and in fact the new medication continues to be very effective.

Existential issues

Existential is defined as "relating to, or dealing with, existence." Schizophrenia is a life experience that puts existential questions right in the foreground. Although schizophrenia is a "no-fault" disease, many patients suffering from the illness struggle with the questions "Why did this happen to me?" and "Why am I here?" Existential questions can arise at any time but seem to be particularly common after the person responds to a new medication. This may be related to the cognitive improvements from new medications that allow the person to reflect on his or her condition in an abstract way.

Patients may have a variety of answers to the "why did this happen to me" question—self-deprecatory answers ("This illness happened because I'm lazy and no good"), blaming explanations ("My parents really screwed me up"), or a spiritual explanation ("God gave me this illness for a reason, but I don't understand it yet"). These struggles to understand can be extraordinarily painful for the patient, and can also be quite painful for others to watch. Because such issues often come to the foreground after the patient's symptoms are much better, others tend to minimize the seriousness of the patient's concerns. However, it is crucial to take these concerns seriously. Achieving some kind of constructive resolution to existential questions can be a matter of life and death. Patients who can't resolve these issues can become very suicidal, especially if they get mired in self-blame and hopelessness. Patients who resolve these existential questions achieve a renewed sense of self-resolve or a new sense of direction.

Helping someone cope

One of the challenges for families and clinicians is to help someone cope with the internal changes brought on by symptom improvements. The first step is to be aware that psychological reactions are common and can profoundly affect the impact of the new medication on the person's life. The hope is that the patient, with the help of family members or mental health clinicians, will be able to adapt to the experience and get on with life with fewer symptoms.

Family relationships

Because of the devastating nature of schizophrenia, many patients require a level of caretaking from their parents that wouldn't otherwise be appropriate. Normal, healthy separation from the parent(s) is not possible because of the persistent symptoms.

Often, the patient's relationship with family members has reached a kind of equilibrium based, in large part, on the effects of the illness. However, a major change in symptoms can have ripple effects on relationships in the family. Families often feel tremendous relief and joy when they see their loved one get better. Families seem most aware, and appreciative of, the re-emergence of the person they knew before he or she got sick. Such a change usually happens shortly after the person responds to the new medication.

But, as the patient recovers, there may be increased tensions at home, especially around issues of autonomy and independence. These issues may already have been there in the background, but the patient was too symptomatic to verbalize these feelings, or too disabled to move toward autonomy. Things change when symptoms improve—the patient is more likely to complain about lack of independence and bristle at any overprotective behavior on the parents' part.

Therefore, as a part of the recovery process, the patient may go through a phase of rejecting his or her family. This seems similar to adolescents rejecting their parents as they try to gain some independence. Rejection may be quite painful for family members because it comes on the heels of symptom improvements. It is naturally very hard for family members to endure this criticism, especially at what should be a joyful time when their relative is finally better.

It is usually best if family members avoid taking such attacks or withdrawal personally and remember that this behavior may be just a temporary phase during the recovery process. Family relationships will improve with the passage of time, as the patient adjusts to the new medication.

Keep expectations realistic. As the recovery continues, there are other possible benefits for the family. The person may be able to function more autonomously, which eases the day-to-day responsibilities for the family members who have had to be caretakers. However, even when the person responds to the new medication right away, changes in autonomy and life functioning take a long time. It is usually a mistake to ask the person who is recovering to take on more responsibilities before a year or so has passed. Trying to rearrange the level of financial or logistic support sooner than that risks backfiring. The person may not be ready to cope with increased responsibilities and may experience a setback if too many new demands are made right away.

After a dramatic improvement, family members frequently hope, often to themselves, that the illness is cured. The danger here is that families may minimize any remaining symptoms or hardships. While this is very normal, it is usually too much to expect, and can cause disappointment down the road when it becomes clear that the person is not "cured," even though the new medication is much better. Also, if symptoms return later on, the family may display a sense of disappointment that the patient could misinterpret as further evidence of failure.

Relationships with friends and intimate partners

As the recovery moves forward, the person may feel an increased need for intimacy, including sexuality. Of course, the need for intimacy may have been there before switching, but wasn't apparent because the person chose to be isolated rather than deal with the increased symptoms or rejection that often follow attempts at closeness. After switching, there can be a long lag time—often over a year—before the person feels strong enough to attempt to re-enter the world of intimate relationships. In the meantime, the person may have to struggle with feeling increasingly lonely, or have to decide how to best go about regaining a social life.

Loneliness can be a big problem for many people with schizophrenia. Having schizophrenia can make it harder to communicate with others, while the stigma associated with the illness makes it harder for people with schizophrenia to go into social situations where they may feel judged or misunderstood.

New demands and expectations. It is sometimes difficult to differentiate between the "growing pains" that can accompany recovery and the irritability that often precedes relapse. As patients recover, they may begin to outgrow the structure, supervision, and rules that were necessary when they were acutely ill. However, they may lack the interpersonal skills needed to diplomatically negotiate the changes that would better match their improved level of functioning.

Alcohol and drug use

The use of drugs and alcohol complicates the recovery of people with schizophrenia. We have already discussed how substance abuse can complicate the switching process (p. 122). Here we discuss how switching antipsychotic medications can sometimes lead to long-term changes in drug, alcohol, and nicotine use. Clinical experience has shown that substance abuse problems sometimes *improve,* while, at other times, a successful switch of medications can paradoxically *worsen* substance abuse. It is difficult to predict what will happen ahead of time.

When a person with schizophrenia has persistent positive and negative symptoms, he or she may not have any reason to stop getting high. The person may not foresee any possibility of having a meaningful life. From this point of view, a momentary "high" from drugs or alcohol might represent the only available source of pleasure or escape. Under these circumstances, getting on a more effective medication might be a turning point for the person, allowing a realization that a better life is possible. However, no matter how effective the atypical antipsychotics may be, by themselves they are unlikely to produce this kind of personal transformation. Participation in a program that actively addresses the person's drug or alcohol problem is almost always also needed.

When the new drug works for negative symptoms, the person may socialize more, which is good. However, increased socializing can also increase the risk for drug and alcohol use.

Medication compliance

It is tempting to assume that the newer medications, with their better side-effect profile, will automatically help people take their medications more regularly. However, clinicians should not automatically assume that the atypical antipsychotics will improve compliance for all patients. The newer medications are more likely to promote better compliance in some cases and worse compliance in others. The compliance benefits of newer medications will probably come primarily from better efficacy, which will allow patients to better manage their medications on their own, and from the increased enthusiasm with which family members and other people in the patient's network will support compliance. Based on our experience, it seems likely that the major new compliance problem will be patients who previously did not want to be on medication but passively complied because they were too ill to put up a vigorous fight. These patients may now have enough energy and sense of purpose to stop their medications.

Atypical antipsychotics may improve compliance by:

- Causing fewer distressing side effects
- More effectively treating negative symptoms (e.g., disorganization) that cause passive noncompliance
- Decreasing the chances of secondary noncompliance because of breakthrough symptoms
- Increasing support for medication from other people
- Decreasing the stigma of taking antipsychotics

Atypical antipsychotics may worsen compliance by

- Switching patients from depot to oral route, which may trigger noncompliance in patients who are unable to comply with oral therapy
- Successfully treating negative symptoms, thus giving patients more energy to be noncompliant
- Providing better relief of symptoms, which can lead to the belief that antipsychotic medications are no longer needed

Symptom recurrence

Positive symptoms may return after a period that is relatively free of symptoms. Symptoms may seem to come "out of thin air," taking the person by surprise. Besides whatever hardships the symptoms cause, they also raise questions about whether the new medication has stopped working. A loss of medication response would be devastating and jeopardize the whole notion of long-term recovery with the newer medications. Fortunately, there is usually another explanation for symptom recurrence after a long remission:

- The person may have been experimenting with stopping or lowering the medication because he or she felt much better and questioned whether medications were still needed.
- The person may have been using recreational drugs or alcohol.
- Because of the person's improved level of functioning, life has become more stressful and the extra stressors are causing the old symptoms to return.

Consider these possibilities before concluding that the medication has stopped working. Ask if the return of symptoms corresponds with better functioning in life. If so, then the medication is still working by allowing the person to do more in life. Patients who "push" themselves as hard as they can only stop pushing when the symptoms come back and they can't push anymore. For those people, any medication, no matter how much better, will appear to have stopped working when the person pushes beyond the "protective" zone.

In the long run, we hope that switching medications will help the person recover. But medications alone are not usually enough. Medications are the cornerstone of recovery that allows the hard work of rehabilitation to happen. The best recoveries usually happen when the person is also in an effective psychological or psychosocial treatment program. As patients improve to a previously unheard of extent, mental health clinicians who treat schizophrenia will increasingly need to focus on the psychological and existential struggles facing patients who have dramatically improved after switching to one of the newer medications. Many psychosocial treatment programs for schizophrenia are geared toward helping the person stay stable in the community and learn to adapt to the vicissitudes of having a severe and persistent mental illness. However, as the use of the atypical antipsychotics becomes more common, many patients will need rehabilitation services that are more than "holding" environments. Unfortunately, many of the currently available programs are not well equipped to work with patients who need help in returning to competitive work or school environments.

The good news is that rehabilitation programs for patients with schizophrenia have been developed that have been shown to be effective for the more ambitious goals of competitive employment. Research on vocational rehabilitation in schizophrenia has shown that certain kinds of supported employment programs can help people regain their ability to work. Unfortunately, these kinds of rehabilitation programs are currently in the minority and are not always readily available to those most in need of rehabilitation.

At least one major study has found that employment rates improve when patients are switched to an atypical antipsychotic. A group of patients assigned to receive either Zyprexa (olanzapine) or Haldol (haloperidol) started off with an employment rate of 10%. In one year, the employment rate doubled to 20% in the olanzapine group and stayed the same for the haloperidol group. One of the authors of this book (PJW) is now investigating the effects of switching to atypical antipsychotics on rehabilitation and vocational outcomes. Although the study is not finished, we can describe some preliminary findings:

- Many individuals who would previously have been too ill to work improve on the newer medications to a degree where meaningful employment becomes a real possibility. However, for patients who have been ill for many years, better medications are necessary but not sufficient. To be able to return to work, the person needs to be in a treatment program that offers "real" vocational rehabilitation.

- The demand for vocational rehabilitation programs will greatly increase over the next few years, and many programs will have to adjust their rehabilitation goals to meet the changing needs of their clients.

- When patients respond to a new drug, improvements in vocational or academic functioning do not happen right away. In fact, short-term outcomes might even seem worse. For example, the first thing people might do when they begin to feel better is to stop going to the rehabilitation program and take a vacation! Or a student who has been struggling with schoolwork might start feeling well enough to date, and his or her grades may go down as a result.

- Long-term improvements in academic or vocational performance seem to happen about a year after the symptoms get better.

Academic and Work Functioning

Schizophrenia is often a disabling condition. Only about one-quarter of patients with schizophrenia are employed. Therefore, people with schizophrenia not only have to deal with the illness itself, but must also contend with the secondary effects of unemployment and underemployment such as poverty and low self-esteem.

A very important question about the atypical antipsychotics is whether these medications can help someone's functioning—that is, increase the chances that someone with schizophrenia will be able to finish school, run a household, or be employed in a competitive job. A related question is whether a disabled person who switches from an older conventional antipsychotic to a newer atypical antipsychotic will be more able to return to work. This basic question goes well beyond symptoms and side effects, and involves the person's educational background, current life goals, current opportunities, and disability rules that may be barriers to vocational recovery. These factors can be difficult to change, even when the person has changed for the better. Very little research has been done on the relationship between the newer medications and functioning, but there are some encouraging early results. One study comparing patients who responded to the newer antipsychotic olanzapine with patients who responded to the conventional antipsychotic haloperidol showed that employment rates doubled from about 10% to about 20% in 1 year among patients receiving the atypical antipsychotic.[1,2] Based on these studies, as well as our clinical experience with the newer medications, we offer some tentative statements on this crucial topic:

- *People can recover their functioning.* Switching to one of the newer atypical antipsychotics—when successful—can lead to meaningful improvements in the person's academic, household, or vocational functioning. This kind of recovery is possible even after someone has been ill for many years.
- *When improvements in life functioning happen, they are gradual.* There may not be any obvious changes right away, and improvements may be noticeable only after about a year or so has passed since the person responded

[1] It seems likely that the other atypical antipsychotics will also improve employment rates. However, the largest long-term study and the most comprehensive database concerning employment and quality of life are available for olanzapine.
[2] These employment rates are lower than the estimated 25% employment rate for patients with schizophrenia. This is probably because the patients who participate in clinical trials tend to have more symptoms than the "average" patient with schizophrenia.

to the new medication. Such a lag time is not really too surprising when you consider how long it takes most people to adjust emotionally to a life *with* schizophrenia. To reverse this process—even if the reversal isn't 100%—also takes time. Time is needed to learn what it's like to live with fewer symptoms or disabling side effects. Time is needed to explore new possibilities and experiment with new options and activities. If the person's initial exploration focuses on socializing, he or she may have little emotional or physical energy left for work or academic pursuits. Setbacks can also happen as the person tries to regain lost functioning; early attempts to improve functioning often end in failure. Time is needed to recover from these new disappointments and regain courage to try again.

- *Better symptom control does not seem to be enough.* Some people have significant improvements in symptoms without any meaningful improvements in functioning, at least for the first few years after switching. It seems that other factors are really important, such as the patient's willingness to endure the hardships of trying to recover functioning, and the presence of a supportive social and professional network.
- *We do not have a clear understanding of why some individuals show more progress in life functioning than others.* Other key factors besides medication response that may affect level of functioning include the person's level of functioning and education before becoming ill, the current level of social support, the quality of psychosocial treatments aimed at improving functioning, and intrinsic aspects of the person such as the nature of his or her life goals, faith in self or religious faith, and ability to endure the inevitable hardships and setbacks that come with attempts to regain functioning.
- *There are economic disincentives to regaining functioning.* As vocational outcomes improve, many more patients will face the possibility of losing their disability benefits and medical/psychiatric insurance (Medicaid) as a result of their better response. This can lead to absurd situations in which the person's response to a newer medication results in the loss of coverage to pay for the medication. In the most extreme cases, the patient may have to go back on an old medication and deteriorate back to the point where disability coverage returns. Obviously, this is unacceptable from a social policy point of view, but until sensible reforms are made in disability regulations, it is important to anticipate such a dilemma *well before it happens.* Because vocational recovery usually begins a year after symptoms improve, there is usually time to try and work out solutions in advance.

- *Many psychiatric rehabilitation programs are not oriented toward true recovery of work or academic functioning.* Until recently, true recovery of functioning for a person with schizophrenia was relatively uncommon, whereas permanent disability was the norm. Many psychiatric rehabilitation programs are oriented more toward a person who is permanently disabled. Someone in the process of recovering functioning may have trouble finding an appropriate recovery-oriented rehabilitation program.

- *There are significant psychological issues involved in returning to work.* Patients with schizophrenia have learned—either by experience or from their clinicians—to lower their expectations in life. In order to adapt to such a serious illness, a person may have had to learn to maintain a sense of self-esteem and self-worth that does not depend on society's expectations of functioning. An improvement in functional capacity can stir up long-dormant feelings of inadequacy and loss, feelings that need to be acknowledged and dealt with.

- *The recovery process can be physically and emotionally grueling.* Regaining functioning is arduous and rehabilitation involves pain and intermittent setbacks. Often there aren't any obvious benefits right away.

- *The process of regaining function can make someone feel more stigmatized.* Many patients who have been ill for long periods of time have found their own niche for themselves. They have found acceptance from their families, are relatively comfortable in psychiatric treatment settings, and are protected from the setbacks and humiliations that might happen when trying to return to a mainstream job or school. Patients may feel socially awkward and aware that they may be different in age or appearance from their peers or colleagues.

Newer Medications and Life Expectancy

Suicide and accidents

People with schizophrenia have a considerably higher mortality rate than the general population because they are more likely to die from suicide, accidents, and cardiovascular disease. The increased rates of suicide and accidental deaths can be linked to the direct effects of persistent psychotic and depressive symptoms in schizophrenia. During the first 10 years of the illness (i.e., during young adulthood), suicide and accidental deaths are far and away the biggest cause of death. It has recently been estimated that about 10% of all patients with schizophrenia die by suicide. Fortunately, there is evidence that the atypical antipsychotics may help reverse this suicide epidemic. A recent epidemiologic study showed that clozapine lowers the risk of suicide. When data on all patients treated at one time or another with clozapine were analyzed, deaths from suicide were found to be much lower during the times when the person was taking clozapine and higher during times off clozapine. It seems quite possible that the risk of suicide may also be lower for patients who do well on other atypical antipsychotics. If so, the epidemiological impact of the majority of people with schizophrenia being treated with one of the atypical antipsychotics would be a reduction in the unacceptably high rates of suicide of recent years.

Chronic medical problems

As patients with schizophrenia get older, the major causes of premature death shift to complications from chronic medical problems, especially cardiovascular disease. Much of the excess mortality in this age group is undoubtedly attributable to the many poor health habits associated with schizophrenia. Compared to the general public, patients with schizophrenia are less active, have poorer diets, smoke more, and tend not to seek medical care for chronic health problems such as diabetes or high blood pressure. These problems result in higher rates of heart attacks, strokes, and pulmonary problems.

- *Impact on obesity*. Most of the atypical antipsychotics cause a certain amount of weight gain over and above what is seen with the conventional antipsychotics. The atypical antipsychotics will probably increase the obesity rate in schizophrenia. As a consequence, rates of medical illnesses that have obesity as a risk factor, including adult-onset diabetes mellitus, hypertension, and high cholesterol, may increase. Therefore, increased attention needs to be paid to diet and physical activity as an essential part of the long-term recovery process.

- *Cigarette smoking* is much more common among patients with schizophrenia than in the general public. There is evidence that the atypical antipsychotics reduce smoking rates in schizophrenia.

- *Physical activity*. Both negative symptoms and EPS from antipsychotics can cause people to reduce their physical activity. Switching to one of the atypical antipsychotics should eventually increase the person's capacity for physical activity. There may be no immediate changes, however, both because of the early sedation caused by some of the atypical antipsychotics and because the person is usually very out of shape and needs to be reintroduced to physical activity slowly and cautiously.

17 Summary of Technical Information

The new medications offer many patients the opportunity to have better lives than was thought possible even a few years ago. However, the choices can be overwhelming at times, and it may be hard to get the kind of information necessary to know what to do or how to do it. Also, no matter how good a medication is in theory, in practice it will have to be given in the right way, and in a way that allows the patient to get the most out of the medication. The technical section has reviewed, in some detail, most of the issues pertaining to the pros and cons of the new medications, what issues are important to think about when considering the alternatives, and the switching process itself. You should consider it a reference, one that you can go back to when you are dealing with a side effect or considering the pros and cons of a particular medication.

In this chapter, we provide a brief summary of the key points covered in the technical section that can be used as a quick reference.

Differences Between the Older and Newer Medications

- The newer atypical antipsychotic medications, as a group, are more effective and have fewer distressing neurologic (EPS) side effects than the older medications.

- The newer medications often work better than the older medications for the negative symptoms of schizophrenia. This has been hard to prove in clinical research trials, but is apparent to almost all experienced mental health clinicians.

- Of the newer medications, clozapine is the one that has been most clearly established to be effective when other medications have failed. Clozapine also has the fewest EPS. However, clozapine can cause many other problems so that it is not used as a first-line atypical medication. Rather, clozapine should be used when other atypical medications fail.

- The other atypical antipsychotics are, on average, roughly equal to the conventional antipsychotics in terms of controlling acute positive symptoms of schizophrenia. In the long run, however, they are more effective in relapse prevention than the conventional antipsychotics.

- It is impossible to predict in advance which medication will work for any individual person.

- One of the major advantages of the older conventional antipsychotics is that some are available in long-acting "depot" injections. This way of giving the medication is essential for some patients who are unable or unwilling to take medication in pill form. None of the newer atypical antipsychotics has the advantage of being available in long-acting preparations.

Differences in Side Effects Between Newer and Older Medications

- Side effects, especially EPS, are one of the biggest problems with the older medications. The newer medications cause far fewer EPS, although they can still cause EPS. There are differences among the newer medications in terms of likelihood of EPS, with clozapine having the least and risperidone the most.

- Anticholinergic side-effect medications are often given to counteract EPS. However, anticholinergics have side effects of their own. Since the newer medications cause fewer EPS, many patients can eventually stop taking anticholinergics and have fewer anticholinergic side effects as well.

- The newer antipsychotics *probably* reduce the risk of developing tardive dyskinesia (TD), but clozapine is the only medication known to be effective in reducing the risk as well as treating tardive dyskinesia after it happens.

- Weight gain is more of a problem with the newer medications. All of the newer medications are associated with weight gain, with clozapine and olanzapine causing more weight gain than risperidone or quetiapine. Ziprasidone, when it becomes available, will be the only atypical antipsychotic without the side effect of weight gain.

- High prolactin levels, which are associated with conventional antipsychotics, cause menstrual irregularities and breast lactation in some women. Most of the newer medications, except risperidone, do not cause high prolactin levels. Menstrual side effects reverse when patients are switched to a newer medication that lowers prolactin.

Switching Antipsychotic Medications

- The decision to switch is a complicated one and should be based on a consideration of all the potential advantages and risks.

- Even though the new medications may be better as a group, on an individual basis there is no way to predict who will do best on what medication. Therefore, there will always be some uncertainty in predicting how any one person's symptoms will respond to a new medication.

- Often the major concern that mitigates against switching is the risk of symptom flare-up during the crossover process.
- To minimize the risk of a symptom flare-up, most doctors recommend a transition period during which both the old and the new medications are prescribed simultaneously. Eventually the old medication is discontinued and the new one takes over.
- Another way to decrease the risk of symptom flare-ups is for clinicians to monitor their patients more closely during the switching period.
- Medication errors are common during the switching period. Methods that minimize the chances of medication errors include patients' getting written instructions, using weekly pill boxes, having extra medication monitoring, bringing pill bottles to appointments, and working with the pharmacist.
- Symptom flare-ups that occur during the first few weeks of crossover do not indicate anything about the person's eventual likelihood of doing better on the new medication. Whenever possible, it is very important to persevere and finish the trial of the new medication.
- Certain problems, especially side effects, that occur during the first week of switching from one medication to another may be withdrawal side effects from the old medication rather than *new side effects* from the new medication.

Assessing Response

- Sometimes, when the patient is talking more or behaving differently after switching, it can be hard to tell if this represents an improvement or a worsening of the patient's condition.
- When the medication switch was made in a stable outpatient for elective reasons (persistent positive symptoms or persistent negative symptoms), it takes up to 3 months at therapeutic doses to tell whether the new medication will be more helpful.
- The 3-month period starts only when the patient has reached a *therapeutic dose* of the new medication, not on the first day the medication is taken.
- There is a big difference between *absolutely no response* at 3 months and *a slight improvement* at 3 months. The new medication should usually be stopped if patients have no improvement at 3 months. The medication should be continued up to 1 year if patients show a little improvement at 3 months.
- In evaluating side effects from the new medication that happen shortly after switching, it is important to know which ones are *early* side effects that usually go away with time and which ones are more likely to persist over time.

- Improvements in EPS are more predictable than improvements in negative or positive symptoms.

Long-term Issues
- It is important to watch for certain problems that might come up after a patient responds to a new medication. In particular, the person may develop a postpsychotic depression after responding and may even be at risk for suicide during this time.
- Many other life changes happen in a delayed fashion or in an irregular pattern. Patients may experience "growing pains" and setbacks during this part of the recovery process.

Final Thoughts

Like most complicated decisions in life, decisions about how best to cope with an illness like schizophrenia are based on information from many sources, including intuition, personal goals and worries, and guidance from other people. The decision of whether to switch antipsychotic medications is almost always a major one. No matter how disappointed the patient or family is with the current medication, it is at least a known quantity. If patients switch medications, they and their families will have to deal with some uncertainty about what is going to happen. We hope that this technical section contains information that will help clinicians, patients, and families better understand the available options and possibilities for the future and make the best decisions possible.

Part III

Paying for Medications

Costs of Atypical Medications

All of the newer antipsychotic medications are much more expensive than the older medications. For example, if you had to pay for the medications yourself, a prescription for a month's worth of any of the newer medications might cost you $300, but a month's worth of an older medication would cost only about $30. This is a huge difference if you have to pay for the medications yourself. Most people cannot afford the newer medications, and will need to have their medications paid for by some kind of insurance benefit program or patient assistance program.

Insurance Programs That May Pay for the New Antipsychotics

Each country has its own system of paying for health care and medications. This section discusses the most common medication payment systems in place in the United States and Puerto Rico.

Does insurance pay for the new antipsychotics?

Medicaid is the program used most frequently to pay for the newer antipsychotic medications. Medicaid is a federal health insurance program in the United States that provides medical assistance for people who do not have much income. Many people with schizophrenia are either on Medicaid or would be eligible for Medicaid.

In many states, Medicaid and most private medical insurance will pay for some or all of these medications. However, each insurance program has its own rules about what medications it pays for and when.

What is the difference between Medicaid and Medicare?

People can apply for Medicaid if they have a disability *and* they have very little money. Anyone on Social Security Income (SSI) automatically gets Medicaid. Some people get enough income from Social Security Disability Income (SSDI) or other sources or have enough money in the bank that they do not qualify for Medicaid.

Medicare is for anyone who has worked in the past and paid into the social security system, and is now disabled or elderly. Someone can get Medicare even if they have lots of money.

People who have worked in the past, are now disabled, and have very little money can get both Medicaid and Medicare.

What if I have too much money to get Medicaid?

People with just a little too much income can qualify for Medicaid by spending enough money on medical expenses to bring their remaining income under the Medicaid limit for their state. Once individuals qualify in this way, they keep their Medicaid coverage for 6 months before again being required to "spend down" their income to below the limit for Medicaid coverage.

Do Medicaid and Medicare cover the same things?

No. Medicaid and Medicare pay for different things. Medicaid pays for most medications that people take outside the hospital. Medicare, however, only pays for medication while you're in the hospital (if you have Medicare coverage during your hospital stay). *It doesn't pay for any medication when you are not in the hospital.* People who have Medicare (and don't have Medicaid too) need to find some other way to pay for medications if they can't afford to buy them (for example, by applying to one of the compassionate need or indigent drug programs offered by various pharmaceutical companies [see p. 157]). The bottom line here is that, when it comes to paying for medications, getting on Medicaid is the way to go.

How do I get on Medicaid?

First, check if you are eligible for Medicaid. Try calling a Medicaid helpline or get advice from your social worker or case manager. There will be an application to fill out and you may have to go to an interview or examination at the Medicaid office. This whole process is stressful and confusing. Very few patients or families can do this on their own. Most hospitals or mental health centers have people who are specially trained in helping you get on Medicaid.

Which medications does Medicaid cover?

The rules are different from state to state. Each state Medicaid agency chooses which medications it will and won't pay for. The medications Medicaid pays for in that state are on the Medicaid formulary—this means they are on the list of approved medications. Some states have Medicaid programs that pay for all the new atypical antipsychotic medications. Other states have programs that only pay for the new medications if your doctor fills in special paperwork. In some states, some of the new medications are not paid for at all.

If you don't know which of the atypical antipsychotics Medicaid will pay for in your state, ask your pharmacist, case manager, nurse, therapist, or doctor.

I'm not on Medicaid now, but I'm told that I'll get on Medicaid soon. Who pays for medications?

Unfortunately, Medicaid only pays for medications at the time you actually get on Medicaid. The waiting time beforehand doesn't count. As you can imagine, sometimes there are long waiting times between the application and actually getting on Medicaid. During that time, you are considered "Medicaid eligible" or "Medicaid pending." Someone else needs to pay for the medications during that time. Sometimes your mental health treatment system picks up the cost, sometimes there are patient assistance programs, or sometimes you or your family will need to pay.

Is it easier to get atypical antipsychotics in the hospital?

Not always. Getting and paying for the new, expensive medications can also be a problem for patients in state or county hospitals. Hospitals have to pay for medications too. If you don't have insurance that pays for the medication, then the cost has to come out of the hospital's budget. Or else the hospital will charge you for the medication and hope you can pay the bill. Sometimes hospitals can't afford to buy the new, atypical medications for very many people.

Figuring Out How to Pay

Figuring out how to pay for medication is a big problem for many people. What's your situation?

__ I have Medicaid
  __ but in my state it doesn't pay for any atypical antipsychotics.
  __ and in my state it pays for some of the atypical antipsychotics.
  __ and in my state it pays for all the atypical antipsychotics.
__ I have Medicare
  __ which won't keep paying for medication after I'm discharged.
  __ which won't pay for medication since I'm not in the hospital.
__ I have private insurance
  __ but it doesn't pay for any atypical antipsychotics.
  __ and it pays for some of the atypical antipsychotics.
  __ and it pays for all the atypical antipsychotics.
__ I don't have any insurance.
__ I don't know.

Is your insurance still active? If you've moved, changed jobs, lost a job, or been hospitalized, you or your family should check to see if you still have active insurance coverage. If you were dropped from your insurance plan because you were too sick to pay or do the paperwork, you may be able to appeal and get your insurance coverage back.

What can people do if there's no way to pay for the medication?

Basically, there are four ways to get medication if you can't afford to pay for it and you don't have insurance that automatically covers it:

1. Use a "prior authorization" process if possible.
2. Talk to your doctor about getting free medication from the drug company. Most drug companies give free medicine to people who can't afford it.
3. Negotiate to get the medication as inexpensively as possible if you or your family are going to have to pay for it.
4. Apply pressure to make it possible for more people to get the new medications.

How can I find out if my doctor is being influenced by insurance or cost pressures not to prescribe the more expensive medications?

If you think a medication isn't being prescribed or suggested because of cost, it might be a good idea to ask the following questions:

- Which antipsychotic medications are already approved by your formulary or program and can easily be prescribed by you?
- Are there any other medications that you think might work for me that are difficult for you to prescribe because of formulary restrictions?
- Do you have to do any extra paperwork to get me on any of the new medications?
- Which antipsychotics can be used *only* with prior authorization? What special rules or restrictions are there for these medications?
- Who makes the rules?
- Is cost a part of the decision process?
- How can the decision be appealed?

While it may be frustrating if the doctor says that there are restrictions or hassles influencing your treatment, at least he or she is being honest. You might want to ask if there is anything you (or your family) can do to make it easier to prescribe a new medication. Perhaps you could fill out some of the paperwork or let him use your session time to fill out forms.

Prior Authorization

What is prior authorization and how does it work?

Prior authorization means that your state Medicaid program or your insurance company has agreed that it will sometimes pay for a particular medication or treatment, but *only* if you get special approval ahead of time. You and your treatment team might have to fill out forms, write letters, send copies of records, or make phone calls to get prior approval.

Who has a prior approval process?

Some state Medicaid programs, managed care insurance programs, and hospitals have a prior approval process for certain medications. They have a list of medications that are expected to be used for most patients. They also have a list of medications that can be used *only* after special requirements have been met. Even if you meet those requirements, you still have to apply for approval.

Does prior authorization mean more work for mental health providers?

Yes. Prior authorization usually means the doctor has to do a lot of extra paperwork. All the extra work often discourages doctors from using some of the new medications—which is, in fact, one of the reasons prior authorization was developed.

Can I always use a prior authorization process to get my medication paid for?

No! You can only use this if you have Medicaid or some other health insurance that pays for outpatient medications *and* if your health insurance company has a prior authorization process set up for the medication that you need.

What else can I do?

It's a good idea to let your treatment team know that you appreciate all the time and extra work it takes to get you on a new medication. Learn all you can and work with your treatment team. Together you may be able to push the system and get the medication your team thinks would be the best choice for you.

What if the prior authorization is denied?

If your application for prior authorization is turned down, you can sometimes work with your treatment team to file an appeal. This means that you and your treatment team take steps (fill out lots more paperwork!) to try to convince the people who made the decision to change their mind. Whether an appeal has any chance of working depends on why the original request was turned down and the rules of your particular medical plan or insurance company. An appeal is a long, slow process that takes a lot of time and work. You and your family should stay involved in this process, help as much as possible, and work with the treatment team to make sure the needed paperwork is filled out and sent in.

Talking with Your Doctor and Treatment Team

What if I've talked with my team, and they won't let me try one of the new medications?

Start by asking your doctor why he or she has decided that one of the new medications is not worth trying. Make sure you understand the reasons for the decision, whether you agree with those reasons or not.

Try to negotiate with your doctor. At times, your case manager or therapist might be able to help you talk with your doctor. Explain what you have heard about the new medications, why you want to give one of them a try, and what you are hoping to get out of a medication change. Listen to the doctor and get educated about both the good things and bad things about the new medications. Also, work to educate the doctor about what you want from your medication, what side effects are the biggest problems for you, and why you think a medication change is a good idea at this time.

What if I can't get my team to let me try one of the new medications, even though I want to?

First, make sure you've discussed it with your team, listened to their opinions, told them clearly what you want, and discussed possible compromises. If you've done that, make sure you understand the team's reasons for not wanting you to switch to one of the new medications.

Most often, the decision not to try a new atypical antipsychotic medication is based on what's best for you, not how much a medication costs. If you think cost is the main reason you aren't able to switch medications, you can discuss with the team how the medications might be paid for, including how to appeal the decision to Medicaid or other payers.

Is it OK to get a second opinion?

At times it might be a good idea to ask for a second opinion from another doctor. It's very important to talk with your treatment team and regular psychiatrist before getting a second opinion. If possible, involve your regular treatment team in helping to set up the second opinion. This doesn't mean switching your treatment to a new doctor. It just means arranging for one meeting with another doctor to get some suggestions and ideas. Getting a second opinion involves making an appointment with a new psychiatrist to review your current treatment and help come up with suggestions of what to try next.

What problems might come up if I get a second opinion?

There are a number of possible problems with a second opinion. Even though a second opinion is common in medicine, it can still annoy your regular clinician or doctor. Also, it might be difficult to arrange a second opinion, especially if you don't have a lot of money or good insurance.

You need to arrange for the new doctor to talk with your regular doctor or get your records so he or she has enough information to make an informed suggestion. Finally, your regular doctor may not listen to the opinion of an outside doctor. Despite all of these problems, sometimes getting a second opinion is the best plan.

What should I do after I get a second opinion?

Ask the doctor to talk with your regular doctor about what you have discussed. Go back to your team and talk with them about what the other doctor recommended. Listen to what they have to say and keep an open mind.

Help from Pharmaceutical Companies

What can I do if I don't have any insurance?

There are, of course, many people without any insurance coverage. If you don't have insurance and you can't afford to pay for medication, you can work with your team to apply for free medication. Almost all the drug companies have a compassionate need or indigent patient program that gives people free medication. They each have their own forms, rules, and steps that have to be followed. Some will ask for a lot of information about your income, your family's income, your medical bills, and lots of other details. Other drug companies won't ask for very much information. In all cases, at least part of the form must be filled out by your doctor.

If your application is approved, the medication is usually mailed to your doctor. Most of the drug companies make you reapply every three months. Some companies have time limits on how long they'll give you free medication.

Can doctors get free samples of any of the atypical antipsychotics?

Yes. Your doctor can get free samples of medication for patients who can't afford to buy it. Even doctors who don't usually get free medication can ask the drug company representative for samples. Most companies give free samples to doctors (although you can't get free samples of clozapine [Clozaril]). Ask your doctor about getting free samples for you.

Phone Numbers for Drug Companies' Compassionate Need / Indigent Patient Programs

Generic Name	Brand Name	Company	Phone Number
clozapine	Clozaril	Novartis	1-800-257-3273
risperidone	Risperdal	Janssen	1-800-652-6227
olanzapine	Zyprexa	Eli Lilly	1-800-545-6962
quetiapine	Seroquel	Zeneca	1-800-424-3727
ziprasidone	Zeldox	Pfizer	1-800-438-1985

How can I get phone numbers for other medications?

Call the drug company directly. Call the national toll-free telephone directory (1-800-555-1212) and ask for the 800 free telephone number for that drug company. The number you are given will be the general telephone number for the company. When you call the company, ask for the number of their indigent patient program.

Negotiating the Best Price

If we can pay for my medication, how can we get the best price?

Some people (or their families) are able to pay for medication. As you know, the cost of medication varies a lot from one pharmacy to another—just like lab costs. Call several pharmacies and compare prices. If you need a weekly blood count as part of being on clozapine, it's worth calling around to several local labs or hospitals with labs to see if you can work out a special deal. Your mental health center may have contracts that let them order medications or lab tests at a lower price. If you're paying for your own medication or lab tests, it might be possible to get the same price.

If we work hard enough and don't give up, can I count on being able to take a new atypical—eventually?

None of these things will work in every situation. The new medications are very expensive because they cost a lot to develop. As more and more people take them, it'll be harder and harder for public and private mental health systems to pay for the medications. Obviously their budgets will need to be increased. However, it will take public awareness about the need for these new medications and political pressure for this to happen.

Are there times when the rules make it impossible to take one of the new medications?

Yes. Sometimes the rules work against people who want to take one of the expensive new medications. The atypicals might not be on the Medicaid formulary or the indigent drug program list of approved medications. Sometimes the rules are written so only a certain number of people can take a new medication at the same time. That's one way to control cost. They might tell you there's not enough money to buy atypical antipsychotics for everyone who wants to take them.

What can be done to change rules that keep people from getting the new medications?

Political pressure, publicity, and working with organizations such as the National Alliance for the Mentally Ill (NAMI) and your local mental health association are some good ways to change the rules. In several states, unreasonable rules that made it hard to get clozapine (Clozaril) have been overturned by political pressure and court action. This may become necessary as the widespread use of new generation antipsychotic medications taxes the budgets of many state agencies and managed care organizations.

This chapter has focused on the hassles and cost barriers to getting on the newer medications. But let's not forget how lucky many people are in the United States to have the opportunity to be on these newer medications shortly after they are approved by the FDA. Compared to other countries, the United States has by far the greatest percentage of use of the newer medications. Much of the credit for this goes to advocacy groups like NAMI and the National Mental Health Association (NMHA). Political advocacy by their dedicated members has been one of the main reasons that the newer medications are covered by insurance and Medicaid. NAMI and other groups have been able to change restrictive medication policies in many states. If you are fortunate enough to have your medications paid for, there is a good chance that you owe it to the efforts of organizations like NAMI and NMHA.

Part IV
Glossary

In this section, we give definitions for some of the terms that are used in this book. We try to explain terms as they are used in the context of situations in which people are treated with antipsychotic medications. Terms printed in bold are defined in the glossary.

You might want to glance over this glossary if you are unfamiliar with what your doctor is saying or when you don't understand the material presented in other sections of this book. The definitions will orient you to the doctor's language and make it easier for you to learn more about your symptoms and treatment.

acute phase (of illness) a worsening of the person's **positive** (psychotic) **symptoms**, often leading to out-of-control or bizarre behavior. Antipsychotic medications are given to eliminate or reduce these symptoms. It often takes 4–6 weeks for the antipsychotic medications to work. The newer and older medications take about the same amount of time to work. Frequently the patient needs to be hospitalized for safety issues during the acute phase.

acute psychotic episode. *See* **acute phase of illness.**

adjuvant medication a second (or third) medication that is *added* onto another medication. The purpose of the second medication is not to replace the first medication, but to boost its benefits. The first medication is still the cornerstone medication and is considered the **primary medication.** The second medication is called an adjuvant to the first medication. It is considered to be an **adjunctive treatment.** The same medication might be used as an adjuvant for one person while being a primary medication for someone else.

adjunctive treatment. *See* **adjuvant medication.**

affinity (for receptors) Affinity means how strongly a medication attaches itself to a **receptor** on the nerve cell. Stronger affinities produce stronger effects. Medications that attach to a receptor in a way that keeps the **neurotransmitter** away are known as **antagonists. Conventional antipsychotics** have strong affinities to the **dopamine** receptor and completely block the dopamine from reaching the nerve cell. **Atypical antipsychotics** have weaker affinities that allow some of the dopamine to reach the receptor. *See also* **agonist.**

agonist a drug or psychiatric medication that works by resembling the neurotransmitter itself. The brain cells behave as if there were more of that neurotransmitter around. An agonist is the opposite of an antagonist. *See also* **antagonist.**

agranulocytosis a potentially dangerous side effect of **clozapine** (Clozaril) that causes people to stop making the white blood cells needed to fight infections. Agranulocytosis occurs in about 1% of people taking clozapine. Agranulocytosis usually occurs in the first 6 months of clozapine treatment, which is why patients starting clozapine have their blood monitored every week for the first 6 months.

akathisia a kind of restlessness or inability to sit still that is caused by medication. Akathisia can cause people to pace, to repeatedly get up and down from a chair, and to have fidgety legs. People describe akathisia as "feeling like I'm jumping out of my skin." Sometimes people have trouble communicating their distress and may not mention akathisia symptoms without being asked. The restless sensation is usually most intense in the upper legs and the trunk. Akathisia waxes and wanes. It may get better when the person is busy or distracted and worse when the person is left alone.

Many psychiatric conditions cause symptoms that are just like akathisia. This can make it difficult to know with certainty whether the problem is due to akathisia or is caused by psychosis, a manic or anxiety state, or drug or alcohol use. *See also* **extrapyramidal side effects**.

akinesia (also referred to as "bradykinesia") a slowing down of movements ("kinesis" is a Latin word for movement"). A person with akinesia may be listless or lifeless. The person's face may lose its usual expressions. Akinesia can sometimes be more of an internal, subjective feeling than actual slowed down movements. A common complaint with akinesia is "I feel like a zombie." Akinesia can closely resemble the **negative symptoms** of schizophrenia or depressive symptoms. It can be difficult, if not impossible at times, to tell the difference between these conditions. *See also* **extrapyramidal side effects**.

alcohol It is well known that alcohol can worsen mood symptoms such as depression. Alcohol can also worsen psychotic symptoms. Continued alcohol use can be an explanation when a new medication does not work as well as expected. *See also* **dual diagnosis**.

allergy While there can be allergic reactions to any medication, allergic reactions to antipsychotic medications are uncommon. When patients report having had an "allergy" to an antipsychotic medication, it is usually a dystonic reaction that is interpreted as an allergy. There is no evidence that schizophrenia or other psychotic conditions are caused by food allergies or other allergic reactions. *See also* **dystonia**.

alpha receptors one of several subtypes of receptors that are receiving sites for the **neurotransmitter norepinephrine**. Some antipsychotics block the alpha receptor. The psychiatric effects of blocking alpha receptors are not fully understood. However, blocking of alpha receptors is the major cause of dizziness during the first few days of starting a new medication. *See also* **orthostatic hypotension**.

amenorrhea to miss menstrual periods. Some of the antipsychotic medications can cause an elevation of the hormone **prolactin**. High prolactin levels fool a woman's hormonal system into "believing" she is pregnant. This side effect of medication can also cause irregular periods and abnormal leakage of breast milk, which is called **galactorrhea**. Amenorrhea in premenopausal in women is often a side effect of the medication, but don't forget that amenorrhea also happens during real pregnancies.

amotivation literally "no motivation." Amotivation can be a **negative symptom** of schizophrenia, a part of **akinesia,** or the result of **depression**. Doctors tend to use this term when they are describing someone's negative symptoms. *See also* **apathy**.

ancillary symptoms symptoms that are not always found in schizophrenia, or happen to other people without a diagnosis of schizophrenia. For example, insomnia is considered an ancillary symptom because it is not really a specific feature of schizophrenia, but is a common and distressing problem for many people with schizophrenia.

anergia literally "no energy." In psychiatry, anergia is used to describe the lack of energy that is one of the negative symptoms of schizophrenia. It may be very hard for doctors to tell the difference between **anergia**, which is a **negative symptom**, and **akinesia**, which is an **extrapyramidal side effect**.

antagonist a drug that blocks the actions of a **neurotransmitter**. The antagonist drug blocks the place on the receptor where the neurotransmitter usually lands. The receptor is "fooled" into believing there is less neurotransmitter around, and that message is then conveyed to the receptor's nerve cell.

antianxiety medications medications that are most commonly used to treat anxiety, whatever the cause. Most antianxiety medications are in the class of medications known as benzodiazepines. These include Ativan (lorazepam) and Valium (diazepam). A related category of medications are the triazolam medications such as Xanax (alprazolam) and Klonopin (clonazepam). Bu-Spar (buspirone) is another kind of antianxiety medication *See also* **adjuvant medication, akathisia, anxiety, insomnia**.

anticholinergic medications medications that counteract many of the **extrapyramidal side effects (EPS)**, especially **dystonia**, **tremor**, and **rigidity**. Anticholinergic medications can sometimes help with **akathisia** and **akinesia**, but they are not effective for **dyskinesia**. Anticholinergics are frequently given along with the **conventional antipsychotics**, either to treat EPS that are there or to prevent EPS from happening. Examples of commonly used anticholinergic medications include Cogentin (benztropine), Akineton (biperiden), and Artane (trihexyphenidyl). Unfortunately, anticholinergic medications have side effects of their own. Fortunately, because they cause far fewer EPS, anticholinergics are not needed nearly as often with the **atypical antipsychotics**. *See also* **anticholinergic side effects**.

anticholinergic side effects Choline is a chemical that nerve cells use to communicate. Many of the medications used to treat the side effects of antipsychotics have strong anticholinergic effects. Some antipsychotics are also very anticholinergic, including Mellaril (thioridazine), Thorazine (chlorpromazine), and Clozaril (clozapine). Common anticholinergic side effects include **dry mouth**, **blurry vision**, **constipation**, and difficulty urinating (**urinary retention**). These problems don't always come from anticholinergics, but if a person is taking an anticholinergic medication, chances are good that such problems are due to the medication.

Anticholinergic problems can be treated in several different ways. Nothing is needed if the problem is mild and not bothersome. Sometimes the passage of time helps resolve the anticholinergic problem on its own. If the problem persists and is bothersome or dangerous, medication adjustments may be needed. These include adding a medication to reverse the anticholinergic effects, decreasing the anticholinergic medication, switching to a less anticholinergic medication, or switching to an antipsychotic medication that is less likely to require an extra anticholinergic side-effect medication.

antidepressant medications medications that work on relieving symptoms of **depression**. They are given as primary medications for people with a diagnosis of major depression. Many of the antidepressant medications are serotonin reuptake inhibitors such as Paxil (paroxetine), Prozac (fluoxetine), and Zoloft (sertraline). For patients with schizophrenia or schizoaffective disorder, antidepressant medications may be added to the antipsychotic to help relieve depressive symptoms. Antidepressant medication should not be taken alone by patients with schizophrenia or schizoaffective disorder. *See also* **postpsychotic depression.**

antiobsessive medications medications that are most commonly used to treat obsessions and compulsions, whatever the cause. Many of the antiobsessive medications are serotonin reuptake inhibitors such as Luvox (fluvoxamine), Paxil (paroxetine), Prozac (fluoxetine), and Zoloft (sertraline). Anafranil (clomipramine) is another antiobsessive medication. In general, antiobsessive medications are safe to take with antipsychotics, although there may be drug-drug interactions, especially when Luvox is given with Clozaril (clozapine). *See also* **obsessive and compulsive symptoms**.

anxiety a normal mood that can also be a symptom in just about any psychiatric condition. As one would imagine, anxiety is a very common symptom when someone has psychotic symptoms—**delusions** and **hallucinations** can be terrifying; having paranoid fears means always feeling like you are under attack. **Akathisia** is a side effect that often causes anxiety. Treatment of anxiety depends on the cause and may include reassurance, adding an antianxiety medication, increasing the dose of the antipsychotic, or treating the akathisia. *See also* **paranoia**.

apathy an indifference to one's environment. There is a kind of dullness to the person's reactions and a sense that the person just doesn't care. Often apathy goes hand-in-hand with having a very low physical energy (**anergia**). Withdrawal from sadness or **depression** is not apathy; rather, apathy is lack of any feeling. Apathy is a common **negative symptom**. Sometimes **extrapyramidal side effects** and severe **sedation** from antipsychotics can also cause apathy. Sometimes problems with drugs or **alcohol** cause apathy. Families and friends may mistake apathy for laziness. *See also* **laziness, substance abuse**.

asociality literally "no social functioning." In psychiatry, it is used to mean the poor social functioning that is due to the **negative symptoms** of schizophrenia.

atypical antipsychotics the newer antipsychotic medications. The newer medications are also sometimes called "novel" or simply "newer." The word "atypical" will soon be outdated, as the atypical medications continue to replace the older medications for first-line use (just like the "New" in New York is outdated!).

The term "atypical" means that the medication belongs to a class of newer medications. If you feel confused about this word, you're not alone! There is disagreement in the medical community about the exact meaning of the word. Sometimes "atypical" refers to the medication's side-effect profile, sometimes to what the medication does in the test tube or in animal models, and sometimes to whether or not the medication affects the **neurotransmitter serotonin**.

Medications considered to be atypical antipsychotics that are currently available in the United States (early 1999) include **Clozaril (clozapine), Risperdal (risperidone), Zyprexa (olanzapine), and Seroquel (quetiapine).** Another atypical antipsychotic called **Zeldox (ziprasidone)** is currently under FDA review, while several others are in earlier phases of testing. At least two other atypical antipsychotics—sertindole and zotepine—are available in other countries but probably will not be available in the United States in the foreseeable future.

avolition lack of volition or will power. This term is used to describe one of the **negative symptoms** of schizophrenia. *See also* **akinesia, negative symptoms.**

"awakenings" term borrowed from a book of the same title by Oliver Sacks. In this book, we use the term to refer to the psychological challenges and changes after a patient with persistent symptoms of schizophrenia responds to one of the newer antipsychotic medications. *See also* **atypical antipsychotics, postpsychotic depression.**

baseline When used by mental health clinicians, "baseline" refers to the state in which a person with persistent symptoms is no better or worse than usual (e.g., "The patient's symptoms were at his usual **baseline** until he changed apartments." *See also* **acute phase, maintenance treatment.**

b.i.d. technical term meaning that a medication should be taken *twice a day*. *See also* **q.d., q.i.d., t.i.d.**

bipolar disorder psychiatric disorder related to problems regulating mood. Also referred to as **manic–depression.** Patients with bipolar disorder have mood swings characterized by periods of **depression** and **mania.** Many, but not all, patients experience psychotic symptoms. Although bipolar disorder differs from **schizophrenia,** doctors often need to distinguish bipolar disorder from schizophrenia when there are psychotic symptoms. Accurate diagnosis is important because **mood stabilizers** (lithium, Depakote, Tegretol) are the **primary medications** for people with bipolar disorder. **Antipsychotics** are often also used during the **acute (manic) phase** either as **adjunctive treatments** with the mood stabilizers or alone for patients who cannot tolerate mood stabilizers. Patients with mood disorders are often more likely to get **extrapyramidal side effects (EPS)** from **conventional antipsychotics.** The **atypical antipsychotics,** therefore, seem to be better adjunctive medications for bipolar disorder because of their better side-effect profile. Also, the atypical antipsychotics seem to have mood stabilizing properties and can be helpful for patients who do not respond to, or cannot tolerate, mood stabilizers.

blurry vision possible side effect of medications that have anticholinergic properties. This side effect often happens early on, when the medication is started or the dosage is raised. The blurry vision will often get better by itself, so it is usually best to wait a few weeks to see if the problem goes away on its own. Other treatments include the medication adjustments discussed under anticholinergic side effects. *See also* **anticholinergic side effects.**

breast milk. *See* **galactorrhea.**

caffeine Caffeine from any source (coffee, colas, "pep pills") can counteract the benefits of antipsychotic medications. Excessive caffeine intake can sometimes be the reason a new medication does not work as well as expected.

cataracts clouding of the cornea (outer layer) of the eye. Some psychiatric medications, including Thorazine, Mellaril, and Tegretol, have been reported to cause cataracts as a very rare side effect. During animal testing, the atypical antipsychotic **quetiapine (Seroquel)** caused cataracts in dogs. Although there is no evidence that Seroquel causes cataracts in people, there is a precaution concerning this in the label for Seroquel.

catatonia a condition in which the person is immobile and extremely withdrawn. Catatonia can be a psychotic symptom and may also be a part of a mood disorder or schizophrenia. However, catatonia can also be a rare but serious side effect of antipsychotic medications. Just as is the case for EPS, the **conventional antipsychotics** are more likely to cause catatonia than the **atypical antipsychotics**.

causes (of psychosis) Research has conclusively shown that psychosis from schizophrenia and bipolar disorders is caused by a brain disorder that ultimately leads to an imbalance in the **neurotransmitters** responsible for the control of thoughts and moods. It is important to know that psychosis is not caused by "bad parenting" or other childhood problems. Also, stress seems to trigger psychosis but not to cause it, just like physical exercise might trigger a heart attack but not actually cause it. **Substance abuse** or **alcohol abuse** can cause psychosis or can trigger a psychotic episode in someone with a psychiatric disorder. The timing of substance abuse or alcohol abuse and the psychiatric symptoms often needs to be carefully sorted out before doctors can make an accurate diagnosis. *See also* **stigma**.

CBC (complete blood count) monitoring periodic blood tests that are needed for patients taking clozapine. The blood is checked for the number of white blood cells that are available to fight infection. Blood tests are done once a week for the first 6 months of taking clozapine and then usually every other week after that. *See also* **agranulocytosis, clozapine**.

cigarette smoking. *See* **nicotine**.

clozapine (Clozaril) the first of the atypical antipsychotics to be introduced and the only one that has been proven to be more effective than the conventional antipsychotics. Clozapine has many drawbacks, including the need for ongoing blood tests, so that its use is limited to patients who have not done well on other antipsychotic medications. Clozapine comes in 25 and 100 mg tablets. *See also* **agranulocytosis, hypersalivation, myoclonus, seizure**.

Clozaril. *See* **clozapine**.

cocaine a substance of abuse that is a dopamine agonist and worsens **positive** (psychotic) **symptoms**. Cocaine use counteracts the protective effects of antipsychotic medications. *See also* **dual diagnosis, substance abuse**.

coffee. *See* **caffeine**.

cognitive problems many patients with schizophrenia have cognitive problems such as trouble concentrating, focusing, or paying attention. With some exceptions, cognitive problems are thought to be caused by the psychiatric condition rather than the medications used to treat the disorder. It is hoped—but not proven—that the atypical antipsychotics may be more effective than the older conventional antipsychotics for these kinds of cognitive problems. *See also* **memory problems**.

compliance. *See* **medication noncompliance**.

constipation a possible side effect of anticholinergic medications, which slow down bowel movements. The person may get constipated and have fewer bowel movements or hard stools. This problem can be annoying for some people. When constipation is severe or happens in an older person, it can be medically dangerous. Mild constipation can be helped by drinking plenty of fluids and eating foods that are high in fiber, such as bran. If the problem is severe or persists, other possible treatments include using laxatives or the medication adjustments discussed under **anticholinergic side effects**. **Clozapine** is an antipsychotic that can cause constipation.

contraindication a medical word meaning a reason *not* to go ahead with a treatment. For example, a recent heart attack is a contraindication for elective surgery. Most of the time, contraindications are weighed against **indications**. An example of a contraindication for switching from an older to a newer antipsychotic medication is when the person needs a long-acting depot antipsychotic medication because he or she has a hard time taking oral medications as prescribed. None of the newer medications are available in a long-acting form.

Before switching antipsychotic medications, it is important to consider possible contraindications. The checklist on page 38 reviews some of the possible contraindications for switching.

conventional antipsychotics the group of antipsychotic medications developed between the 1950s and 1970s; also referred to as "neuroleptics" or "traditional" or "classic" antipsychotics. These medications include haloperidol (Haldol), fluphenazine (Prolixin), chlorpromazine (Thorazine), thioridazine (Mellaril), and perphenazine (Trilafon). They work by blocking the nerve cells that receive the neurotransmitter dopamine. In general, they are effective for **positive** (psychotic) **symptoms** and less effective for **negative symptoms** of schizophrenia.

crossover used in this book to refer to the process of switching from one antipsychotic to another. This process may involve a period of time during which the old antipsychotic medication and the newer antipsychotic medication are prescribed simultaneously.

delusions believing things that no one else believes, such as an unshakable belief that the CIA is following you when no one else thinks this is happening or believing that you are Jesus. *See also* **positive symptoms**.

denial of illness a term used to mean that the person is not aware of (or does not acknowledge) having a psychiatric condition. Not surprisingly, patients who deny their illness are less likely to take recommended medication as prescribed. Denial of illness can be a vexing problem for family members of patients with schizophrenia, especially when the person does much better on medication. For patients who tend to deny their illness all the time, switching medications does not seem to change the person's point of view.

depot therapy (also referred to as "depot route") a long-acting form of antipsychotic medication that is given by an injection into a muscle approximately every 2–4 weeks. It is called "depot" because the medication is stored in the muscle for several weeks, just as a bus depot stores buses. Other types of medications such as hormones and antibiotics also come in depot forms. Only two long-acting depot antipsychotic medications are available in the United States today: Prolixin (fluphenazine) and Haldol (haloperidol). Both are older, high-potency, conventional antipsychotics. None of the newer atypical antipsychotics are currently available in long-acting depot form. It seems likely that some of the newer medications will eventually come in long-acting forms, but this won't happen anytime soon. Some antipsychotic medications can also be given in short-acting injections, but these are not depot medications.

depression a very common psychiatric disorder. When a depressive disorder occurs by itself without other psychiatric disorders, it is called "unipolar depression." Treatment for unipolar depressive disorders includes antidepressant medications and/or certain kinds of psychotherapy. Unless the depression is very severe or the person has psychotic symptoms, antipsychotics are not needed.

Patients with schizophrenia also have very high rates of depression. Depression in schizophrenia has to be treated very differently from unipolar depression. In evaluating depressive symptoms in schizophrenia, the doctors need to evaluate the patient's **positive symptoms** and side effects before making a final diagnosis of depression. One common form of depression in schizophrenia is called **postpsychotic depression.**

diagnosis A doctor makes a psychiatric diagnosis by evaluating the person's current psychiatric symptoms and past history of symptoms. The doctor also examines the results of laboratory tests and the physical examination to rule out medical problems that might be causing the symptoms. The doctor then uses the information to give a name to the person's symptoms (a diagnosis). To do this, the doctor often compares the person's problems with the diagnostic criteria for disorders that are listed in *DSM-IV.* Much of the time, there is no lab test or x-ray that pinpoints the diagnosis, so that the accuracy of the diagnosis depends to a great extent on the accuracy of the information the doctor gathers. Therefore, the doctor will want to interview the family as well as the patient. One of the hardest parts of accurate diagnosis is figuring out whether the problems could be caused by **substance abuse;** therefore, it is important to be truthful about drug and alcohol habits.

dietary precautions There are no dietary restrictions for patients taking antipsychotic medications (however, there are dietary restrictions for people taking a rarely used type of antidepressant known as monoamine oxidase inhibitors [MAOIs]). Most of the newer medications (with the exception of Zeldox) can be taken either with food or on an empty stomach. Weight gain can happen after switching to one of the newer atypical antipsychotics. If this is a concern, it is a good idea to be very careful about maintaining a healthy diet during the switching period. *See also* **weight gain.**

dopamine a neurotransmitter in the brain. Both conventional and atypical antipsychotics slow down (antagonize) dopamine's ability to transmit messages between nerve cells in the brain. *See also* **antagonist.**

drooling. *See* **hypersalivation.**

drug–drug interactions changes in the metabolism or blood levels of one drug when a second drug is added. Most drug interactions in psychiatry are safe for medically healthy adults, but there are exceptions. Because this is a very complicated area, for the most part we have not discussed drug-drug interactions in this book.

dry mouth a common **anticholinergic side effect.** People with persistent dry mouth are more likely to have dental problems. One way to help mild dry mouth is to chew sugarless gum or suck on sugar-free candy.

DSM–IV *Diagnostic and Statistical Manual of Mental Disorders, 4th Edition,* published by the American Psychiatric Press, Washington, D.C., in 1994. *DSM-IV* contains the major diagnostic system that is used by psychiatrists in the United States. In *DSM-IV*, all major psychiatric conditions are described and the clinical criteria used to make the **diagnosis** are outlined for each condition.

dual diagnosis literally the presence of two diagnoses at the same time. When one is speaking of psychotic disorders, the term is usually used to mean a person who has both a major psychiatric disorder, such as schizophrenia, and a **substance abuse** or **alcohol** problem.

dyskinesia abnormal muscle movements that are most common in the face, mouth, tongue, and hands. The movements usually look like writhing or wriggling and tend to come and go. The person is often not aware of these movements, which are often discovered by other people who spend time with the person. There are many different types and causes of dyskinesia. Two types of dyskinesia are commonly caused by antipsychotic medications:

- **withdrawal dyskinesia** is a temporary dyskinesia that occurs when antipsychotic medication is stopped
- **tardive dyskinesia** is a dyskinesia that persists over a long period of time

It is impossible to identify the type of dyskinesia simply by observing the abnormal movement. The exact diagnosis is usually based on information about all the medications the person is taking or has recently taken.

dystonia an uncontrollable muscle spasm. Anyone who has had writer's cramp has actually experienced a dystonia. Patients starting medication may experience a dystonia, which could look like a neck or jaw spasm or cause a rolling up of the eyes. Anxiety tends to trigger dystonic reactions. Dystonic reactions come and go, so that they may not actually be witnessed by any mental health professional. Sometimes acute dystonia is misdiagnosed as part of the psychiatric condition, especially when the person is psychotic or has trouble describing his or her symptoms accurately.

early side effects side effects that happen within days to weeks after starting a new medication. Early side effects tend to go away on their own over time. For example, sedation can be an early side effect of starting a new medication but often goes away in a few weeks.

early warning signs symptoms or behaviors that happen before a person has an acute psychotic episode (relapse). Many people have a telltale pattern of early warning signs, which can help alert them and their families and clinicians that a crisis may be coming. In such situations, the hope is to rapidly treat the symptoms ("heading them off at the pass") so that a full-blown relapse can be avoided.

ejaculatory problems difficulties with ejaculation as part of normal male sexual functioning. Ejaculation may be too rapid or too delayed.

epilepsy. *See* **seizures.**

erectile problems difficulty or inability to achieve or maintain an erect penis as a part of normal male sexual functioning.

extrapyramidal side effects (EPS) a series of neurological side effects of antipsychotics that involve a disruption of the part of the brain known as the extrapyramidal system. The disruption involves the neurotransmitter dopamine. Disruption of dopamine in this brain area can cause disorders that affect normal movement. EPS include akathisia, dystonia, tremors, muscle rigidity, and akinesia. Taken together, EPS are one the most serious problems with the older **conventional antipsychotics**. One of the major breakthroughs with the newer **atypical antipsychotics** is that they are much less likely to cause EPS.

formulary Most insurance plans have a list of preferred medications. This list is called a "formulary." Doctors are encouraged to prescribe medicines that are "on formulary" and discouraged from prescribing medications that are "off formulary." Medications that are "off formulary" are much harder for the doctor to prescribe and may not be covered. (Many Veterans' Administration Medical Centers still have restricted formularies that do not include all of the newer antipsychotics.) Some plans have not included all of the newer medications in their formularies and/or make it harder for the doctor to prescribe one of the newer medications. Because we do not know ahead of time who will do best on which medication, these formulary restrictions lead to lost opportunities for many patients. *See also* **Medicaid**.

galactorrhea abnormal leakage of breast milk. *See also* **amenorrhea**.

half–life the length of time a drug will stay in the blood stream. It refers to the amount of time it takes for half (50%) of the drug to be eliminated from the body. A medication with a short half-life (for example, under 12 hours) needs to be taken more frequently than a medication with a longer half-life (for example, longer than 24 hours).

hallucinations changes in your senses, such as hearing voices or seeing unusual things that are not there. *See also* **positive symptoms**.

herbal therapies Herbal remedies have become increasingly popular in the United States for many emotional and medical problems. For example, the extract of a plant called St. John's Wort is used as a home remedy for depression and a plant called Valerian is used for insomnia. People sometimes believe that herbal therapies are always safe or don't have side effects. *This is not true; herbal treatments do have side effects.* Many of these herbs can make psychotic symptoms worse. Unlike prescription medications that are carefully tested and approved by the FDA, herbs are not regulated and are sold without careful testing or research.

It is very important for patients to be truthful about the herbal treatments they are taking. They should also discuss this issue with their doctor before starting a herbal treatment. In general, people with major psychiatric disorders such as schizophrenia or bipolar disorder should avoid herbal therapies. *See also* **megavitamin therapy.**

histaminic receptors receiving sites for the **neurotransmitter** histamine. Some of the antipsychotics block histaminic receptors. The psychiatric effects of blocking histaminic receptors are not fully understood. However, like antihistamines taken for colds, antipsychotics with antihistaminic effects can cause sedation.

hypersalivation increased salivation, drooling. Hypersalivation is a common side effect of **clozapine**.

indication a reason to go ahead with a treatment. For example, appendicitis is an indication for abdominal surgery. Most of the time, indications are weighed against **contraindications**. In the context of switching antipsychotic medications, an example of an indication for switching from an older to a newer antipsychotic medication is when the person continues to have persistent **extrapyramidal side effects** despite efforts at treating them with side-effect medications.

Before switching antipsychotic medications, it is important to consider the indications for switching. Often, this includes reviewing with the doctor the **"target symptoms"** for the newer medication. The checklist on page 35 reviews some of the reasons to switch medications. *See also* **contraindications**.

insomnia trouble getting to sleep, a common symptom of many psychiatric problems. For patients with psychotic disorders, insomnia can be a symptom of

paranoia, which makes the person afraid of being killed or harmed while asleep. Insomnia can also be a sign of too much **caffeine** or can be caused by **akathisia** at bedtime. Waking up too early in the morning can be a symptom of **depression**, especially if the person wakes up feeling very depressed.

laziness Persistent **negative symptoms** can be confused with laziness. Generally speaking, people need to be very cautious about judging a person with schizophrenia as "lazy." Most of the time, the person is incapacitated by the illness and/or side effects. *See also* **akinesia, apathy**.

loneliness a normal emotion that comes from the distressing sensation of being disconnected to, or isolated from, other people. People with schizophrenia can be lonely because of the consequences of their symptoms or because of stigma. However, there can be a surprising lack of loneliness among some people with schizophrenia who remain isolated but not lonely. This lack of connection between someone's life circumstances and their internal experience is probably a result of **negative symptoms**, especially indifference. The negative symptom factor may explain why some patients experience more loneliness after their negative symptoms get better.

long-acting shot. *See* **depot therapy**.

maintenance treatment a phase of treatment during which medication is used to control ongoing symptoms and to prevent or delay relapse. For patients with schizophrenia, ongoing antipsychotics are needed to prevent or delay recurrence of acute symptoms, even when the person has been free of any symptoms for a long time.

mania a period of abnormally elevated, expansive, or irritable mood. The person may have an inflated sense of self-esteem or grandiose ideas, feel a decreased need to sleep, be more talkative than usual, feel that his or her thoughts are racing, be easily distracted, start a series of new projects, and become involved in risky activities (such as unrestrained shopping sprees or sexually indiscrete behavior). *See also* **bipolar disorder.**

manic–depression *See* **bipolar disorder, mania.**

Medicaid a health insurance program that is federally funded by the United States government. It is available to citizens of the United States with low incomes who are disabled by a medical or physical illness. Most individuals suffering from severe mental illness are disabled by their illness and are eligible for Medicaid. *Medicaid almost always pays for the newer medications. See also* **formulary, Medicare**.

Medicare Like **Medicaid**, Medicare is a federally funded health program. It is for people who have worked in the past or whose spouses have worked. Most elderly, retired people are in the Medicare program, but people with schizophrenia who once worked may also receive Medicare. Although Medicaid and Medicare sound similar, the way they cover prescription medications is very diffferent. *Unlike Medicaid, Medicare does NOT pay for prescription medications. See also* **formulary**.

medication crossover. *See* **crossover**.

medication noncompliance not following a doctor's recommendation. Noncompliance is very common among patients who are supposed to be taking antipsychotic medications. In part, this isn't any different from other medical conditions, such as high blood pressure, where noncompliance is also very, very common.

There are some additional factors that make noncompliance very common among patients with schizophrenia. First of all, many of the symptoms of psychosis make it impossible for the person to know that treatment is needed. For example, by definition, patients are not aware that paranoia is a symptom of their illness. Another common reason that patients may not take their medication is the distress caused by **extrapyramidal side effects**, especially from the older **conventional antipsychotics**. Finally, taking medications for a mental illness is very stigmatizing. It is therefore hardly a surprise that it is very difficult for many people to accept such a stigmatizing diagnosis.

One approach that can help patients who are not compliant with their antipsychotic medication is trying a long-acting depot antipsychotic. Unfortunately, none of the newer antipsychotics come in long-acting forms. The only depot medications now available are older conventional antipsychotics. Another approach is to minimize distressing side effects by routinely using the newer atypical antipsychotics. Doctors often have to balance the pros and cons of these options to try and come up with the best plan for the individual. *See also* **denial of illness, depot therapy, stigma.**

megavitamin therapy A minority of mental health practitioners believe that schizophrenia should be treated with very high doses of vitamins or minerals, but most psychiatrists do not find megavitamin treatment helpful. Whatever else, megavitamin therapy is not a substitute for antipsychotic medication in the treatment of psychosis. Rather, such treatments might supplement antipsychotic medications. *See also* **herbal therapies.**

memory problems Some medications can cause memory problems. In particular, **anticholinergic medications** and lithium have been shown to cause memory difficulties for some people, even at "normal" therapeutic doses. *See also* **cognitive problems.**

missed periods. *See* **amenorrhea.**

mood disorders a set of psychiatric diagnoses in which the major problem is mood regulation. Mood may be too low (**depression**), too high (**mania**), or too high at some times and too low at others (bipolar disorder, which is also referred to as manic-depression). For a patient with a mood disorder, mood symptoms are the **primary symptoms.**

mood stabilizers a class of medications that reduce mood swings (the "highs and lows" associated with **bipolar disorder** (also called manic-depression). Examples include lithium, Depakote (divalproex), and Tegretol (carbamazepine). The last two medications were initially marketed as anticonvulsants for **seizure** patients, but were accidentally discovered to have mood stabilizing properties. Mood stabilizers are also used to boost the effects of antipsychotic medications in patients with schizophrenia or schizoaffective disorder. *See also* **adjuvant medications.**

muscarinic receptors a subtype of cholinergic receptor (the other subtype are **nicotinic receptors**). **Anticholinergic medications** reduce extrapyramidal side effects (EPS) by blocking the muscarinic receptors in the basal ganglia part of the brain. However, anticholinergic medications have their own side effects which are caused by their ability to block muscarinic receptors in other parts of the body. *See also* **anticholinergic side effects, extrapyramidal side effects.**

muscle rigidity. *See* **rigidity.**

muscle spasm. *See* **dystonia, extrapyramidal side effects, myoclonus.**

myoclonus a sudden jerky movement of the arms that often happens right before falling asleep (which is normal). However, if myoclonus happens during the day in a person taking clozapine, it may be a warning that there may soon be a **seizure**. *See also* **clozapine**.

National Alliance for the Mentally III (NAMI) a grassroots advocacy organization whose goal is to improve the lives of those suffering from schizophrenia. For further information call 1-800-950-NAMI, or see the resource section at the end of this book.

negative symptoms the abilities and motivation that people lose when they have a mental illness. They are called "negative" because the person has lost abilities and interests they once had. People with negative symptoms may have less energy, lose interest in things they once enjoyed, withdraw socially, and have difficulty concentrating. There is no single negative symptom, and some patients have more of one type of negative symptom than another. Sometimes it can be difficult or impossible to distinguish negative symptoms from internal preoccupation, **depression**, or an **extrapyramidal side effect** known as **akinesia**. While not a cure, the **atypical antipsychotics** are often more effective than the **conventional antipsychotics** for treating persistent negative symptoms. *See also* **avolition, apathy, asociality, laziness**.

neuroleptic malignant syndrome (NMS) a rare but very serious condition caused by antipsychotics. Signs of NMS include severe rigidity and elevated levels on a blood test called CPK. The main treatment for NMS is to stop the antipsychotic medication for at least 2 weeks. The **atypical antipsychotics** are not as likely as the **conventional antipsychotics** to cause NMS, but it is still a possibility. *See also* **catatonia, extrapyramidal side effects**.

neuroleptics a term sometimes used to refer to **conventional antipsychotic** medications because they cause neurological (**extrapyramidal**) side effects. Because the newer atypical antipsychotics are much less likely to cause EPS, this term is not usually used to refer to the newer medications.

neurotransmitter a chemical that is used to transmit a message between nerve cells in the brain. Nerve cells store neurotransmitters in nerve endings. When a nerve impulse is sent to the nerve ending, neurotransmitters are released into the space between the cells. The neurotransmitter then attaches itself to a part of a nearby nerve cell that is designed to receive that specific chemical. The part of the nerve cell that receives the neurotransmitter is called a **receptor**. These receptors can figure out the concentration of that neurotransmitter and help translate this message back into a new nerve impulse.

There are many different kinds of neurotransmitters. Two neurotransmitters that are very important in the treatment of schizophrenia are **dopamine** and **serotonin**. Antipsychotics work by blocking the receptors that measure the concentration of neurotransmitters. All antipsychotics block dopamine receptors to some extent. All the **atypical antipsychotics** (and some of the **conventional antipsychotics**) also block serotonin receptors. In addition, some antipsychotics block other neurotransmitter receptors, including **alpha, histaminic, muscarinic**, and **nicotinic receptors**.

nicotine and nicotinic receptors Nicotine is the psychoactive component of cigarettes. There are neurotransmitters in the brain that receive nicotine. It seems that stimulating nicotine receptors actually helps normalize some of the brain abnormalities in schizophrenia and also helps antipsychotics work better. In other words, nicotine from cigarettes may help alleviate some of the symptoms of psychosis. This may partly explain why so many patients with psychosis smoke cigarettes.

nonresponse to medication The medication has not worked for the person's symptoms. What is considered nonresponse depends on what benefits the doctor expected from the medication.

In this book, nonresponse is used to mean that the medication did not work, not that something else was interfering with the medication's effectiveness. Several other things can interfere with a medication working. The person may not take the medication as prescribed or may be using alcohol or drugs. The dose may be too low, or enough time may not have been allowed for the medication to take full effect. When someone is not doing well on a new medication, it is very important to distinguish between true nonresponse (the medication is not working for that person) and these other factors. *See also* **partial response**.

norepinephrine a neurotransmitter. *See also* **neurotransmitter**.

"novel" or "newer" antipsychotics another term for the **atypical antipsychotics**.

nutrition Many people with psychotic disorders have poor nutrition, living on junk foods and fast foods. Only under extreme circumstances will poor nutrition *cause* psychosis, but poor nutrition probably makes it harder for the antipsychotic medications to work properly. Patients should try to avoid "junk food" diets; if that is unrealistic, the diet should be supplemented with once-a-day multivitamins.

obesity. *See* **weight gain**.

obsessive and compulsive symptoms predominant symptoms in a psychiatric disorder known as obsessive-compulsive disorder (OCD). Antiobsessive medications, such as Anafranil, Luvox , Paxil, Prozac, or Zoloft, are the primary treatment for a person with OCD. Patients with schizophrenia or schizoaffective disorder may also have secondary OC symptoms in addition to positive or negative symptoms. These OC symptoms sometimes improve when an antiobsessive medication is added to an antipsychotic. One puzzling observation is that the newer medications help decrease OC symptoms in some patients, but may actually worsen them in others.

olanzapine (Zyprexa) one of the newer atypical antipsychotics. It is made by Eli Lilly and was approved by the FDA in the fall of 1996. Olanzapine comes in 2.5, 5, 7.5, and 10 mg tablets.

orthostatic hypotension a drop in blood pressure upon sitting or standing. Symptoms of orthostatic hypotension can range from mild to severe. Mild symptoms include dizziness and lightheadedness when standing; severe symptoms include loss of consciousness and falling. Some antipsychotics cause more orthostatic hypotension than others; the amount of orthostatic hypertension a medication causes seems to depend on how strongly it blocks **alpha receptors**. Orthostatic hypotension is usually an *early* side effect.

For medically healthy adults, early orthostatic hypotension can be a nuisance but is usually not dangerous. For older people, or patients with other medical (especially cardiac) problems, orthostatic hypotension can be a serious health risk because of the medical consequences of sudden drops in blood pressure and the danger of sudden falls.

paranoia unfounded belief or fear that others are trying to cause harm. Often paranoid thoughts are a part of a person's delusion(s). Paranoid symptoms can cause overwhelming anxiety or can lead to harmful actions. *See also* **positive symptoms**.

parkinsonism extrapyramidal symptoms (tremors, muscle rigidity, and **akinesia**) resemble the symptoms of Parkinson's disease. *See also* **extrapyramidal side effects, rigidity, tremor**.

partial response The person is showing some signs of improvement on a new medication, but the doctor considers the degree of the improvement inadequate. Like nonresponse, partial response is a relative concept and depends on the doctor's expectations. It can sometimes be difficult to distinguish between nonresponse and partial response. However, this distinction is very important because the doctor is more likely to recommend that someone with a partial response remain on the new medication for an extended period of time. *See also* **nonresponse to medication**.

polypharmacy the use of more than one drug to treat a patient. Many patients taking psychiatric medications are prescribed more than one medication at a time. The term "polypharmacy" is also used in a more narrow sense to mean the long-term use of two or more antipsychotic medications at once.

positive symptoms changes that mental illness makes in a person's perceptions (five senses), thoughts, feelings, and behavior. Positive symptoms are often called "psychotic symptoms." They are called "positive" because they mean that the person has behaviors and experiences that one would not normally expect them to have. Positive symptoms include **delusions, hallucinations, paranoia,** and **thought disorder**.

postpsychotic depression depression that occurs shortly after a psychotic episode gets better. The person's psychotic symptoms may be gone or much better. However, in postpsychotic depression, the person gets increasingly depressed and may report feeling despondent, hopeless, or worthless. Suicidal thoughts and even suicide may happen during this phase. The first step in the treatment of postpsychotic depression is to recognize it for what it is. Postpsychotic depression often appears after other "improvements" have occurred, so that the doctor and family are caught off guard. Suicidal ideas should be taken especially seriously during this time.

Medication treatment includes adding an antidepressant to the antipsychotic medication. The antidepressants used to treat postpsychotic depression are exactly the same as those used to treat other kinds of depression. *See also* **antidepressant medications, depression**.

potency (of medication) as used in this book, the number of milligrams of medication needed to achieve a certain amount of antipsychotic effectiveness. The fewer the milligrams needed to achieve a certain effectiveness, the higher the potency of the drug.

As an example, let's compare two antipsychotic medications. It has been shown that 100 mg of Thorazine (chlorpromazine) has, on average, the same effectiveness as 2 mg of Haldol (haloperidol). Because it takes a smaller amount of Haldol to get the same effect, Haldol is an example of a high-potency medication and Thorazine is a low-potency medication.

It is easy to mix up potency with how well the drug works (which is called its efficacy). People often get worried or frightened when they switch to an antipsychotic medication with a different potency. When a person goes from a high-potency medication to a low-potency medication, they sometimes worry that too much is being prescribed. On the other hand, going from a low-potency to a high-potency medication can cause concern that the dose of the new medication is way too low.

primary medication the medication or medication class that is most important for an individual. Patients often receive more than one class of psychiatric medication at once. For example, a person who is taking an antipsychotic, antidepressant, and an antianxiety medication at the same time is taking three different classes of medication. For patients with schizophrenia or schizoaffective disorder, the antipsychotic medications are usually the primary treatment and other medications are the adjunctive, or secondary, treatments. For a person with bipolar disorder, a mood stabilizer such as lithium or Depakote would be the primary treatment and an antipsychotic might be considered adjunctive. *See also* **adjuvant medication**.

primary symptoms the symptoms that are most relevant to making a psychiatric diagnosis. For the diagnosis of schizophrenia, positive and negative symptoms are the primary symptoms. Notice that primary symptoms aren't necessarily the worst symptoms. For example, someone with schizophrenia may be more distressed by anxiety or depressive symptoms, even though they are not primary for the diagnosis.

prolactin elevation an increase in the levels of the hormone prolactin. Prolactin is a hormone that is released from the pituitary gland into the bloodstream. Its normal role is to start milk production and stop menses in women who have just given birth.

Some antipsychotics cause the pituitary gland to release more prolactin, which can cause prolactin elevations in some people. This prolactin elevation can cause menstruation to stop or lead to milk leakage in the breasts. Prolactin elevation is detected by a blood test. It is not medically dangerous, and high prolactin levels return to normal when the medication is stopped, or the person switches to an antipsychotic medication that does not elevate prolactin. *See also* **amenorrhea, galactorrhea**.

psychiatric diagnosis and antipsychotic therapy Antipsychotics work to control psychotic symptoms regardless of cause. Improvement on antipsychotic medications does not tell you the underlying cause of the psychosis. Antipsychotics are most often used for patients who have a psychiatric **diagnosis** of **schizophrenia, schizoaffective disorder**, or bipolar disorder. Antipsychotics are also used in some kinds of depressive disorders, especially when psychotic symptoms are present. In addition, antipsychotics are often used to help control behavioral problems that occur in dementia or developmental disabilities. *See also* ***DSM-IV*, mood disorders**.

psychotic symptoms. *See* **delusions, hallucinations, positive symptoms**.

quetiapine (Seroquel) one of the newer atypical antipsychotics made by Zeneca. It comes in 25 mg, 100 mg, and 200 mg tablets (other dose strengths are expected to be available soon).

q.d. technical term meaning that a medication that should be taken *once a day*. *See also* **b.i.d., q.i.d., t.i.d.**

q.i.d. technical term meaning that a medication that should be taken *four times a day*. *See also* **b.i.d., q.d., t.i.d.**

receptor a protein lying on the membrane layer of a nerve cell. Receptors are designed to receive **neurotransmitters**. Each receptor receives a specific neurotransmitter. Receptors are very sensitive to the concentration of the specific neurotransmitter they receive, while at the same time they ignore other neurotransmitters. Medications often work by changing the sensitivity of a receptor to its specific neurotransmitter. *See also* **receptor profile**.

receptor profile a particular pattern of receptor binding. Many of the psychiatric medications discussed in this book have effects on more than one **neurotransmitter receptor**. In fact, some antipsychotics bind to (block) more than five neurotransmitters. No two medications have the exact same pattern of receptor binding. In fact, each medication has a unique "fingerprint" of specific binding patterns. *See also* **affinity, dopamine, serotonin**.

refractory positive symptoms positive symptoms that have not responded to a number of different treatments. *See also* **nonresponse to medication, positive symptoms**.

rehabilitation Just as patients with heart conditions regain functioning with cardiac rehabilitation, patients recovering from psychosis often need psychiatric rehabilitation to regain work and social functioning. The newer **atypical antipsychotics** seem to help many patients enter rehabilitation.

relapse. *See* **acute phase**.

residual symptoms any symptoms that remain after the person has been stable on a medication for a long period of time. Residual symptoms are sometimes called **baseline** symptoms.

restlessness. *See* **akathisia**.

rigidity an increase in the general tenseness of muscles that is not caused by anxiety or exercise. This rigidity causes muscles to tire more easily and can also make it more difficult to perform repetitive movements precisely. Muscle rigidity can occur as part of the **extrapyramidal side effects (EPS)** of certain antipsychotics. A reliable sign that the muscle rigidity is due to EPS is a decreased arm swing while walking.

Risperdal. *See* **risperidone**.

risperidone (Risperdal) the second atypical antipsychotic introduced after clozapine. It is made by Janssen and comes in 1,2, 3, and 4 mg pills, as well as in a liquid form.

schizoaffective disorder a disorder in which the person has the symptoms of both a major mood disorder, such as major depression or bipolar (manic-depressive) illness and schizophrenia. Sometimes, the person has the symptoms of schizophrenia when mood symptoms are not present. The pharmacologic treatment of schizoaffective disorder is usually very similar to that of schizophrenia—that is, antipsychotics are the **primary medication** for schizoaffective disorder. All the advantages of the **atypical antipsychotics** are the same for patients who have a diagnosis of schizoaffective disorder.

schizophrenia Schizophrenia usually begins during adolescence or young adulthood. It is rare for schizophrenia to begin "out of the blue" after age 30. To make a diagnosis of schizophrenia, the person has to have had **positive (psychotic) symptoms** (such as **delusions** or **hallucinations**) for a significant period of time. Usually there is evidence of other serious trouble in the person's life such as difficulty working or going to school. Often the person was always a loner or became much more isolated after the illness started. There is no blood test or x-ray that can confirm a diagnosis of schizophrenia. Rather doctors make the diagnosis by talking to the person and his or her family to evaluate current and past symptoms.

To make the **diagnosis**, doctors must eliminate other conditions that can look like schizophrenia. They look especially for **alcohol** or **substance abuse** or for a possible **depression**. The doctor must be trained in psychiatric diagnosis in order to tell these conditions apart, because many patients with schizophrenia have depressive symptoms, while many patients with mood disorders have psychotic symptoms. If the psychotic condition is fairly recent, even the best doctors may be uncertain about the person's actual diagnosis. Then, the patient, doctor, and family have to take a "wait and see" approach.

Antipsychotics are the cornerstone of treatment for schizophrenia, even if the person has had only one episode (assuming the doctors are sure of the diagnosis). The person needs to continue taking antipsychotics even after the worst psychotic symptoms improve—otherwise the chances of relapse are extremely high. *Almost every expert in schizophrenia believes that one of the newer* **atypical antipsychotics** *should be used for someone experiencing a first episode of schizophrenia.* *See also* **DSM-IV**, **negative symptoms.**

sedation an effect of medication that makes a person feel sleepy or tired, or harder to stay awake. Sedation can be an early side effect in the first few weeks of trying a new antipsychotic medication, but may also be a long-term problem for some patients. Whether sedation is helpful or a problem depends on the person and symptoms. Some antipsychotics are more sedating than others.

seizure a sudden convulsion. Antipsychotic medications sometimes trigger seizures in patients who already have seizure problems or are vulnerable to seizures. With the exception of **clozapine,** if the person is not already at risk for seizures, it is very rare for an antipsychotic to cause a seizure out of the blue. In contrast, about 5% of patients treated with **clozapine** will get seizures. Risk factors for clozapine include the actual dosage level (higher dose = greater risk) and how quickly the dose is raised. **Myoclonus** may be an early warning sign of future seizures in patients treated with clozapine. Even if the person does have a seizure, clozapine can often be continued if the dose is lowered and/or an antiseizure medication such as Depakote or Klonopin is added.

Seroquel. *See* **quetiapine.**

serotonin a **neurotransmitter** involved with many brain functions, including sleeping, mood regulation, and appetite. Many psychiatric medications affect serotonin regulation. All the newer antipsychotics affect serotonin transmission by blocking serotonin **receptors** of nerve cells that "catch" the serotonin being released from nearby nerve cells. One of the leading theories about why the newer drugs seem more effective and/or have fewer neurologic side effects is that they affect the serotonin system as well as the **dopamine** system.

sertindole a newer atypical antipsychotic that is not currently available in the United States because of concerns about possible cardiac problems. However, it is available in Great Britain and some other European countries.

sleepiness. *See* **sedation.**

"split" personality Many people confuse schizophrenia with "split" personality. Actually, these are very different problems. "Split" personality is called multiple personality disorder or dissociative identity disorder and is quite a rare psychiatric condition. People with schizophrenia have only one personality, but have other characteristic symptoms of **schizophrenia.**

stigma Many patients who suffer from psychosis, as well as their families, feel very stigmatized by the condition. The effects of stigma on self-esteem and morale can be as damaging as the illness itself. However, there are ways to counter some of the stigma. Organizations like the **National Alliance for the Mentally Ill (NAMI)** fight stigma on a national level. Joining such an organization often decreases the isolation that comes from stigma. Treatment with one of the newer **atypical antipsychotics** can help reduce stigma by taking away some of the "medicated" look that was frequently present when people were treated with the older **conventional antipsychotics**.

substance abuse It is important to know that substance use is not the same as substance abuse. Many people use drugs without getting into trouble. A diagnosis of substance abuse is given when there is a repeated pattern of (illicit) drug use that gets the person into trouble. The problem drug is usually a "street" drug like marijuana or cocaine, but could also be an over-the-counter or prescribed medication, as in the case of psychosis from diet pills. Because people with mental illness are very sensitive to the dangerous effects of these substances, they are very vulnerable to the problems drug use can cause and can easily get into trouble with comparatively little use. Therefore, many people with schizophrenia also have a substance abuse diagnosis simply because it takes very little use to cause major symptoms or problems. Unfortunately, active substance abuse problems make the antipsychotic medications much less effective. *See also* **alcohol, caffeine, dual diagnosis**.

suicidal behavior. *See* **depression, postpsychotic depression.**

taper a dosing schedule in which a medication dose is lowered. When stopping medications, it is usually safer to go down slowly over a period of time rather than to "cold turkey" a medication suddenly. (However, tapering may not be possible when the person is having a dangerous reaction to the medication and the medication has to be discontinued suddenly. Some examples of dangerous reactions in which the medication needs to be stopped right away include low white blood count (**agranulocytosis**) from clozapine, **neuroleptic malignant syndrome**, or severe overheating.) Tapering a medication reduces the chances of withdrawal reactions. A medication taper can be used either to go off a medication completely or to go to a lower dose by several steps rather than in "one fell swoop." *See also* **crossover, target dose, withdrawal syndromes**.

target dose a doctor's best guess about the dose the person will eventually take, barring any problems that would call for a revision—either up or down—in dosing. Medications are often started at small doses to avoid side effects or to see how the person adjusts to a new medication. The dose is then raised. Doctors base their target dose recommendations on a variety of factors, including the person's treatment history, medical condition, and results of dosing studies. Target doses are also adjusted based on the response to the medication, any side effects, and, for some medications, the results of blood tests that monitor how much medication is actually in the bloodstream.

target symptom the symptom or symptoms doctors hope will improve when they prescribe a new medication, adjust the dose, or switch from one medication to another.

tardive dyskinesia. *See* **dyskinesia.**

therapeutic range the range of daily doses of a medication found to be effective. Remember that these are average ranges. Some people do fine on lower doses, while others may need larger doses. Therapeutic ranges may also need to be adjusted based on the person's diagnosis, age, and medical condition.

Nonetheless, the therapeutic range is a good starting point for understanding what a person's dose means in terms of usual doses, and can be helpful when a person is not doing as well as was hoped. *See also* **nonresponse, partial response**.

thought disorder changes in how a person thinks, such as having trouble thinking clearly, becoming easily confused, or having trouble concentrating. *See also* **positive symptoms**.

t.i.d. technical term meaning that a medication should be taken *three times a day*. *See also* **b.i.d., q.d., q.i.d**.

titration schedule adjustments in the dose of medication (frequency taken and amount) as the person goes on a new medication (dosage increases are sometimes called "up-titration") or as the person goes off a medication ("down-titration"). As a general rule, faster titrations are more likely to cause side effects as the dose is being increased or withdrawal reactions as the dose is being lowered. *See also* **crossover.**

tremor repeated to-and-fro shaking movement of the muscles. The movements have a regular interval, which distinguishes them from the irregular movements characteristic of dyskinetic movements. Tremors are most often seen in the hands, but can also occur in other areas such as the legs, neck, head, mouth, and tongue. Tremors can occur on only one side of the body (unilateral tremor). Tremors sometimes happen when the muscle is in one position and go away when the muscle changes position (postural tremor). The shaking can be very rapid in some kinds of tremors, and slow in other kinds (fast and slow tremors). Finally, some hand tremors get worse when the person tries to do some activity (action or intentional tremors), while others are worse when the hand is at rest (resting tremors).

The most common kind of tremor from antipsychotic medication is a *slow, resting tremor*. In contrast, other causes of tremors, such as lithium or alcohol, tend to cause *fast, intentional* tremors. Any kind of tremor can come and go. Most tremors get worse when the person is anxious or physically tired. *See also* **parkinsonism**.

urinary retention (inability to urinate) urinary problems that can be caused by anticholinergic medications. Symptoms include difficulty urinating (i.e., the person has the urge to urinate but has trouble starting urination or cannot completely empty the bladder). Sometimes there is a need to urinate frequently (although frequent urination can also be caused by a bladder infection or increased water intake). When severe, urinary retention can cause a complete blockage of bladder functioning, which is a medical emergency requiring immediate attention. *See also* **anticholinergic side effects**.

urination (excessive) a possible sign that the person has been drinking excessive amounts of water. When this happens in schizophrenia, it is called "psychogenic polydipsia," which can be a very dangerous problem. The **atypical antipsychotics**, especially **clozapine**, may be helpful for this problem. Lithium can also cause excessive urination.

Viagra (sildenafil) a medication used to treat erectile dysfunction problems. Viagra seems to be effective for erectile dysfunction that is due to any cause. Therefore, while it has not been studied, Viagra may be effective for erectile difficulties caused by psychiatric medications. Viagra is not indicated for loss of sexual desire or sexual difficulties in women. Viagra should not be taken with certain cardiac medications.

vitamin E Some studies suggest that taking vitamin E might reduce symptoms of tardive dyskinesia (while other studies have not found this). Patients who wish to take vitamin E need to take 1200–1600 IU daily along with their antipsychotic (three or four 400 IU capsules in divided doses). *See also* **dyskinesia, nutrition, vitamins.**

vitamins Many people with schizophrenia have vitamin deficiencies because of poor diet and nutritional habits. A single multivitamin taken once a day can be helpful and safe. Vitamins are a nutritional supplement, not a treatment of psychosis. *See also* **megavitamin therapy.**

WBC (white blood cell count). *See* **agranulocytosis, clozapine.**

weight gain a common side effect of both the older **conventional antipsychotics** and the newer **atypical antipsychotics.** In general, weight gain is more of a problem with the newer antipsychotic medications (both in terms of likelihood and number of pounds). Some of the newer medications tend to cause more weight gain than others.

withdrawal dyskinesia, withdrawal side effects. *See* **dyskinesia, withdrawal syndromes.**

withdrawal syndromes symptoms or problems that arise directly from discontinuing a medication. Depending on the person and the type of medication that was stopped, withdrawal symptoms can be physical (such as nausea or muscle stiffness) or emotional (such as restlessness or malaise). Withdrawal syndromes usually happen within the first few weeks of stopping a medication. Withdrawal problems can be confused with (1) side effects of any new medication being given, or (2) symptoms of the person's psychiatric condition.

Zeldox. *See* **ziprasidone.**

ziprasidone (Zeldox) will probably be the fifth atypical antipsychotic introduced in the United States.

Zyprexa. *See* **olanzapine.**

Part V
Resources

Support Groups

NAMI

*The National Alliance for the Mentally Ill (NAMI) is the national umbrella orga-
nization for more than 1,200 local support and advocacy groups for families and
individuals affected by serious mental illnesses. There are NAMI support groups
in all 50 states, the District of Columbia, Puerto Rico, and Canada. To learn more
about NAMI or locate your state's NAMI affiliate or local support groups, write to:*

NAMI
200 N. Glebe Road, Suite 1015
Arlington, VA 22203-3754
703-524-7600 or call the NAMI Helpline at 800-950-NAMI (800-950-6264)

*Most local branches of NAMI are listed in the telephone book under NAMI and
the name of the local chapter.*

*Several other organizations can also help you find support groups and informa-
tion:*

NDMDA
National Depressive and Manic-Depressive Association
730 N. Franklin Street, Suite 501
Chicago, IL 60610-3526
800-82-NDMDA (800-826-3632)

NMHA
National Mental Health Association
National Mental Health Information Center
1021 Prince Street
Alexandria, VA 22314-2971
800-969-6642

National Mental Health Consumer Self-Help Clearinghouse
1211 Chestnut Street, 11th floor
Philadelphia, PA 19107
800-688-4226

Recovery, Inc.
802 N. Dearborn Street
Chicago, IL 60610
312-337-5661

Web sites   http://www.nami.org

Web page for the National Alliance for the Mentally Ill. Provides information on NAMI resources and up-to-date information about treatments and political issues relating to mental disorders.

http://www.schizophrenia.com

An excellent, noncommercial site that provides a monthly newsletter service, as well as many bulletin board and discussion areas for people whose lives are affected by schizophrenia—consumers, families, and clinicians. This site was established by Brian Chiko and is dedicated to his brother John.

http://freenet.msp.mn.us/ip/stockley/mental_health.html

A good general starting place for finding mental health resources on the Internet.

http://www.cmhc.com/guide/pro22.htm

A Web page of pharmacology references that provides basic information about prescribed medication.

http://www.mentalwellness.com

This is a Web site sponsored by Janssen (makers of Risperdal) that offers general information about experiences of having a mental illness oriented for consumers and their families.

http://www.psychguides.com

Site for the Expert Consensus Guideline Series for the treatment of mental disorders. Order a copy of the clinicians' guidelines for the treatment of schizophrenia or download the handout for patients and families (which is available in English and Spanish).

http://www.samhsa.gov

Substance Abuse and Mental Health Association (SAMHSA) is a federal agency whose mission is to improve the quality and availability of prevention, treatment, and rehabilitation services from substance abuse disorders and mental illness. The site has an excellent bibliography on issues related to evaluation of support and psychosocial treatment services for persons with schizophrenia.

http://uhs.bsd.uchicago.edu/dr-bob/tips/tips.html

The Psychopharmacology Tips page is an indexed archive of the psychopharmacology discussion group. It provides information about current innovative use of medications and the recognition and treatment of side effects. It is based on the contributors' clinical experience, not on research, and it must be used with this in mind.

http://www.libertynet.org/mha/cl_house.html
National Mental Health Consumers' Self-Help Clearinghouse.

http://www.HealthAtoZ.com

HealthAtoZ—The Search Engine for Health and Medicine. Although this is a commercial site with drug ads, it offers free Medline searches.

For More Information   The following materials provide more information on schizophrenia and its treatment. Books that are available through NAMI are indicated. To obtain a copy of the *NAMI Resource Catalogue*, write NAMI or call 703-524-7600 or the NAMI Helpline at 800-950-6264.

Books about Schizophrenia

American Psychiatric Association. *Diagnostic and Statistic Manual of Mental Disorders, 4th Edition (DSM-IV)*. American Psychiatric Association, 1994
The *DSM-IV* contains the major diagnostic system that is used by psychiatrists in the United States. In the *DSM-IV*, all major psychiatric conditions are described and the clinical criteria used to make the diagnosis are outlined for each condition.

Backlar, P. *The Family Face of Schizophrenia*. JP Tarcher, 1994
A family member's story of coping with schizophrenia that will be especially helpful to anyone first encountering the illness in his or her family. Includes comments, insight, and advice of highly qualified mental health and legal professionals. Available from NAMI.

Keefe, R., Harvey, P. *Understanding Schizophrenia: A Guide to the New Research on Causes and Treatment*. Free Press, 1994
Basic introduction for individuals interested in understanding schizophrenia, including the prevailing research.

Moller, M., Murphy, M. F. *Recovering from Psychosis: A Wellness Approach*. Available from Psychiatric Nurses, Inc., 12204 W. Sunridge Drive, Nine Mile Falls, WA 99026, 509-468-9848.

Moller, M., Murphy, M. F. *Symptom Management: A Wellness Expedition*. Available from Psychiatric Nurses, Inc. 12204 W. Sunridge Drive, Nine Mile Falls, WA 99026, 509-468-9848.

Mueser, K. T., Gingerich, S. *Coping with Schizophrenia: A Guide for Families*. Harbinger, 1994
Highly readable, good, all-around guide for coping strategies. Includes many helpful tables, worksheets, and short topic summaries. Special chapter includes sibling relationships. Available from NAMI.

Torrey, E. F. *Surviving Schizophrenia: For Families, Consumers, and Providers (3rd edition)*. Harper & Row, 1995
Schizophrenia in understandable terms with practical suggestions for families. Available from NAMI and most bookstores.

Psychiatric Patient and Family Education Materials

Acher-Svanum, H., Krause, A. *Psychoeducational Groups for Patients with Schizophrenia: A Guide for Practitioners*, 1991. A practical manual that provides all the basics for educating patients about schizophrenia. Available from Therapeutic Resource Company, 1-888-331-7114.

Bisbee, C. *Educating Patient and Families about Mental Illness*, 1997. A comprehensive manual for patient and family education classes. Medication pages have been updated to include the latest antipsychotics and antidepressants. Over 450 pages in a three-ring binder (easy photocopying of handouts). Lessons include: What is Mental Illness?, Causes of Mental Illness, Medications Used to Treat Mental Illness, Management Skills, and more. Available from Partnership for Recovery, 888-IDEAL TX (888-433-2589).

Lefley, H. P., Wasow, M. *Helping Families Cope with Mental Illness*. Harwood, 1994.

Moller, M., Murphy, M. *Recovering from Psychosis: A Wellness Approach*, 1997.
A collection of useful, ready-made material that can be used for patient edu-

cation classes. Available from Psychiatric Rehabilitation Nurses, Inc., 12204 W. Sunridge Drive, Nine Mile Falls, WA 99026, 509-468-9848.

Murphy, M., Moller, M., Billings, J. *My Symptom Management Workbook: A Wellness Expedition*, 1997. Another collection of useful, ready-made material that can be used for patient education classes. Available from Psychiatric Rehabilitation Nurses, Inc., 12204 W. Sunridge Drive, Nine Mile Falls, WA 99026, 509-468-9848.

NAMI Family-to-Family Education Program, 1998. As free education and support for families with relatives with mental illnesses, this 12-week course is taught by trained family members. The curriculum focuses on schizophrenia, bipolar disorder, panic disorder, clinical depression, and obsessive-compulsive disorder. Discussed are the clinical treatment of these illnesses and the knowledge and skills that family members need to cope. Also available in Spanish. Available from NAMI.

Scheifler, P., Bisbee, C. *Beat Mental Illness: An Educational Board Game*, 1986. A fun way to teach and learn basic information about serious mental illnesses. Can be played in less than an hour by up to 16 people. Eighty question cards teach information about symptoms, treatment, and illness management. The rule book provides all the answers. Ten blank cards can be used to create your own questions. Available from Partnership for Recovery, 888-IDEAL TX (888-433-2589).

Scheifler, P. *When Mental Illness Invades the Family: Developing Practical Communication Skills*, 1990. This 1-hour video that presents 15 ideas that families and front-line staff can use to better communicate with people who have a severe and persistent mental illness. Available from Huntsville NAMI, 256-534-2628.

Weiden, P., Gever, M., Scheifler, P., McCrary, K., et al. *TeamCare Solutions*, 1997. A series of 10 workbooks, an instructor's manual, and a videotape. Titles include: Getting the Best Results from Your Medicine, Helping Yourself to Prevent Relapse, Understanding Your Illness, Managing Crisis and Emergency Situations (a guide for families and friends), and more. Very reasonably priced. Available from Eli Lilly & Co., 888-997-7392.

Personal Accounts

Beers, C. *A Mind that Found Itself*. University of Pittsburgh, 1981. A classic account of the impact of mental illness and the pivotal influence of treatment providers. An important autobiography that should be read by patients and mental health providers. First published in 1908, it remains compelling and clinically accurate. A story about recovery and triumph of the human spirit. An unforgettable eye-opener into the world of mental illness.

Burke, R. *When the Music's Over: My Journey into Schizophrenia*. Penguin, 1996. A rare window into the mind of a person with paranoid schizophrenia. An intense, colorful account of the delusional, chaotic world of mental illness that is exacerbated by persistent use of street drugs and alcohol.

Duke, P., Hochman, G. *A Brilliant Madness: Living with Manic-Depressive Illness*. Bantam, 1992. Patty Duke recounts her temper tantrums, crying jags, hospital stays, suicide attempts, spending sprees, and crushing depressions. Chapters detailing her roller-coaster life with manic depression alternate with chapters that educate readers about the illness. An excellent combination of autobiography and education.

Jamison, K. *An Unquiet Mind: Memoirs of Moods and Madness.* Knopf, 1995. A woman's experience with bipolar disorder and how it shaped her life. A remarkable personal testimony and a moving, exhilarating memoir. A good example of persistent denial resulting in repeated relapses which finally break through to acceptance and recovery.

North, C. *Welcome, Silence: My Triumph over Schizophrenia.* Avon, 1989. Dr. Carol North's battle against an illness that dominated her life for almost 20 years. A moving story about one woman's struggle and triumph over schizophrenia.

Schiller, L. *The Quiet Room: A Journey Out of the Torment of Madness.* Warner, 1996. A woman's experience with schizophrenia, its devastating effect on her life, and how she finally learned to understand and cope with her illness. Available from NAMI.

Medication and Research

Bernstein, J. G. *Drug Therapy in Psychiatry* (3rd edition). Mosby, 1995. A good, standard psychopharmacolgy textbook, well written and well referenced.

Bentley, K. J., Walsh, J. M. *The Social Worker and Psychotropic Medication: Toward Effective Collaboration with Mental Health Clients, Families, and Providers.* Brooks/Cole, 1996. An important resource for social workers involved with the mentally ill, especially pertinent because social workers are increasingly involved in medication management in both inpatient and out-patient settings. This text provides useful information for those who may not have received such training professionally. Available from NAMI.

Bouricius, J. K. *Psychoactive Drugs and Their Effects on Mentally Ill Persons.* NAMI, 1996. New, expanded edition that provides an excellent and up-to-date description of the uses, side effects, and interactions of drugs used in psychiatric practice. For families and consumers. Available from NAMI.

Brown, T., Stoudemire, A. *Psychiatric Side Effects of Prescription and Over-the-Counter Medications.* American Psychiatric Press, 1997.

Diamond, R. J. *Instant Psychopharmacology.* W.W. Norton, 1998. A handy guide to the indications, contraindications, and side effects of the five major classes of psychotropic drugs.

Drug Facts and Comparisons. Facts and Comparisons, 1997. A compendium of all prescribed medications with indications and side effects, including very useful summary tables. It covers the same material as the *Physicians' Desk Reference (PDR)*, but is much more readable. It is also much more expensive.

Gelenberg, A. J., Bassuk, J. G. *The Practitioner's Guide to Psychoactive Drugs (4th edition).* Plenum, 1997. An excellent general handbook.

Gitlin, M. J. *The Psychotherapist's Guide to Psychopharmacology (2nd edition).* Free Press, 1996. A book designed for the nonphysician. It is very readable and includes a lot of clinical wisdom about medication as well as technical information. It includes a good general overview of biological psychiatry theory as well as pharmacology. Excellent for general understanding, but somewhat less useful as a rapid reference book.

Gorman, J. M. *The Essential Guide to Psychiatric Drugs.* St. Martins, 1995. An excellent book written for clients and families as well as nonmedical professionals. It is very readable and well organized and can serve as a detailed reference as questions arise. It contains much more information on more medications than other consumer-oriented psychopharmacology books. Available from NAMI.

Gorman, J. M., Editor. *The New Psychiatry: The Essential Guide to State-of-the-Art Therapy, Medication, and Emotional Health*. St. Martins, 1996. A consumer-friendly book designed to educate consumers and help them get good medical care. It presents well-defined goals of treatment and describes how consumers can determine whether these goals are being reasonably met. Available from NAMI.

Janicak, P., Davis, J., Preskorn, S., Ayd, F., Jr. *Principles and Practice of Psychopharmacotherapy (2nd edition)*. Williams & Wilkins, 1997. An excellent, very current, more technical psychopharmacology text. It is very well referenced and includes research support for findings.

McEvoy, J. P., Weiden, P. J., Smith, T. E., Carpenter, D., Kahn, D. A., Frances, A. The Expert Consensus Guideline Series: Treatment of Schizophrenia. *Journal of Clinical Psychiatry, 57 (supplement 12B)*, 1996 (also available on the Internet; see above).

McEvoy, J. P., Scheifler, P. L., Frances, A., et al. The Expert Consensus Guideline Series: Treatment of schizophrenia, 1999. *Journal of Clinical Psychiatry*, in press.

Physicians' Desk Reference (PDR) (53rd edition). Medical Economics, 1999. This book lists every prescription medication marketed in the United States, along with indications, approved dose ranges, and side effects. It has indexes for medications by trade name, generic name, and drug category. Unfortunately, it is difficult to interpret information in this book. For example, it lists every reported side effect without giving information about which side effects are common and which have been reported only once, which are serious and which are trivial. *Drug Facts and Comparisons* (see above) covers similar information in a more user-friendly format, but the *PDR* is much more commonly available.

Perry, P. J., Alexander, B., Liskow, B. I. *Psychotropic Drug Handbook (7th edition)*. American Psychiatric Press, 1997.

Schatzberg, A. F., Cole, J. O., DeBattista, C. *Manual of Clinical Psychopharmacology (3rd edition)*. American Psychiatric Press, 1997. A very good handbook, very recently updated.

Schatzberg, A. F., Nemeroff, C. *Textbook of Psychopharmacology*. American Psychiatric Press, 1995. The current definitive textbook on psychopharmacology. It is large, detailed, very well referenced, and very readable. It is also very expensive.

Coping Strategies for Families

Adamec, C., Jaffe, D. J. *How to Live with a Mentally Ill Person: A Handbook of Day-to-Day Strategies*. Wiley, 1996. Offers self-help style advice to caregivers. Includes sections on personal experiences, education, stigma, coping, and the mental health system. Available from NAMI.

Hatfield, A. B. *Coping with Mental Illness in the Family: A Family Guide*. NAMI, 1991. A handbook for families. Available from NAMI.

Hatfield, A., Lefley, H. P. *Surviving Mental Illness: Stress, Coping, and Adaptation*. Guilford, 1993. The subjective experiences of people with different diagnoses, including schizophrenia, bipolar disorder, and major depression. Available from NAMI.

Lefley, H. P. *Family Caregiving in Mental Illness*. Sage, 1996. An excellent and timely examination of patients' rights and treatment needs from the point of view of all those involved. Focuses on family burden and research and theoretical perspectives that influence mental health professionals. Available from NAMI.

Waslow, M. *The Skipping Stone: The Rippling Effect of Mental Illness in the Family*. Science & Behavior, 1995. Brings home the powerful effects of severe mental illness on immediate and extended family members. This book is valuable to anyone who must live with or treat mental illness. Available from NAMI.

Woolis, R. *When Someone You Love Has Mental Illness: A Handbook for Family, Friends, and Caregivers*. Tarcher/Perigee, 1992. Practical, comprehensive, and clearly written. Excellent for families recently stricken with severe mental illness. Available from NAMI.

Wrobleski, A. *Suicide: Why? 85 Questions and Answers about Suicide*. SAVE, 1989. Available from NAMI.

Videos about Schizophrenia

The following two videos may be ordered from: Division of Social and Community Psychiatry, Box 3173, Duke University Medical Center, Durham, NC 27710.

Burns, B. J., Swartz, M. S., Executive Producers; Harron, B., Producer and Director. *Hospital without Walls*. Department of Psychiatry, Duke University, 1993.

Swartz, M. S., Executive Producer; Harron, B., Producer and Director. *Uncertain Journey: Families Coping With Serious Mental Illness*. Department of Psychiatry, Duke University, 1996.

Wheeler Communications Group, Producers; Bilheimer, R., Director. *I'm Still Here: The Truth about Schizophrenia*. Sponsored by Janssen Pharmaceutica. A superb and moving video portraying the impact of schizophrenia on four different consumers and their families. To order, see their Web site, www.wheelercom.com.

American Psychiatric Association, *Critical Connections: A Schizophrenia Awareness Video*. Sponsored by Zeneca Pharmaceuticals. This 30-minute videotape is designed to help consumers and families cope with schizophrenia. In the video, people describe how the new medications have helped them do better in their lives. To order, call 888-357-7924, ext. 6140.

The following four videos, produced by Mary Moller, may be ordered from: NurSeminars, Inc., 12204 W. Sunridge Drive, Nine Mile Falls, WA 99026 (509-468-9848).

Understanding and Communicating with a Person Who Is Hallucinating
Understanding and Communicating with a Person Who Is Experiencing Mania
Understanding Relapse: Managing the Symptoms of Schizophrenia
Understanding and Communicating with a Person Who Has Delusions

Specific Medications, Side Effects, and Other Treatment Issues

Risperidone

Person-to-Person is an educational and support service for patients who are taking risperidone (Risperdal). It is sponsored by Janssen, the maker of risperidone. The *Person-to-Person* program provides counselors who can help link consumers with their local services and, if desired, provide practical day-to-day assistance such as appointment reminders. For more information about this program, call 800-376-8282.

Marder S, Meibach R. Risperidone in the treatment of schizophrenia. *American Journal of Psychiatry, 151,* 825–835, 1993

Peuskens, J. Risperidone in the treatment of patients with chronic schizophrenia: A multi-national, multi-centre, double-blind, parallel group study versus haloperidol. *British Journal of Psychiatry, 166,* 712–726, 1995

Umbricht, D., Kane, J.. Risperidone. *Schizophrenia Bulletin, 21,* 593–606, 1995

Clozapine

Breier, A., Buchanan, R. W., Irish, D., Carpenter, W. Clozapine treatment of outpatients with schizophrenia: Outcome and long-term response patterns. *Hospital and Community Psychiatry, 44,* 1145–1149, 1993

Essock, S., Hargreaves, W. A., Dohm, F. A., et al. Clozapine eligibility among state hospital patients. *Schizophrenia Bulletin, 22,* 15–25, 1996

Kane, J., Honigfeld, G., Singer, J., et al. Clozapine for the treatment-resistant schizophrenic: A double-blind comparison with chlorpromazine. *Archives of General Psychiatry, 45,* 789–796, 1988

Yesavage, J. *Clozapine: A compendium of selected readings (4th edition).* Sandoz Pharmaceuticals, 1995. Nice compendium that includes most important topics on clozapine use.

Olanzapine

Beasley, C., Tollefson, G., Tran, P., Satterlee, W., Sanger, T., Hamilton, S. Olanzapine versus placebo and haloperidol: Acute phase results of the North American double-blind olanzapine trial. *Neuropsychopharmacology, 14,* 111–23, 1996

Tollefson, G. D., Beasley, C. M., Jr., Tamura, R. N., Tran, P. V., Potvin, J. H. Double-blind, controlled, long-term study of the comparative incidence of treatment-emergent tradive dyskinesia with olanzapine or haloperidol. *American Journal of Psychiatry, 154,* 1248–54, 1997

Tollefson, G. D., Beasley, C. M., Jr., Tran, P. V., Street, J. S., Krueger, J. A., Tamura, R. N., Graffeo, K. A., Thieme, M. E. Olanzapine versus haloperidol in the treatment of schizophrenia and schizoaffective disorder and schizophreniform disorders: Results of an international collaborative trial. *American Journal of Psychiatry, 154,* 457–65, 1997

Tollefson, G. D., Sanger, T. M. Negative symptoms: A path analytic approach to a double-blind, placebo- and haloperidol-controlled clinical trial with olanzapine. *American Journal of Psychiatty, 154,* 466–74, 1997

Weiden, P. J. Olanzapine: A new "atypical" antipsychotic. *Journal of Practical Psychiatry and Behavioral Health, 3,* 49–53, 1997

Quetiapine

Arvanitis, L., Rak, I. Efficacy, safety, and tolerability of 'Seroquel' (quetiapine) in elderly subjects with psychotic disorders. *Schizophrenia Research, 24,* 196 (abstract), 1997

Arvanitis, L., Rak, I. The long-term efficacy and safety of 'Seroquel' (quetiapine). *Schizophrenia Research, 24,* 196 (abstract), 1997

Goldstein, J., Arvanitis, L. 'Seroquel' (quetiapine) is not associated with dose-related extrapyramidal symptoms: Overview of clinical results. *Schizophrenia Research, 24*, 198 (abstract), 1997

Small, J., Hirsch, S., Arvanitis, L., et al. Quetiapine in patients with schizophrenia: A high- and low-dose double-blind comparison with placebo. *Archives of General Psychiatry, 54*, 549–57, 1997

Weiden, P. J. Quetiapine ('Seroquel'): A new "atypical" antipsychotic. *Journal of Practical Psychiatry and Behavioral Health, 3*, 368–73, 1997

Switching Antipsychotics

Borison, R. Changing antipsychotic medication: Guidelines on the transition to treatment with risperidone. *Clinical Therapeutics, 18*, 592–607, 1996

Ereshefsky, L., Toney, G., Saklad, S. R., et al. A loading-dose strategy for converting from oral to depot haloperidol. *Hospital and Community Psychiatry, 44*, 1155–1161, 1993

Shore, D. Clinical implications of clozapine discontinuation: Report of an NIMH workshop. *Schizophrenia Bulletin, 21*, 333–337, 1995

Weiden, P. J. Using atypical antipsychotics. *Journal of Practical Psychiatry and Behavioral Health, 1*, 115–119, 1995

Weiden, P., Aquila, R., Standard, J., Dalheim, L. Switching antipsychotic medications. *Journal of Clinical Psychiatry, 58*, 63–72, 1997

Yadalam, K. G., Simpson, G. M. Changing from oral to depot fluphenazine. *Journal of Clinical Psychiatry, 49*, 346–348, 1988

Acute Extrapyramidal Side Effects

American Psychiatric Association. *Diagnostic and Statistical Manual of Mental Disorders (4th edition).* American Psychiatric Association, 1994 (see pages 678–680 and 735–751 for information on medication-induced movement disorders)

Frances, A. J., Weiden, P. J., Ross, R. Medication-induced movement disorders. In T. A., Widiger, A. J. Frances, H. A. Pincus, et al. (Eds.), *DSM-IV Sourcebook: Vol. 1* (pp. 495-504). American Psychiatric Association, 1994 (see chapters 30–35 for information on specific movement disorders)

Lieberman, J. The effects of clozapine on tardive dyskinesia. *British Journal of Psychiatry, 158*, 503–510, 1991

McEvoy, J. P. The clinical use of anticholinergic drugs as treatment for extrapyramidal side effects of neuroleptic drugs. *Journal of Clinical Pharmacology, 3*, 288–302, 1983

Sachdev, P. The epidemiology of drug-induced akathisia. *Schizophrenia Bulletin, 21*, 431–462, 1995

Tardive Dyskinesia

Jeste, D. V., Yassa, R. Neuroleptic-induced tardive dyskinesia. In T. A., Widiger, A. J. Frances, H. A. Pincus, et al. (Eds.), *DSM-IV Sourcebook: Vol. 1* (pp. 573-582). American Psychiatric Association, 1994

Kane, J. M., Jeste, D. V., Barnes, T. R. E., et al. *Report of the American Psychiatric Association Task Force on Tardive Dyskinesia.* American Psychiatric Press, 1992

Other Side Effects

Stanton, J. Weight gain associated with neuroleptic medication: A review. *Schizophrenia Bulletin, 21*, 461–472, 1995

Newsletters and Journals

The Advocate, National Alliance for the Mentally Ill. This is a bimonthly newsletter published by NAMI. It is one of the benefits of NAMI membership. It covers new medications, current research, state and federal political and advocacy issues, book reviews, legal issues, and more. Available from NAMI.

Biological Therapies in Psychiatry Newsletter, A. Gelenberg (editor), Mosby Year Book. One of the best newsletters for medication-oriented psychiatrists. Requires fairly sophisticated knowledge of psychopharmacology; not for beginners.

The Decade of the Brain, National Alliance for the Mentally Ill. This is a quarterly publication for presenting research, clinical practices and advances, services, and policy relevant to serious mental illnesses. Although the articles are written by leaders in their fields, they are written in language accessible to a lay audience. Available from NAMI.

Psychiatry Drug Alerts, J. Roche (executive editor), MJ Powers & Co.

Primary Psychiatry, MBL Communications, Inc., 665 Broadway, New York, NY 10012-2302. This is a journal oriented to family practice and other primary care physicians. It has excellent reviews of basic psychopharmacology, with extremely useful charts and very good summaries of current medications. It is practical, and despite its focus on physicians is very readable. It is available free to primary care physicians. Psychiatrists can also request a subscription.

Schizophrenia Bulletin, Office of Scientific Research, NIMH, U.S. Dept. of Health and Human Services. This is a journal dedicated to advancing knowledge about the causes and treatment of schizophrenia. It is an excellent source of current knowledge and trends among researchers in schizophrenia. For information call 202-512-1800.

Part VI
Handouts

If you or someone you care about has been diagnosed with schizophrenia, you may feel like you are the only person facing the difficulties of this illness. But you are not alone. Schizophrenia is a serious medical illness that affects almost 3 million Americans. Although widely misunderstood and unfairly stigmatized, schizophrenia is actually a highly treatable disease of the brain. Left untreated, however, schizophrenia can devastate the lives of individuals and families. Fortunately, new medications are improving the outlook for those who suffer from this illness. With new treatments, people with schizophrenia are increasingly able to lead independent and productive lives. Here are answers to commonly asked questions about schizophrenia.

What is schizophrenia?

Let's start with what schizophrenia isn't. Schizophrenia is *not* split personality. Schizophrenia is *not* caused by bad parenting. Schizophrenia is *not* caused by personal weakness. Schizophrenia *is* a brain disorder. Like seizure disorders (epilepsy), it is a brain disorder that isn't detected by X-ray. The diagnosis is made by a careful review of symptoms and behavior.

Schizophrenia is a brain disorder that interferes with the ability to think clearly, know what is real, manage emotions, make decisions, and relate to others. Scientists don't know exactly what causes schizophrenia, but research is on the verge of finding just which problems in brain functioning are responsible for the symptoms.

When does schizophrenia begin? Schizophrenia can affect anyone at any age, but three-quarters of those with the disease develop it between the ages of 16 and 25. Most cases develop before age 30 and new cases are quite rare after 40.

What are the diagnostic symptoms of schizophrenia? There are certain symptoms that need to be present for a diagnosis of schizophrenia to be made. These are positive symptoms and negative symptoms.

Positive symptoms are not "positive" in the sense of being a good thing. Positive symptoms are sometimes called "psychotic" symptoms since the patient has lost touch with reality in important ways.

- *Delusions.* People with schizophrenia may have ideas that are strange, false, and out of touch with reality. They may believe that people are reading their thoughts or plotting against them, that others are secretly monitoring and threatening them, or that they can control other people's minds.
- *Hallucinations.* People with schizophrenia may hear voices talking about them, often saying very negative things. Less commonly, they may see objects that don't exist.

- *Confused thinking and disorganized speech.* People with schizophrenia may have trouble communicating in coherent sentences or carrying on a conversation.

Negative symptoms include emotional flatness or lack of expression, an inability to start and follow through with activities, speech that is brief and lacks content, and a lack of pleasure or interest in life. Although not as dramatic as positive symptoms, negative symptoms can interfere significantly with the person's functioning.

- *Flat or blunted emotions.* Schizophrenia can make it difficult for people to know what they are feeling or to clearly express their emotions. They show less emotion, laugh less, cry less, worry less.
- *Lack of motivation or energy.* People with schizophrenia often lack energy and have trouble starting projects or following through with things once begun. At the extreme, they may have to be reminded to do simple things like taking a bath or changing clothes.
- *Lack of pleasure or interest in things.* People with schizophrenia may not take much pleasure or interest in the things around them, even things they used to find enjoyable. "The world feels flat as cardboard." They may feel that it is not worth the effort to get out and do things.
- *Limited speech.* People with schizophrenia often do not have many thoughts. Their minds may feel empty much of the time. Because of this, they may have trouble carrying on a continuous conversation or saying anything new.

To be diagnosed with *schizophrenia*, a person must have had delusions or hallucinations and trouble functioning for at least 6 months.

What other problems are sometimes confused with schizophrenia? Before diagnosing schizophrenia, it is important for the doctor to rule out these other problems that may resemble it:

- Psychotic symptoms caused by the use of drugs. Drug abuse, especially of cocaine, LSD, or PCP, is the most common cause of symptoms like schizophrenia. The doctor will usually do a urine and blood screening test for these drugs.
- Psychotic symptoms caused by medical illnesses.
- Major depressive episode or manic episode with psychotic features. Psychotic symptoms occur only during mood episodes.
- Schizoaffective disorder. Features of both mood disorder and schizophrenia.

This handout from *Breakthroughs in Antipsychotic Medications* (W. W. Norton & Company, 800-233-4830) may be reproduced.

- Delusional disorder. Only delusions, but no other positive, disorganized, or negative symptoms as in schizophrenia.

Medication Treatments

Medications used to treat schizophrenia are called antipsychotics. They help relieve the hallucinations, delusions, and thinking problems associated with the disease. These medications seem to work by correcting an imbalance in the chemicals that help brain cells communicate with each other.

A number of new medications have recently been developed for schizophrenia. These are called *atypical antipsychotics* because they are less likely to cause extrapyramidal side effects (EPS), which are the most disabling and distressing side effects associated with the conventional antipsychotics (see below). Also, many patients experience better positive and/or negative symptom control with the atypical antipsychotics. Examples of atypical antipsychotics are:

- clozapine (Clozaril) approved in 1990
- risperidone (Risperdal) approved in 1993
- olanzapine (Zyprexa) approved in 1996
- quetiapine (Seroquel) approved in 1998

At least one other atypical antipsychotic (ziprasidone [Zeldox]) might be available in the United States in the near future.

Because of side-effect problems, clozapine is reserved for situations in which other antipsychotic medications have failed. All of the other atypical antipsychotics can be used at any time for the appropriate reason(s).

Antipsychotics that have been in use for a long time are called *conventional antipsychotics.* Some of the most common conventional antipsychotics are:

- chlorpromazine (Thorazine)
- fluphenazine (Prolixin)
- haloperidol (Haldol)
- thiothixene (Navane)
- trifluoperazine (Stelazine)
- perphenazine (Trilafon)
- thioridazine (Mellaril)
- loxapine (Loxitane)

How are antipsychotics given? Antipsychotic drugs are usually taken daily in tablet or liquid form. Fluphenazine (Prolixin) and haloperidol (Haldol) can also be given in "depot formulations" by injection at 1–4-week intervals. With depot formulations, medication is stored in the body and slowly released. This can be especially helpful for patients who have a hard time sticking with their treatment.

Unfortunately, as yet, none of the newer atypical antipsychotics are available in long-acting form. Risperidone (Risperdal) is available as a liquid, and ziprasidone (Zeldox) may have a short-acting injection form available when it comes out.

Selecting medications for a first episode of schizophrenia. Most experts suggest treating the first episode of schizophrenia with one of the newer atypical antipsychotics. This is to decrease the overall side-effect burden for the patient. There is no agreement, though, on which of the first-line atypicals should be tried first; each of these medications has its own strengths and weaknesses relative to the others. It is too early to tell for sure whether starting with the newer medications will improve the prognosis for first-episode patients with schizophrenia, but many doctors are optimistic that the newer antipsychotics will help many patients do better than had ever been thought possible on the older medications.

Selecting medication for later, recurrent episodes. The first thing the doctor will want to find out is whether the patient has been taking the medication in the recommended doses and if not, why not. Very often breakthrough episodes result from medication noncompliance, which is often related to troubling EPS. If the patient stopped medication because of side effects, the doctor may consider switching to an atypical antipsychotic that has fewer EPS than the previous medication. If the noncompliance is due to problems other than side effects, such as a lack of insight into the illness, the doctor may suggest switching to a depot formulation of a conventional antipsychotic.

Medications for patients who continue to have symptoms. There are a lot of choices for patients who don't respond to the first antipsychotics tried. The newer medications can often help patients whose symptoms do not respond completely to the conventional antipsychotics. Patients who don't respond to one of the newer medications will often respond to one of the other newer antipsychotics. There is no agreement yet on which "first-line" atypical antipsychotic—olanzapine, quetiapine, risperidone, or ziprasidone—to try first. Should other medications fail, clozapine should be tried eventually.

If clozapine is so helpful, why don't doctors try it first? Unfortunately, clozapine has a number of serious side effects that are uncomfortable and can even be fatal. The other atypical antipsychotics do not have this problem and therefore are used first.

Medication during the recovery period. It is very important that patients stay in treatment even after recovery. If patients stop taking their medications after a first episode of schizophrenia, four out of five will have another relapse within one year. Even first episode patients who fully recover from their acute episode should stay on antipsychotic medication for at least 12 months. If patients have more than one episode of schizophrenia or have not recovered fully from a first episode, treatment will usually continue indefinitely. Patients with schizophrenia have to take their medications for a long time, frequently all their lives.

How successful are treatments for schizophrenia? Schizophrenia is a highly treatable disease. Like diabetes, a cure has not yet been found, but the symptoms can usually be controlled with medication. Prospects for the future are constantly brighter through the pioneering explorations in brain research and the development of the newer medications described in this book. To achieve these results, however, patients must stick to their treatment, take medicine as directed, and avoid substance abuse. *Even if you have felt better for a long time, you can still have a relapse if you go off your medication.*

What are the possible side effects of antipsychotic medications? Because people with schizophrenia have to take their medications for a very long time, often for their whole life, it is very important to recognize and try to treat any side effects they may have from these medications.

Of most concern are a group of side effects known as extrapyramidal side effects (EPS). EPS are much more of a problem with the older conventional antipsychotics. Antipsychotics can make patients feel slowed down and stiff, or shake with a tremor. They can also make people feel so restless that they walk around all the time and cannot sit still. Long-term use of antipsychotic medications can sometimes cause a side effect called *tardive dyskinesia,* which is a writhing movement often in the tongue or mouth. Fortunately, although there still are some EPS problems, the newer atypical antipsychotics are much less likely to cause EPS.

After discharge. When patients are discharged from inpatient care, they are usually not fully recovered. This can be a difficult time with increased risks for relapse, substance abuse, and suicide. Medications are almost always recommended for after discharge. Inpatient staff will provide the patient with enough medication to last until the first outpatient appointment. They will usually schedule this appointment for the patient, ideally within a week after discharge.

During the maintenance phase of treatment, outpatient staff should provide education for patient and family about the illness. The outpatient staff should also teach the family skills for coping with the difficulties of having a relative with schizophrenia and encourage them to recognize early warning signs of relapse.

Psychosocial Rehabilitation

Psychotherapy by itself is not effective in treating the symptoms of schizophrenia. However, individual and group counseling can provide those who suffer from the disease and their families important support, skill building, and friendship. Psychotherapy focuses on teaching the patient about the illness and helping him or her resume usual activities and responsibilities. Research shows that patients who stick with their medications, have families who are educated about the illness, and who get psychosocial rehabilitation have the best long-term recoveries.

The kind of outpatient care needed depends on how well patients have responded to treatment and how reliable they are in taking their medication. Often, medication visits are scheduled monthly. Vocational rehabilitation is important for stable patients who need help with resuming gainful employment. For *patients who don't take their medication regularly,* more active interventions are likely to be needed to be sure the patient takes medications. For patients whose symptoms continue despite the best treatment, residential treatment or at least frequent attendance at the day hospital may be needed.

What can a patient do for a better recovery?

You will benefit by learning as much as possible about how to live with schizophrenia. Here are the most commonly asked questions about lifestyle changes.

Is there anything I can do to help improve my chances for a good recovery? The answer is a resounding yes. You should try to learn as much as possible about the disorder and its treatments. There are also a number of other things you can do to help cope with the illness and avoid relapses.

- *Avoid alcohol and illicit drugs, and limit caffeine.* The use of these substances provides a short-term lift but they often have a devastating effect on the long-term course of the illness.

- *Become familiar with early warning signs of a relapse.* Each individual tends to have his or her own "signature" signs that warn of a coming episode. Learn to identify your own warning signals. When these signs appear, speak to your doctor as soon as possible so that your medication can be adjusted.

- *Do not stop your medication on your own.* It is normal to have occasional doubts and discomfort with treatment. Be sure to discuss your concerns and discomforts with your doctor, therapist, and family. If you feel a treatment is not working or you are having trouble with side effects, tell your doctor—don't stop or adjust your medication on your own.

What can families do to help?

A diagnosis of schizophrenia can be very difficult, not only for the person who is ill, but also for the family. Because so many people are afraid and uninformed about the disease, many families try to hide it from friends and deal with it on their own. If someone in your family has schizophrenia, you need understanding, love, and support from others. No one causes schizophrenia, just as no one causes diabetes, cancer, or heart disease. Your are not to blame—and you are not alone.

Help the patient find appropriate treatment. The most important thing you can do is to help that person find effective medical treatment and encourage him or her to stick with it. To find a good doctor or clinic, you may want to ask your own physician for a referral or contact the psychiatry department of a university medical school or the American Psychiatric Association. You can contact the National Alliance for the Mentally Ill to consult with others who have a family member with schizophrenia.

Paying for treatment is difficult for many people with schizophrenia and their families. Private health insurance coverage generally does not provide comparable benefits for psychiatric illnesses as for other medical disorders. Public programs such as Medicaid and Medicare may be available to finance treatment. Social workers or case managers may be able to help you through the difficult red tape, but you may also have to contact your local Social Security or social services office directly. Then you may need to help the ill person through the application process.

Learn about the disorder. Learn all you can about the patient's illness and its treatment. Talk to the patient's doctor if possible.

Encourage the patient to comply with treatment, see the doctor, and avoid alcohol and drugs. The most important factor in keeping patients with schizophrenia out of the hospital is having them take their medications regularly. Sometimes long-acting injectable forms of medication are used when patients cannot be relied upon to take a pill. Some patients allow a family member to help him or her remember to take the medicine.

Handling symptoms. Try your best to understand what the afflicted person is going through and how the illness causes upsetting or difficult behavior. When people are hallucinating or delusional, it's important to realize that the voices they hear and the images they see are very real to them and difficult to ignore. If you notice these signs, you should not argue with them, make fun of or criticize them, or act alarmed.

Learn the warning signs of suicide. Take any threats the person makes *very seriously.* Seek help from the patient's doctor and other family members and friends. Call 911 or a hospital emergency room if the situation becomes desperate. Encourage the person to realize that suicidal thinking is a symptom of the illness.

Learn to recognize warning signs of relapse. Learn the warning signs of a relapse. Stay calm, acknowledge how the person is feeling, indicate that it is a sign of a return of the illness, suggest the importance of getting medical help, and do what you can to help him or her feel safe and more in control.

Don't expect too much during recovery. When patients are recovering from an acute psychotic episode, let them approach life at their own pace. Don't push too hard. At the same time, don't be too overprotective. Try to do things *with* them, rather than *for* them, so they are able to regain their sense of self-confidence. Also, make priorities. For example, patients with schizophrenia often smoke a lot and may have problems with excessive weight gain. Although you can encourage the patient to try to control these problems, it is important not to put a lot of pressure on him or her. The first priority is controlling the illness.

How to Cope

To survive schizophrenia, one of the most important steps you can take is to join an advocacy or support group. More than 1,000 such groups affiliated with NAMI (800-950-6264) are now active in local communities in all 50 states. Members of these groups share information and strategies for everything from coping with symptoms to finding financial, medical, and other resources.

Schizophrenia poses undeniable hardships for everyone, but it does not have to destroy you or your loved ones. To deal with it in the best possible way, it's particularly important for you to take care of yourself and do things you enjoy, and not allow the illness to consume your life. The newer medications are already a big improvement and new research discoveries should bring even more effective treatments in the future.

This handout is adapted with permission from McEvoy, J.P., Weiden, P.J., Smith T.E., Carpenter, D., Kahn, D.A., Frances, A. The Expert Consensus Guideline Series: Treatment of Schizophrenia. *Journal of Clinical Psychiatry,* 57 (supplement 12B), 1996: pp. 51–58.

This is a brief guide to the medications used to treat psychotic symptoms (hallucinations, delusions, disorganized behavior). Doctors treat these symptoms with medications known as *antipsychotics*. This handout reviews the pros and cons of different antipsychotics to guide your choice of medications and your decision about whether to switch medications. *This guide will not help with figuring out whether you need an antipsychotic medication. Also, this guide cannot replace talking to your doctor about your treatment.*

Definitions

Older antipsychotic medications (called *conventional antipsychotics)* have been available for many years. These older medications are also called *neuroleptics* because they cause neurologic side effects. Examples are Prolixin, Haldol, Trilafon, Mellaril, and Thorazine. Side effects called *extrapyramidal side effects (EPS)* are a major problem with the conventional antipsychotics. Examples of EPS are *akinesia* (being slowed down, "feeling like a zombie"), *akathisia* (body restlessness), and *tardive dyskinesia* (writhing movements). Newer medications are now available. They are called *atypical antipsychotics* because they don't cause nearly as many EPS as the conventional antipsychotics. Examples are Clozaril, Risperdal, Seroquel, and Zyprexa.[1] Although conventional antipsychotics usually do a good job with psychotic symptoms, they generally don't do a good job on negative symptoms, such as low energy levels or being very isolated from others. The atypical antipsychotics work much better for some people, even though they still don't cure negative symptoms.

Which antipsychotic medication should you pick?

There is no right answer to this question, but there are some important issues to think about. First, you need to know some things that apply *to all the antipsychotic medications:*

- It is impossible to know for sure ahead of time how well an antipsychotic will work for any individual person.
- It is much easier to predict side effects.
- Antipsychotic medications don't work right away. To be effective, they have to be taken the right way for long enough.

When you are taking an antipsychotic for the first time

Most doctors believe that you should try a newer atypical antipsychotic (Risperdal, Seroquel, Zeldox, or Zyprexa)[2] rather than an older medication because the newer medica-

tions have fewer EPS and are easier to take. Even though Clozaril is the most effective antipsychotic, doctors avoid using it right away because it has some serious side effects.

There are reasons why someone might be started on an older conventional antipsychotic first. Only the older medications come in short-acting and long-acting injections. The doctor may need to give an injection to someone who is out-of-control, or might recommend taking antipsychotics by long-acting injection to help with medication compliance. Older medications might also be used because they are much less expensive.

Starting an antipsychotic after being off medication

When restarting an antipsychotic medication, the doctor and patient need to consider the person's past experience—both good and bad—with antipsychotic medications. The general rule is to continue the previous medication when there was a good response and few side effects. A different medication should be tried when the past medication did not work well or there were serious side effects. In real life, unfortunately, the past history is often unclear and the doctor makes a judgment call with very little to go on.

When a new medication is tried, most of the time it should be one of the atypical antipsychotics, even if the person has already tried another atypical antipsychotic. *Not doing well on one of the atypical antipsychotics doesn't mean that another one won't work. Many patients need to try several antipsychotics before finding the one that works best. If the person has not done well on many different antipsychotics, consider Clozaril.* The major exception is when the person has a pattern of stopping medications and then getting psychotic. Then, the best choice might be to start a conventional antipsychotic that can be changed to a long-acting depot form.

You are on one of the older medications: Should you stay or switch?

Take your time deciding. Switching under these circumstances is usually not an emergency and you can choose the time that's best for you. Get the opinions of your friends, family, and treatment team. Think about what you might gain by switching from a conventional to an atypical antipsychotic.

- If you are doing well, don't switch medications! But make sure that you are doing as well as you think. Other people may notice problems that could be helped with another medication.

---

[2] Zeldox is expected to be available soon. There is no general agreement between doctors on which one of these medications to try first.

[1] Others are being developed and may be available soon.

This handout from *Breakthroughs in Antipsychotic Medications* (W. W. Norton & Company, 800-233-4830) may be reproduced.

• If you have distressing or embarrassing EPS, chances are very good that switching to an atypical antipsychotic will help.

• If you have persistent symptoms of schizophrenia, switching to a newer medication might help, but no one can guarantee you will do better.

Switching medications won't work for problems that aren't caused by medications. Street drugs or alcohol cause persistent positive and negative symptoms. Switching won't help unless the substance abuse issue is addressed.

Consider switching if:

• You take your medications regularly and don't have a drug or alcohol problem.

• Your medication isn't helping as much as you had hoped, because you have persistent symptoms of schizophrenia or distressing EPS.

• You are willing to go through the hassle and uncertainty of switching medications. (It can take a while for the medication to work, so you may feel worse before you feel better).

You should probably hold off on switching if:

• You and your family are satisfied with your current medication.

• You or your doctor prefer a long-acting depot medication.

• You aren't sure if your insurance will pay for the new medication.

• Even if you found a medication with fewer side effects, you still wouldn't want to take *any* medication.

• You can't afford the hassle of switching medications right now.

• You aren't able to make the time commitment (usually 6 weeks or more) to trying a new treatment.

You are already on one of the newer medications: Should you try another one?

Most of the reasons for switching are pretty much the same when you are on one of the newer medications: bothersome side effects or persistent symptoms. There are some side-effect differences among the newer medications. If you are having one of the following problems, consider asking your doctor about other atypical antipsychotics.

• Although EPS are less likely to occur with the newer medications, they still can happen. If you have bothersome EPS on one of the newer medications, consider trying another that might have fewer EPS.

• If you have gained too much weight on one of the newer medications, try another that might be less likely to cause weight gain.

• Other side effects that may decrease with another atypical include persistent sedation, loss of normal menstrual cycle, dry mouth, and blurry vision.

What if a new medication doesn't work well for you? While it is disappointing whenever a medication doesn't do its job, the good news is that another medication might work very well! Don't give up. There is some debate about how many atypical antipsychotics to try before trying Clozaril, but all doctors agree that Clozaril often helps for persistent positive symptoms when none of the other medications work.

Other issues to consider

• Changing medications can be tricky. Make sure you do this carefully, and know ahead of time who to contact should problems come up.

• When you change medications, pick a time when there aren't other major changes in your life. When you switch, make it your priority! Remember, the time you put in now may give you a lifetime of benefits!

• It can take up to 3 months to know whether a new medication will work. Don't be disappointed if it doesn't help right away. You may just need more time.

• When changing antipsychotic medications, keep your expectations realistic. It is better to hope for smaller gains and be pleasantly surprised than to be disappointed because you expected too much.

Summary

There are new medications for psychosis that, for many people, work much better and are much less bothersome than the older ones. You now have choices that weren't there a few years ago. However, with new choices come new challenges. The challenge with atypical antipsychotics is to get the most out of the medicines with the least risk possible.

Antipsychotic medication greatly reduces the chance that patients with schizophrenia will relapse. Unfortunately, about half of patients recovering from a relapse stop medication within 1 year. This handout explains some reasons patients with schizophrenia stop their medication and suggests ways families can help.

If medications are so helpful for schizophrenia, why do patients stop taking them?

People with mental illness aren't the only ones with compliance problems. Medical patients often stop medication when symptoms get better or the benefits of treatment seem far off. Likewise, many patients with schizophrenia don't see any day-to-day benefits from antipsychotics; there can also be a long lag time between stopping medication and the resulting relapse.

Certain features of schizophrenia cause greater compliance problems than are usually seen in other serious medical conditions. Probably the biggest cause of noncompliance in schizophrenia is denial of illness. More than half of those with schizophrenia don't admit they are ill or need medications. The following problems can lead to denial.

- *Psychotic (or "positive") symptoms.* Paranoia, grandiosity, and disordered thinking can cause people to refuse medication because of a lack of insight. This can lead to a vicious "catch-22" cycle—psychotic symptoms lead to noncompliance which leads to more symptoms. Fortunately, when "positive" symptoms are properly treated, the person will often (though not always) become more cooperative with medication treatment.

- *Cognitive and disorganized symptoms.* Disorganization and trouble learning from experience make it harder for patients to realize they are ill or that medications can help prevent relapse.

- *Embarrassment.* Having a mental illness is very stigmatizing. Medications are a daily reminder of being ill or different from others.

- *Side effects.* Many antipsychotic side effects are very unpleasant. Akinesia is a state of feeling or being slowed down "like a zombie." Akathisia is a feeling of restlessness that causes jitteriness or a need to pace. Even if these or other side effects aren't a problem right now, past episodes of side effects can make people unwilling to ever take antipsychotic medications again. The good news is these side effects can be effectively treated.

- *"Negative" symptoms.* People with schizophrenia often have low energy and motivation, which can make it very hard for them to get medications without help or follow instructions reliably. In such cases, the person isn't really against taking medication, but needs help to follow the prescribed regimen.

- *Alcohol or street drug use.* Drug or alcohol use can make people too "stoned" or intoxicated to follow through with medication. Many patients have also been told that it is risky to mix prescribed medications with street drugs or alcohol and will stop antipsychotics before using drugs or alcohol. Patients should stay on their antipsychotics even when they are using drugs or alcohol.

- *Family or therapist opposition.* Patients may stop antipsychotics if a family member does not want them to take them or if their psychotherapist or substance abuse counselor is opposed to psychiatric medications.

- *Changes in social network, supervision, or treatment system.* If a person was taking medication because of the influence of a family member or mental health professional, disruptions in that relationship may cause the person to stop. There is also a high risk of noncompliance when a person who was getting medication in a supervised setting goes to an unsupervised setting.

Recognizing noncompliance

Sometimes it is obvious a person has stopped medication; at other times it is harder to tell. Often patients hide their noncompliance because they will get in trouble if people find out. Mental health professionals often miss the fact that their patients have stopped medication, so you cannot rely solely on their assessment. Still, maintain contact with the doctor to discuss compliance and other issues. Double-check what the doctor has actually recommended. Patients sometimes hear what they want to hear and believe a professional recommended stopping the medication, when it was actually the patient who insisted on stopping.

Talking about compliance

First, when should you not talk to your relative about compliance? Don't push the issue if your relative gets inflamed or agitated, especially if he or she is getting psychotic. An understanding of the need for medications tends to "go out the window" when acute symptoms return and no amount of convincing may work. In this situation, contact the treatment service or a crisis team immediately. *Do not get into a direct confrontation about medicine, especially when your relative is getting sick. Not only will a confrontational approach be counterproductive, it can also be very dangerous.*

Otherwise, it is usually OK to ask about compliance. If you suspect your relative may be noncompliant, ask—but in a way that is not judgmental or threatening. Discuss noncompliance as something normal, perhaps mentioning a time when you did not comply with medication. If you find out there is noncompliance, don't punish or scold your relative or it may be the last time you get an honest report. Gently ask the person why medicines are being rejected without trying to argue about it.

If your relative is noncompliant, the next step is to do something about it. Take your time deciding what to do. First, try to get your whole family to agree on the need for medication. Otherwise, the person you are trying to convince will naturally seek out and value the opinion of the family member most opposed to medications (a problem more common in divorced families). Have the family member who is most influential do the talking—usually, the spouse or boy/girlfriend, followed by friends, siblings, and (last, of course) parents.

Next, figure out what to say. Avoid starting with a "strong arm" approach, which can lead to unproductive power struggles. Rather, try to persuade your relative to take medication by finding a perspective you can both agree on. Focus on *day-to-day benefits* (e.g., better sleep, antianxiety effects) rather than adopting a "scare the daylights" approach. If you want to discuss how medications help prevent relapse, ask the person if a relapse would make it hard to achieve his or her goals. The connection between preventing relapse and meeting life goals may not be apparent to the person being asked to take medication. If the person is denying psychotic symptoms, avoid a head-on confrontational approach. Sometimes, what seems to be "denial" is really embarrassment about being ill or is part of a healthy desire to appear well. Be sensitive and understanding about how difficult it must be to admit that you are "mentally ill."

If your relative complains of side effects, be sympathetic. Ignoring complaints about side effects won't make them go away and indifference may make your relative feel neglected or misunderstood. However, don't complain about side effects or the need for medicine in front of your relative—this can erode his or her willingness to stick with any medication regimen. Instead, discuss your concerns with the doctor.

If persuasion does not work, it is better to have the doctors or treatment system do the "arm twisting." If all else fails, you may have to resort to involuntary commitment or a mobile crisis team evaluation. While painful, this is far better than directly confronting your relative about compliance during a crisis.

Other things you and the doctor can do about noncompliance

- Help your relative find a doctor who communicates well with families and has a strong focus on side-effect management.

- Ask the doctor about switching from an oral to a long-acting injectable antipsychotic (depot therapy). While depot therapy does not guarantee improved compliance, it makes it much easier to track compliance and shifts the medication power struggle out of the home and into the clinic, where it belongs.

- If side effects are a major cause of noncompliance, ask the doctor about switching to one of the newer atypical antipsychotics. Sometimes there is a trade-off between giving the older medications by long-acting injections and starting one of the newer medications, which currently come only in pill form.

- Patients with schizophrenia often have a hard time following a complicated drug regimen. Ask the doctor about simplifying the drug regimen. The pharmacist can be a major ally in this kind of situation.

- Finally, maintain hope. People can change. Never give up!

Reprinted with permission from the *Journal of Practical Psychiatry and Behavioral Health.*

April 1999

Sun	Mon	Tue	Wed	Thu	Fri	Sat
				1	2	3
4 *Easter*	5 *1 Atypical** 3 Haldol 1 Cogentin*	6	7	8 *Therapist 10 A.M.*	9	10
11	12	13	14	15	16 *Case Manager 3 P.M.*	17
18	19 *2 Atypical 2 Haldol 1 Cogentin*	20	21	22 *Phone con-tact with therapist*	23	24
25	26 *3 Atypical 1 Haldol 1 Cogentin*	27	28 *Doctor 1 P.M.*	29	30	

Recovery Is a Journey......Not a Destination

* Doses will vary depending on the medications and the titration schedule.

This handout from *Breakthroughs in Antipsychotic Medications* (W. W. Norton & Company, 800-233-4830) may be reproduced.

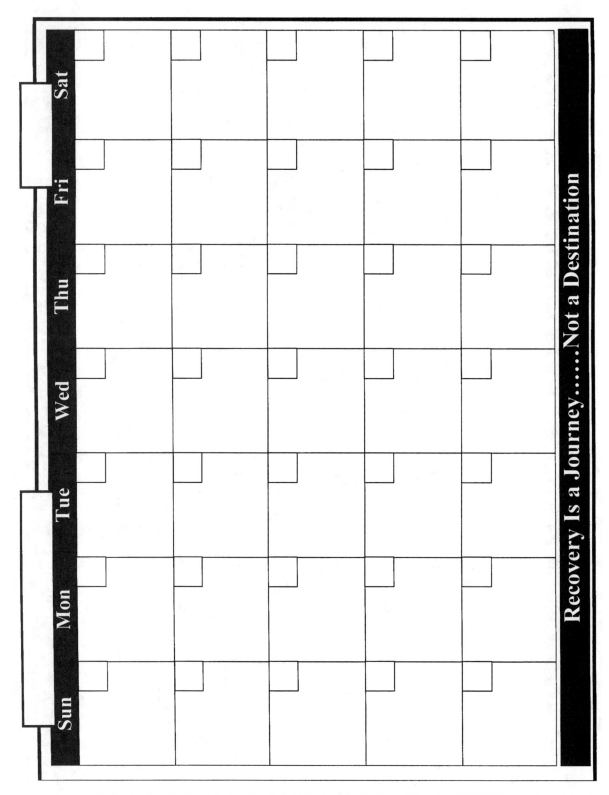

This handout from *Breakthroughs in Antipsychotic Medications* (W. W. Norton & Company, 800-233-4830) may be reproduced.

Directions: Read each statement carefully.
Mark the best answer for each one.
Mark only one answer for each.
If you don't know an answer, take a guess, don't leave it blank.

1. Being an active partner in your own recovery means that medication decisions:
   A. Are up to the doctor; just take what the doctor tells you to
   B. Are usually made with your input
   C. Should never be discussed with the patient or family
   D. Are none of your business

2. The main job of antipsychotic medications is to:
   A. Help people sleep better
   B. Get rid of depression
   C. Stop or block psychotic symptoms
   D. All of the above

3. Examples of positive symptoms include:
   A. Hallucinations, delusions, and not speaking unless spoken to
   B. Paranoia, confused thinking, and not feeling pleasure anymore
   C. Not showing feelings, not cleaning house, not showering very often
   D. Hallucinations, delusions, and paranoia

4. Antipsychotic medications help stop or reduce psychotic symptoms by:
   A. Correcting the chemical imbalance in the brain
   B. Increasing ventricular size
   C. Decreasing amitriptyline in the brain
   D. All of the above

5. Dopamine and serotonin are:
   A. Atypical antipsychotic medications
   B. Brain chemicals that are connected to symptoms of schizophrenia
   C. Conventional antipsychotic medications
   D. None of the above

6. Examples of atypical antipsychotic medications include:
   A. Seroquel, Trilafon, and Zyprexa
   B. Clozaril, Risperdal and Seroquel
   C. Zyprexa, Serentil, and Zeldox
   D. Navane, Stelazine, and Clozaril

7. Compared to old antipsychotics, the new atypical antipsychotic medications:
   A. Work on negative symptoms but not positive symptoms
   B. Are more likely to cause restlessness and dry mouth
   C. Usually do a better job on negative symptoms
   D. All of the above

8. An example of a good reason to consider switching to an atypical medication is:
   A. I'm stable and my symptoms are under control
   B. I need a shot because it's too hard for me to remember to take pills
   C. I have EPS that bother me a lot
   D. None of the above

9. An example of a good reason for *not* switching medication is:
   A. My last relapse was over 6 months ago and I still have lots of symptoms
   B. I just got out of the hospital a month ago
   C. My family and doctor recommend switching
   D. All of the above

10. The best time to switch medication is when:
    A. I'm about to start a job, return to school, or move
    B. I'll be taking a trip with my family
    C. I don't want to put up with any hassles or extra symptoms
    D. I can make switching a priority over other things for a while

11. When choosing which atypical medication to switch to it is important to:
    A. Consider the most frequent side effects of each medication
    B. Realize it doesn't matter which one you take; they're all the same
    C. Expect the doctor to know for sure which one will work well for you
    D. Remember that if one doesn't work, the other ones won't either

12. Most of the time a medication switch is done by:
    A. Stopping the old medication as soon as the new one is started
    B. Taking the new medication along with the old one for a little while
    C. Taking both the new and old medication together for up to a year
    D. None of the above

13. After they switch to an atypical antipsychotic medication, most people find that:
    A. They will always need a side-effect medication to control EPS

This handout from *Breakthroughs in Antipsychotic Medications* (W. W. Norton & Company, 800-233-4830) may be reproduced.

B. Their side-effect medication can slowly be discontinued about a month after they finish the switch

C. They have more EPS for up to a year

D. They have a much higher risk of TD

14. The best way to make sure you follow the switching plan correctly is:

A. Listening and trying to remember the main points

B. Insisting on doing it on your own because you don't need help

C. Using a switching calendar and a pill box

D. Refilling your pill box on different days each week

15. The problem people sometimes have while switching medications is:

A. A temporary increase in symptoms

B. Side effects because of going off the old medication

C. Early side effects of the new medication

D. All of the above

16. The best thing to do if you start having problems during a medication switch is:

A. Stop taking the new medication, but keep taking the old one

B. Take extra medicine and see if you feel better

C. Go to the hospital

D. None of the above

17. Working with your treatment team during a medication switch includes:

A. Canceling your appointments if you're doing fine

B. Not talking about problems so you won't end up in the hospital

C. Talking with someone on your team about problems or concerns

D. Skipping doses whenever you're feeling OK

18. When switching medication, it's very important to remember that:

A. If you have trouble during the switch, the new medicine won't work

B. The starting dose will probably be enough to do a good job

C. It usually takes about 2 days to see if a new medicine will help you

D. It can take up to 3 months to know how much the new medicine will help you

19. The best thing to do if the medicine you switched to doesn't work well is:

A. Stop taking the new medicine until you see the doctor again

B. Talk with your doctor about trying another atypical antipsychotic

C. Go to the hospital

D. Take extra pills and stay in bed for a few days

20. If you've tried some of the atypicals and none have worked very well for you:

A. Consider switching to Clozaril if you haven't tried it yet

B. Give up, nothing will work

C. Just keep taking what you're on now, they all work the same

D. Drink more caffeine and see if it helps

21. There is a higher risk of relapse when switching from:

A. Zyprexa to any other medication

B. Risperdal to Seroquel

C. Clozaril to another antipsychotic medication

D. None of the above

22. Many people find that after they switch to an atypical medication:

A. They are cured

B. Their persistent positive and negative symptoms improve

C. They don't need any medication after their symptoms go away

D. They don't have any side effects

23. Getting better after a medication switch may lead to new problems such as:

A. Wanting to leave the illness behind or coping with feelings of loss

B. Trying to do too much at once or making up for lost time

C. Feeling disconnected from people or wanting to be sexually active

D. All of the above

24. Postpsychotic depression:

A. Is least likely to happen after symptoms improve

B. May be a psychological reaction to getting better

C. Is always dangerous and requires hospitalization

D. Is never treated with antidepressant medication

25. The main message of "Medications are the keys to recovery" is:

A. Hope, faith, and connecting with other people are never helpful

B. If the medicine you're taking doesn't work, just keep taking it

C. All antipsychotic medications are the same

D. Try each medicine until you find one that works well for you

Knowledge Assessment, continued

Answer Key

Question	Answer	Question	Answer	Question	Answer
1.	B	10.	D	18.	D
2.	C	11.	A	19.	B
3.	D	12.	B	20.	A
4.	A	13.	B	21.	C
5.	B	14.	C	22.	B
6.	B	15.	D	23.	D
7.	C	16.	D	24.	B
8.	C	17.	C	25.	D
9.	B				

This Knowledge Assessment was developed for use in classroom settings to evaluate participants' progress toward learning the key points covered in this guide. It is designed to be used as a "pretest" to measure people's knowledge before reading the material, and as a "post-test" after completing the guide to measure knowledge acquisition.